Trouble
with Jesus

Trouble with Jesus

**Women, Christology,
and Preaching**

L. Susan Bond

Chalice Press
St. Louis, Missouri

All scripture quotations, unless otherwise indicated, are from the *New Revised Standard Version Bible,* copyright 1989, Division of Christian Education of the National Council of Churches of Christ in the USA. Used by permission.

Cover Design: Lynne Condellone
Cover image: 13th century Macedonian icon of the crucifixion published by the Aries Verlog in Munich. Reproduced by permission.
Interior Design: Wynn Younker
Art Director: Michael A. Domínguez

This book is printed on acid-free, recycled paper.

Visit Chalice Press on the World Wide Web at
www.chalicepress.com

10 9 8 7 6 5 4 3 2 1   99 00 01 02 03 04

Library of Congress Cataloging–in–Publication Data

Bond, L. Susan
    Trouble with Jesus: women, christology, and preaching / by L. Susan Bond
        p. cm
    Includes bibliographical references and index.
    ISBN 0-8272-3635-2
    1. Jesus Christ—Person and offices. 2. Feminist theology.
3. Preaching. I. Title
    BT205.B56   1999   99–38564
    232'.082—dc21   CIP

Printed in the United States of America

Contents

Preface

To friends and family and colleagues who have supported this project, I give deep thanks. To former colleagues at Lexington Seminary Sharyn Dowd, Sharon Warner, Tony Dunnavant, and Michael Kinnamon, I appreciate encouragement when this project was just a glimmer in my mind. To Lexington students, especially Kris Bentley, Becky Zelensky, and Debbie Vaughan, I give thanks for hours of discussion, homiletic brainstorming, and letters. To Vanderbilt colleagues David Buttrick, Victor Anderson, Peter Hodgson, and Arliene Dearing, thanks for believing in this project and offering strong support. Women students at Vanderbilt have also been supportive, particularly those in the class "Women, Christology, and Preaching." Thanks to Terry Strachan Terrell, Melitta Padilla, Alison Caple, Tonya Burton, Leslie Linder, Cindy Nelson, Neely Williams, and the lone brave male student, George P. Lee III. Gail Davidson has been a devoted conversation partner whose honest questions helped develop the soteriological metaphor of salvage in chapter 4. Carl Gabrielson was a research assistant during the early phase of writing, and I thank him for his dogged and inspired pursuit of elusive articles. Teresa Lockhart Stricklen, a fine homiletician, has combed through the text to provide a helpful index. The faith communities of Vine Street Christian Church and Edgehill United Methodist Church have provided spiritual strength and insight to my ongoing work.

Distant friends and colleagues Ron Allen and Rufus Burrow, Jr., at Christian Theological Seminary, have been mentors and tormentors without whose encouragement I would have been sorely hampered. John McClure, at Louisville Presbyterian Theological Seminary, has read portions of the rough draft and has been a strong advocate for my research. Marjorie Suchocki has read the entire manuscript and offered helpful commentary. The women's group within the Academy of Homiletics has offered the kind of strength and confidence that characterizes the uppityness of women preaching. Jon L. Berquist at Chalice Press has been an excellent friend and editor. His concrete suggestions, along with those of David Polk, helped me focus clearly on the task. Their conversations were invaluable. To all, many thanks.

Finally, I offer my deepest thanks to my daily living companions, Matthew Bond, Megan May, and J. Coffey May. Beyond the saying of it, I appreciate their ability to embody the immediacy of grace and mercy.

Introduction

This project began to take shape during my first three years of teaching homiletics, first at Lexington Theological Seminary and later at Vanderbilt Divinity School. At Lexington I began to be aware of the problems women students had with feminist types of christology as they tried to apply them to biblical texts for preaching. A strange pattern emerged; women tended to preach deeply christological texts in ways that trivialized Jesus and valorized women. Regardless of the narratives, parables, or discourses they selected, they tended to portray Jesus as either a sexist Jew or a thoroughgoing anti-Jewish feminist, and they tended to portray the women figures as heroines. Interpretive approaches were severely gendered, elevating women to epistemological genius and relegating men to literary foils and hapless fools. There was so little variety in their approaches that I could begin to predict exactly where and how the rhetorical strategies would appear. On occasion, a woman student would seek me out, perplexed as she tried to wrest the text into conformity with a canonical woman's theology. Similar problems emerged in introductory courses on worship design. Women students had an almost universal antipathy to developing eucharistic liturgies that had any relationship to the traditional symbols of body and blood. Jesus had become a problem for many of them.

My curiosity was further provoked upon reading Christine Smith's impressive work in *Preaching As Weeping, Confession, and Resistance: Radical Approaches to Radical Evil*. Smith is committed to homiletics as a theological endeavor, and her book explored incarnational models of community. While her book was not overtly christological, her chapter on classism used the cross as a primary reflective category. Smith rejected sacrificial atonement thinking as a strategy that benefited the haves at the expense of the have-nots.[1] What particularly interested me, however, was her recognition that the use of christological categories and interpretive strategies varied significantly across races and cultures. Smith had noted this divide between white women and women of color in an earlier work but couldn't account for the difference.[2] Contemporary with Smith's work was Jacquelyn Grant's book *White Women's Christ and Black Women's Jesus*, which articulated the differences and suggested that atonement theories were at the heart of the matter. Somehow, the suffering of Jesus was not the problem within some marginalized ethnic communities that it was among white mainstream feminists. I began to wonder how it was that white women feminists had so much trouble with Jesus and that women of color did not have trouble with Jesus in the same way. And most particularly, I wondered at the way these differences played out homiletically. Did different christologies and soteriologies result in different styles of prophetic preaching? How were christologies related to the types of sermonic claims and illustrations that students used in classes? What rhetorical strategies were necessary to overcome the differences between texts, classical doctrines, and liberating proclamation?

At Vanderbilt my fascination with the Jesus problem deepened. I met with the school's women students group for informal discussion of Rebecca Chopp's book *Saving Grace*. We were discussing her theological metaphor of "warming quilt" when I pressed the small group to an experiment. I asked them to reflect how they could communicate the theological claims of "warming quilt" to a traditional group of laywomen. What christological ideas did warming quilt convey? What familiar beliefs about Jesus and the Jesus story were analogous to Chopp's metaphor? There was an awkward silence. The small group of women bowed their heads and avoided eye contact with me. I tried again, pointing out that women preachers had to find common ground in the traditional symbols of the faith. "What does a warming quilt image convey about Jesus?" Again, an awkward silence. Finally, one woman lifted her eyes and said very softly, "A lot of us have trouble with Jesus."

During this time span (1993–1997), the Jesus Seminar was in full swing. Some academics and some laypeople were interested in the work of the Jesus Seminar, but it was curious to me that there was little formal attention to this work beyond hysterical news reporting. No one in the academy seemed to care as much about Jesus as the Jesus scholars did. Over lunch one day, a frustrated colleague startled me by articulating exactly this attitude. "Who cares about christology? No one really pays attention to that anymore." That moment was a haunting reminder of a comment that the late Dr. Samuel Proctor had made as a visting professor at Vanderbilt. "Ladies and gentlemen," he announced to an introductory class, "I have come to the conclusion that Jesus is no longer very popular."[3] While I didn't doubt the accuracy of his statement with regard to mainstream theological education, I was struck by how alien this viewpoint would seem to the average congregation.

At the same time that my colleague was exclaiming over the irrelevance of Jesus, I was teaching a continuing education class at two local congregations. It was a month-long multimedia class called "Faces of Jesus," which used slides of Christian art through the centuries along with music from each major historical period. I structured the classes around historical controversies and shifts in the tradition's christological thinking and with reference to philosophical debates, rationalism and scientific method, romanticism and the individual, and the legacy of the Enlightenment. I discovered that there was an avid interest in christology, in theological reflection, and in making sense of Jesus. People were taking notes and asking for reading assignments! If some theologians consider christology obsolete, ordinary Christian communities certainly do not. Preachers who do not address christological issues within contemporary congregational life may be missing one of the richest teaching opportunities available.

This book explores the peculiar "trouble with Jesus" that contemporary women preachers and theologians have inherited. This is not a formal text on christology or on women's theology, epistemology, or hermeneutics. I am neither a guild theologian, nor do I pretend to excel in matters christological. Readers who hope for full-blown theological expertise of the academic kind are advised to look elsewhere.

So, some readers will wonder why a homiletician doesn't just stick to her area of expertise: exploring strategies and methods of sermon construction. There is a popular assumption that the real work of homileticians involves extensive biblical studies for the purposes of "unlocking the Bible" for contemporary preaching. However, as homileticians are increasingly rediscovering, homiletics is a theological enterprise. Theological content and homiletic form are integrally related, as my anecdotal experience with women students suggests. And to the extent that the average congregation learns any historical, systematic, or constructive theology, they learn it primarily from preachers. If preachers do nothing more than replicate the theological biases of texts or the theological biases of contemporary theologians, their parishoners will probably be bewildered at the variety of christologies offered from Sunday to Sunday. As a discipline, homiletics is moving away from its two-hundred-year captivity to biblical studies and biblical theology, and the "how-to" mindset that reduces preaching to religious communication. Homiletics is beginning to reclaim its traditional dialogue partners of theology, philosophy, and rhetoric.

Part of the homiletic task is to weigh the different christological options and offer some coherent approach that persists through time—at least from one Sunday to the next. Preachers need to be able to ask and articulate what is at stake with particular approaches, and they need to locate themselves theologically so that parishoners can develop theological thinking themselves. Although it may sound strange to some ears, it is probably necessary for preachers to know what they believe or what they take to be theologically appropriate as they approach the preaching task. At the very least, proclamation must offer rhetorical strategies that suggest how Christians can adjudicate the strengths and weaknesses of particular theological postures.

This project explores the theological aspects of interpretation and proclamation relative to a particular pair of issues: women and christology. My own work could not have proceeded without the groundwork established by a generation of courageous women theologians. Three have been particularly figural in the preparation of this book. Elisabeth Schüssler Fiorenza's work in New Testament scholarship has been helpful in establishing the historical plausibility of egalitarian communities within the earliest church and in calling for a "basileia bias" in interpreting the Christian scriptures. Beyond that, though, her work in apocalyptic symbols and in rhetorical critical approaches to interpretation are absolutely foundational for the claims I make here. In a similar vein, Sallie McFague's work in metaphorical theology and constructive feminist theology undergird much of my own constructive work in chapter 4. Her attention to body metaphors and the way they relate to ecofeminism and the body politic run implicitly throughout this project. Finally, Marjorie Suchocki's feminist process theology is implicit in my own proposal for a theology of salvage. I assume that God is always working within a particular context, against the weight of evil and entropy, to bring about the best that is possible. Suchocki's own "church-friendly" scholarship provides a truly feminist type of theology: practical, accessible, and concerned with the corporate lives of actual communities.

Other influences need to be noted. David Buttrick's work in homiletic theory is singular for its reclamation of poetics and rhetoric. His implicit christology and ecclesiology have contributed significantly to this work, along with his iconoclastic style. Another colleague, Victor Anderson, has influenced my own turn toward the language of "practices" as a way to explore the real theological commitments of communities. By exploring practices, I have been able to discuss the ecclesial practices of ritual and missionary outreach within a single metaphorical paradigm, and to make use of ritual studies to explore attitudes and acts toward bodies and the "other." The turn toward practice has allowed me to use Mary Douglas' work on the symbolism of dirt as a primary organizing category for a theology of salvage that must come in contact with what is considered unclean. For introducing me to the work of Douglas, ritual theorists, and social phenomenologists (especially Alfred Schutz), I thank colleague Howard Harrod. However, I alone am accountable for any mistakes or blunders within this text.

This project explores several major theological shifts that conspired to produce contemporary christological problems. Part of my overall strategy is to reclaim a demythologized primitive christology, the dramatic *christus victor* theory of atonement. One advantage of this reclamation is that it is extremely compatible with homiletic interpretations of New Testament texts. The primitive status of the theory does not itself grant immediate authority, but it does have the practical advantage of being more plausible and coherent with the early church's understanding of Jesus and his ministry. And, demythologized as a contemporary social critique of power, the primitive theory has significant possibilities for revitalizing the church's proclamation and its ministries of compassion toward the world. By contrast, each major shift away from primitive theories either introduces or reinforces a theological blunder. While this primitive theory is not without problems, it doesn't suffer from the accumulation and interaction of later blunders and may be more easily appropriated for homiletics.

The first chapter explores the context of parish preaching, the relationship of proclamation to a sacramental setting, and the particular "christological crisis" of contemporary ordained women in parish ministry. The discussion reconnects homiletics with rhetoric and with sociological disciplines, directing homiletic reflection toward its communal setting. This chapter also outlines the major concerns and themes of contemporary women's theology: suffering, bodies, sexuality, community, and experience. I also propose a heuristic or reflective tool I call "the icon of the battered woman" to address the current concerns about the reality of suffering. I also explore various methodological strategies and make suggestions for a homiletic method of christological reflection.

Chapter 2 explores several problems within the classical tradition that must be addressed in homiletical christologies. The assumptions behind this chapter are twofold: first, that ordinary congregations actually operate with one or more versions of classical atonement theory and christological doctrine; and second, that preachers who don't know better will reinforce disasters they could avoid. The sections are divided according to major paradigm shifts, whether they are in christology, soteriology, or another systematic category. The major shifts are from resurrection to incarnation, from human to divine, from rescue to retribution, from risk to safety, from contact to avoidance. One of the primary metaphorical oppositions is that of purity and pollution, which, if misunderstood or misappropriated, reverses theological meanings. Using metaphorical categories (dirt, stain, purity, cleanliness) is particularly productive for homileticians who must make sense of metaphors that function within the tradition and within contemporary culture. (Readers may also want to skip between this chapter and the purity/ pollution section on rituals in the last chapter.) This chapter is intended to offer more than just a summary; it explores the way metaphorical understandings shape and sometimes distort theological meaning and ethical practices if they are literalized. At the end of each major historical section is a section on contemporary homiletical implications for reflection.

The next chapter explores the family resemblances within several contextual christologies. I have attempted to avoid the common problem of describing "the womanist understanding" or "the Asian approach to christology." Each contemporary option is represented by at least three women for the purpose of showing diversity within each perspective, as well as common concerns. As a white, middle-class, Protestant academic, I don't pretend to represent all of these positions from the "inside." I do firmly believe, however, that women are accountable to each other, at least to be familiar with and respectful of other positions. I have limited the contemporary options to Sophia christologies, womanist christologies, mujerista christologies, incarnational christologies, and Third World christologies. It would be fascinating to add a discussion of post-Christian and goddess perspectives, but such a direction would be more than just adding another section. The questions raised by Western forms of neopaganism and alternative (or indigenous) spiritualities are best reflected on as a dimension of interfaith dialogue in chapter 5.

Chapter 4 establishes guidelines for a contemporary woman's christology, using critiques from the contemporary options and combining them with traditional claims that should be incorporated. The center of this chapter is my development of a metaphorical christology of salvage, drawn from contemporary literature and explored with reference to traditional symbols of cross, resurrection, and incarnation. Within this discussion, I reclaim a primitive christus victor christology/soteriology, reconstrue Chalcedonian claims metaphorically, and attempt to reverse the purity/pollution oppositions with a theology of "dangerous contact." From this risky position, I construct a communal vocation of salvaging what the world has rejected, and we revisit the icon of the battered woman.

Chapter 5 develops an approach to community practices that derive from a theology of salvage. Ritual practices help congregations rehearse their contact with the world and should have some consistency with the world-oriented practices of justice that proclamation undergirds. Of particular interest to women studying christology are the world-oriented practices of interfaith dialogue and interaction. One of the major sections of this chapter is the discussion of purity/pollution patterns within traditional approaches to ritual behavior, and how those "clean" and "unclean" categories operate inclusively or exclusively. In keeping with the previous chapter, I develop sacramental and world-oriented understandings that require dangerous contact instead of avoiding it. Finally, I offer a public homiletic christology "confession" or "credo" that summarizes the constructive development throughout.

I do not know if the preaching ministry is in crisis or not. Nor do I know about the overall health of Christianity worldwide. I am fairly convinced that women in the parish need homiletical help for a problem they can feel but hardly articulate. For all women preachers who feel a strange ambivalence toward Jesus, this book is an attempt to pay attention to your lived experience and to take your misgivings seriously.

Chapter 1

The Christological Crisis
of Women Preachers

Problems arise however, once she is finally ordained and begins to work in the reality of the pastorate. For she is not a perfect stereotype either of the artificial feminine or of the sacrificial Jesus...The internalized stereotypes of the woman minister are shared by her congregation who often, quite unconsciously, project impossible expectations upon her. These projections are gender specific.[1]

Suddenly, everybody is talking about Jesus. The Jesus Seminar has produced a flurry of scholarship, weekly newsmagazines profile the major breakthroughs, and bookstores pack the shelves with the latest theories about the historical Jesus. In theology, new reflections on christology confront us with an embarrassment of riches. We have Asian christologies, African christologies, womanist, mujerista, sophia, and lesbian christologies.

Certainly all this attention to Jesus and to christology is good for the academy and good for the church. However, few of the writers have turned their attention toward the practical questions of the parish minister. How do these new theories and reflections affect the local pastor who must still preach, prepare for worship, and shape congregational ministry? More particularly, how do women pastors appropriate christological scholarship for resources that shape their understandings of weekly preaching, worship, and the mission of the church?

Since Rosemary Radford Ruether asked, "Can a male savior save women?" women theologians and pastors have recognized that our images of God-in-the-flesh can be a practical problem. Beyond the immediate questions of aiming hermeneutical suspicions at scripture, christology raises all kinds of other questions. The local pastor, and most particularly the female pastor, recognizes what many academic theologians seem to overlook. Once you begin to tinker with Jesus you can expect repercussions in all dimensions of ministry. The problem goes far beyond the inclusive language debates to our deepest theological claims. How do we understand the nature of the Trinity in our creeds and confessions? How do we understand the divinity or the humanity of Christ? How do we celebrate the eucharist if sacrificial models are corrupt? How do we shape congregations for ministry if suffering servanthood is no longer a viable paradigm for Christian vocation?

In many ways, all pastors and their earliest congregations go through a replay of what I'd call "seminary shock" or "dislocation." First-year students come into theological education with unformed and uncritical theological ideas, and the first semester or two of school is startling. The instructors use a completely different vocabulary from the confessional language of the parish. New divinity students are dislocated and disoriented by the language and the ways of thinking, and they frequently feel ignorant because they don't know the difference between existential and ontological. By the time students graduate, they have more or less weathered the crisis by learning the new language and styles of discourse. As new theologians they have learned to demythologize and to reflect on praxis; they are confident that the symbol of Jesus can point to "a proleptic vision of eschatological redemption." Surviving theological education has confirmed the necessity for the church to be transformed toward the future.

But survival has been costly. The new theologians have learned a new language, but they have forgotten the language of the church and their mentors in the faith. Most students leave seminary having more or less rejected the old confessional language and anachronistic metaphors of the tradition. Like hostages in real-life crisis situations, divinity students have become more and more sympathetic with their "captors." They have forgotten how dislocated they were at the beginning and have traded the mother tongue of the faith for the alien discourse of theology.

For many women pastors the tension is simply ignored, and theological integrity suffers. We may engage in a variety of practical schizophrenias. In one part of a Sunday service we preach a Jesus who liberates, and in another we celebrate a meal whose main character is a willing victim. Or we may systematically eradicate sacrificial metaphors from our liturgy and our sermons but can't seem to communicate with the lay folk who still want to sing "draw me near the Cross." We more or less recognize that the traditional language and images are at odds with our theological claims, but we can't find any common ground with our congregations. In some situations the sense of unease hovers around the edges of congregational life but never emerges with any real vigor. Pastor and parishioners silently negotiate a fragile truce. They make peace with their lack of communication and honor a conversational "don't ask, don't tell." Pastors gather in monthly clergy meetings and lament the theological anachronisms of their folk, while the lay members mutter over coffee, wondering why the minister can't just preach about Jesus.

Sometimes the situation is far more serious and borders on what Julie Hopkins has called a "christological crisis" among women clergy. This crisis begins with formal theological education and becomes even more intense and painful than the fragile truce. Women of all colors, social locations, and sexual orientations have been encouraged to challenge understandings of a suffering savior, blood sacrifice, and pie-in-the-sky second comings. They have been encouraged—in fact, trained—to "have trouble with Jesus." When new pastors shift from theological education to the parish, they start preaching this gospel of liberation to their congregations. Women pastors are especially subject to problems because they feel a compelling allegiance to various women's theologies. For all their commitment to contextualizing and community, women pastors begin putting their congregations through the same kind of theological hazing they endured. And congregations don't get it. They still think that ministers should be like Jesus; that is, the Jesus these wised-up women have left behind.

With regard to women pastors, the christological problem is compounded by cultural ideas of romantic femininity and the cult of ideal womanhood. Women preachers are asking for enough trouble just being in the pulpit, let alone trying to take Jesus away from the folk. These cultural prejudices against women in ministry make their bold and "bossy" claims of the revised Jesus particularly suspect. The combination of women's christology and the romantic notion of women as "Christlike" (with regard to passivity, nurturing, supportiveness, and self-sacrifice) conspires to form a particularly toxic local situation. Women ministers, all fired up and ready to change the world, are sabotaged by two dynamics: by their own confessional amnesia and by the bewildered resistance of congregations. Women ministers, with more at stake than their male counterparts, are the least able to break through the stereotypes to change the stereotypes.[2]

Hopkins is perhaps the only woman theologian to consider the christological nature of the women's crisis in parish ministry, but even she overlooks the compounding of the crisis that results from the problem of alien discourse. If we continue to think of the crisis in terms of language or forms of discourse, then the problem is more easily addressed. As theologically educated pastors, we have ways of thinking about the faith that congregations need. But we must speak their language to do it. We have to become bilingual. Imagine a denominational mission board preparing to send folks overseas, where folks speak a different language. The first thing the mission board does is to prepare its missionaries with a crash course in the indigenous language. We would be appalled at the thought of sending missionaries in to insist that the indigenous folks learn the missionaries' language. Yet that's frequently the consequence of liberal theological education. Inadvertantly, we strip folks of their mother tongue and never help them become interpreters, negotiating between the indigenous culture and new knowledge.

This interpretive rhythm is one of the primary issues in preaching. I am not recommending a conservative "good-old-days" mentality that insists on a nostaligic restoration of confessional faith language. Such a postliberal approach is theologically and ethically insufficient, since it maintains the status quo without critique. And it is also a problem because it doesn't engage congregations in any kind of critical discernment process with regard to their own practices and commitments.[3] I am, however, insisting that our preaching language must begin with a respect for the language that congregations find familiar. Most laypeople learn theology from preachers, and if we want to transform folks theologically, we will have to begin with the language and symbols they already know. Ada María Isasi-Díaz insists that theology be accessible to the everyday beliefs and practices of ordinary religious folk. "The challenge in this is always how to start with…everyday beliefs and religious practices, how to keep them up-front and center even as I use the language of the academy."[4] Isasi-Díaz refers to this commitment as being grounded in "lo cotidiano," the everyday life of believers.[5] Patricia Hill Collins makes a similar observation about academic scholarship in general, reminding us of the hubris and unknowing violence we perpetuate by silencing these ordinary discourses.

> I could not write a book about black women's ideas that the vast majority of African-American women would not read and understand. Theory of all types is often presented as being so abstract that it can be appreciated only by a select few. Though often highly satisfying to academics, this definition excludes those who do not speak the language of elites and thus reinforces social relations of domination.[6]

Elisabeth Schüssler Fiorenza claims that the familiar language of the Bible and of everyday faith contain possibilities for transformation that we frequently overlook. In fact, claims Schüssler Fiorenza, we should focus more attention on the transformative possibilities within our symbolic language than on attempts to abandon that language or displace it with another. We should not abandon traditional languages and metaphors, but transform them from the inside out.

The Community Context of Preaching

Let's imagine a Sunday morning service where the preacher, an ordained Episcopal woman, has just finished preaching a sermon based on the woman at Bethany who anoints Jesus with oily perfume. Our preacher, the Reverend Ms. Jones, has developed the homiletical strategy that the woman was a boundary violator, a courageous and uppity woman who wouldn't let anything come between her and an act of devotion. She is heroic in the sense that she will not be submissive. She refuses to be a victim of the social order, and Jesus commends her for her resistance. Reverend Jones is quite pleased with her ability to wrestle some liberation out of this text and to demonstrate to her flock that the scriptures, properly approached, support social transformation agendas.

Now Reverend Ms. Jones takes her place behind the eucharist table and begins the liturgy of the sacrament. As we eavesdrop on the service, we realize that everything she has just woven together in her sermon is about to come unraveled. Whether she is celebrating the older rite or the newer rite, she will liturgically reinscribe the virtues of willing sacrifice, obedience unto death, and the merits of vicarious suffering. In the eucharistic liturgy, Christ becomes a victim on our behalf. The Jesus who approved *resisting victimization in the sermon* is displaced by the Jesus who *embraces victimization in the liturgy*. Christ, our Passover, is sacrificed for us. As the bread is broken and the wine is poured, we join Jesus in presenting our own bodies, souls, and selves as living sacrifices to God. Without missing a beat, the Reverend Ms. Jones shifts from one christology to another and subverts her own proclamation.

Since proclamation and the sacraments occur within the same community, and within the same brief time frame, contradictions between the theological claims can frequently be jarring. Or, if their oppositions are not noticed by congregations, lay members internalize the contradictions as if they were not contradictory. Sociologists of religion call this process rationalization, where bits and pieces of information are integrated within some overarching conceptual scheme to provide meaning. Pieces that fit within overall patterns will simply be integrated, some pieces will be tacked on or adjusted until they fit, and other pieces will be rejected as strange. These negotiations happen both formally and informally as congregations come to some shared understanding of their beliefs and their commitments. Congregations are social communities of people who gather voluntarily to perform certain types of religious or moral activities. Sociological approaches can inform homiletic perspectives by illuminating the nature and function of moral communities, how they form and maintain themselves, and how they transform or negotiate new understandings. At a generic level, they are what sociologists call collectivities, groups of humans who function as communities engaged in moral activity and critique, which operate from a base of socially constructed symbolic meanings and narrative history. A moral community is a group of people who think about moral activities for the purpose of engaging in common projects. They have an identity that is based on some story or stories they tell themselves and certain symbolic figures or acts that inform their stories. Some secular moral communities we know about might include Greenpeace, Amnesty International, and the National Association for the Advancement of Colored People (N.A.A.C.P.). They meet the general criteria: using narrative histories and symbolic systems to engender moods and motivations, to change or support certain types of behavior, and to interface with other structures of society.

Religious moral communities are like generic moral communities, with a significant difference. The religious moral community refers to a relationship with a transcendent reality, or some reality that is taken to be greater than the sum of bio-social experience. This is what Clifford Geertz identifies as the cosmic or "general order of existence" category, or what Emil Dürkheim refers to as the supernatural realm. Religious moral communities are distinguished by their explicit identification of an ontological or transcendent authority for their symbolic systems and their consequent ordering of human life. Religious moral communities point to something outside of their communities and beyond their own bio-social experience to warrant or justify their symbolic systems of belief.

This warranting is always related to a tradition of narrative and symbol. Historic continuity with primary symbols and narratives is what we could call the center of a moral community. Sociologists of religion call this the "sacred canopy" or "symbolic universe." Even though such narratives and symbols may be continually reinterpreted, their presence and maintenance as symbols and narrative structures are critical to the identity of a religious moral community. Narratives, symbols, and symbolic activities (ritual or liturgy) have both durability and resiliency. Symbols, ritual acts, and narratives endure, and they provide the nucleus around which moral community is ordered and through which critique is possible.

This tradition-constituted nature of moral community is its primary and most identifiable core of strength.[7] Whether at the level of symbols, narratives, ritual, or moral discourse, the tradition-core of a moral community provides for continuity with both its predecessors and successors. Within the academic community of theological discussion, Alasdair MacIntyre, James Gustafson, Stanley Hauerwas, H. Richard Niebuhr, and others note this necessity for a moral community to be in narrative continuity and to share at least a common cluster of symbols that provide origin, identity, and trajectory for the community. Within the anthropological study of religion, Geertz suggests this narrative and symbolic core will be the dimension of the moral community that must either resist or transform to engage specific contextual situations. Although the biblical tradition of both testaments (Hebrew Bible and Greek scriptures) holds many common narrative and symbolic elements, Jews and Christians do not identify the same narratives and symbols as primary or constitutive: They are distinct moral communities with distinct identities.

The key symbols, activities, and narratives will provide a locus around which the moral community gathers and structures its life. As a center, the narratives and symbols will need to provide enough content to be distinct from other moral communities (Jesus and Moses are two such centers) but fluid enough to include a number of different interpretations of the key symbols and narratives. The crucifixion and resurrection of Jesus is an example of a symbol and narrative core that delimits Christianity from the Jewish or Muslim tradition but that allows for Baptists and Methodists and Catholics to understand themselves as part of the same moral community (even if their interpretations of the meaning of the symbol-narrative core are vastly different). In this way, utter relativism is checked (though a certain degree of relativism is countenanced), and the symbol and narrative system allows for differing moral visions to be mediated by reference to a common symbol-narrative core. To the extent that the members of a moral community can embrace the key symbolic and narrative core, there will be common ground for communication and moral discourse.

The narrative and symbol core must mediate not only among the members and have meaning relative to the ultimate referent (supernatural, transcendent, ontological). The moral community will engage its symbols and narrative as the level of ordering the moral activity of the members. This means that moral communities negotiate their corporate projects (whether you call this Christian ethics, church outreach, or political activity) with reference to their sacred canopy.

The tension contained within symbols between the ontological indicative and the existential imperative provides much of the discerning activity involved in internal and public moral discourse. A religious moral community must always be engaged in the activity of moral discourse, both for the purposes of defining and reinterpreting its own activity, and for the purpose of negotiating the meaning of its own narrative-symbol structure. Geertz's case studies demonstrate that this kind of moral discourse is ongoing where the religious tradition is vital. There is a level of engagement that involves the constant questioning of the tradition (a hermeneutic of suspicion) as well as a constant interpretation of that tradition within changing situations (a hermeneutic of trust). This dialectic activity of discernment is moral discourse that engages the symbols at the level of reference and at the level of their appropriated sense. As Geertz suggests, the understanding of this ongoing interstructured activity of meaning-making is fruitful for dialogue within the tradition and across traditions. MacIntyre sees this dialectic of tradition-constituted inquiry as the pattern that is most productive of internal integrity and public accountability.

Within contemporary American Christianity, two distortions of this dialectic operate. A more conservative and literalistic segment of American Christianity has been unable to engage the dialectic between its inherited meanings and the ongoing interpretation necessary. Plausibility structures have fallen apart. To some extent, this distortion is represented by the narrative theologians and narrative homileticians themselves. Strict narrative approaches that operate in isolation from public discourse and critique result from communities who engage a closed conversation between themselves and the tradition. As Ronald J. Allen puts it, this postliberal posture is circular.

> The chief virtue of postliberalism is its thoroughgoing Christian orientation. It warns the preacher against easily accomodating to prevailing worldviews. [But] the assumption that the Bible and Christian doctrine normatively name the world sometimes makes it difficult for postliberals to deal with texts (or doctrines or practices) that are theologically or morally problematic.[8]

A position that reduces theological reflection to a highly encoded private conversation risks not only irrelevancy, but also distortion, since it categorically eliminates accountability to public inquiry.

A more liberal and progressive segment of American Christianity has abandoned the symbolic forms (due perhaps to their lack of plausibility in contemporary culture) of its inherited tradition and has lost its ability to discern between the claims of the moral community and the secular community. This is at least one reason that narrative theologians like MacIntyre and Hauerwas call for a return to the narrative identity of the Christian faith; they see that the claims of a secularized postmodern humanism have become the prevailing assumptions by which Christian communities engage moral discernment. In its most extreme form, this is the deconstructive position that rejects all authority and acknowledges no universals. Deconstructive approaches provide the necessary hermeneutic of suspicion that helps preachers guard against idolatry, religious pride, and authoritarianism. This radical position encourages us to recognize the limits of all forms of human knowledge and to recognize our own interpretive biases. Deconstructive suspicion is essential to women's theological projects, but it does not substitute for a constructive theological vision. The suspicion of worldviews is not, in itself, a defensible position. MacIntyre reminds us that "there is no standing ground, no place for enquiry, no way to engage in the practices of advancing, evaluating, accepting, and rejecting reasoned argument apart from that which is provided by some particular tradition or another."[9]

Without this ongoing relationship between the traditional symbols and narratives and with the general culture at large, a moral community will lose its ability to make moral discernments based on a core of beliefs. The tension between a core of religious beliefs and the desire to include a broad spectrum is simply part of the reality of a moral community. The more definitive and rigid the core of beliefs, the smaller the community. The more undefined and flexible the core of beliefs, the more pluralism is encouraged, not only within the community but among other communities of enquiry. One of the advantages of symbol and narrative is that they allow a reasonable amount of flexibility with regard to interpretation, but they always demand that interpretation be done within the bounds of the symbols and narratives. A religious moral community, related to a tradition of symbols and narrative, gathers authority for its beliefs and activities with reference to an ultimate reality beyond mere bio-social life, understands this relationship with an ultimacy that indicates patterns (norms or principles) for engaging in moral activity, and engages itself actively in levels of public and internal moral discourse relative to its inherited tradition of symbols and narrative.

Preaching, at its best, reflects a community's conversation as it reinterprets the communal symbols and narratives relative to its own social location. Preaching is on-your-feet (or seat-of-the-pants) theologizing. Preaching engages the community's own symbols and narratives to suggest interpretations that disclose meaning. Preaching is the constant renegotiation of meaning within a particular tradition and its own context. Preaching is rhetorical theology, arguing for a highly contextualized understanding of God's presence and redemptive activity. Preaching names God's presence, and names it into a particular place and time. Preaching is both epistemic (revelatory) and invocational.

With regard to a worship context, preaching will also wager about the meaning of ritual life and how a liturgy is to be understood. Liturgical practices, like strict narrative approaches, can become closed systems of meaning. In part, that is the beauty of liturgical practices: They conserve and hold the primitive narratives and symbols for our regular engagement. In ritual, we act out or rehearse our beliefs, reinforcing our common understandings. But liturgy is subject to the same reduction of meaning that narrative approaches contain. Preaching must not simply reinscribe the narrative or the primitive meanings of liturgy. Preaching offers direction, teleological pointers, a breath of current spirit into the acted-out beliefs of the faith communty. Preaching is a rhetorical and theological commentary, a negotiation of what it means that we believe and act out certain shared values.

At the most precise level, it means that preaching happens within a group of peculiar people who operate within certain narratives and symbols and within certain ritual practices. Preaching is an activity that starts with the most basic symbols and narratives of a faith community and structures them toward production of meaning. This is what Ricoeur, along with Aristotle and Augustine, claims to be the productivity of imaginative discourse. Preachers offer a structure of reflection, suspicion, trust, and understanding that forms a community's shared way of knowing. We do, through preaching, structure a communally shared understanding of dynamic faith that is related to the tradition, to the daily life of decision making of believers, and to the ethical projects of the church.

Preaching as Theology

The particular practice we will explore is the theological practice of preaching. Most homileticians would agree that preaching is best done as a theological endeavor, yet few can articulate precisely how preaching is theological. Even to insist that preaching is a *practical* theology is ultimately not instructive. For some, preaching is theological in the sense that it is the pedagogical vehicle for conveying doctrine; preaching is theological by virtue of its content. For others, preaching is theological in the sense of interpreting biblical texts; it is theological by virtue of its interpretive approach to discerning religious meaning. For others, preaching is theological in the sense of applying certain theological positions or strategies to texts or doctrines. In this mode, preachers "apply" feminist or liberationist theological strategies to texts or claims. None of these approaches is what I mean when I claim that preaching is theological. All of these are derivative approaches that reduce preaching to the communication of an idea, doctrine, text, or position.[10]

Homiletic theology is a method of theological negotiation whereby the preacher "talks through" the possibilities of Christian faith for this particular community at this particular time. It is, as Lucy Atkinson Rose has it, a theological wager about truth. Preachers theologize in front of particular congregations, engaging in highly contextualized and tailor-made theological wagers. They do this theologizing out loud to a group of people.

Consequently, preaching has much more to do with sociology and rhetoric than with psychology and communication. The turn to sociology and rhetoric reflects a recent homiletic return to the hearers, asking how people will hear and understand what is at stake theologically. Sociology is more suited to homiletics than is psychology, for the simple reason that we are not working with individual thought but with the common thought processes of highly contextualized groups. Sociology studies group behavior and the means by which group behavior is shaped or changed. Rhetoric is the logical partner of sociological approaches, since it deals with structures of argument and persuasion for oral presentations to groups. Rhetoric is more suited to homiletics than communication theory, since it attends more to the audience's modes of hearing than to ways of packaging ideas for consumption. Homiletics is a rhetorical theology that pays high regard to the way groups are persuaded by oral presentation. Preaching is a rhetorical theological wager, structured to persuade a group of people in a particular social location. Preaching is much more than applied theology, biblical hermeneutics, or communication theory. Preaching is theological by virtue of its method, arguing for a particular vision of truth within a particular group of people, in order that that group will shape its common identity and projects around that particular vision of truth. Preaching invents a theological rhetorical strategy to construct what Walter Brueggemann calls an "alternative consciousness," a hermeneutical position through which to view the world.[11]

Preaching is like systematic theology in its endeavor to project a coherent mode of viewing the faith. Preaching is like constructive theology in that it builds a theological foundation from which communities can operate. Preaching is quite distinct from either systematics or constructive theology in its contextual messiness and its rhetorical setting. Homiletic theology must always take account of the "common ground" of the audience, addressing its oral presentation to real people located in a time and place. When divinity students ask their professors, "How will this preach?" they are usually not asking for theological clarification, but for rhetorical clarification. The homiletic question of "how" is the rhetorical question of particular audiences. Homiletic theology cannot bracket out folk religion, television evangelism, Charles Colson books, or the latest angel craze. Homiletic theology is constantly renegotiating its truth wagers in light of popular beliefs, symbols, narratives, and myths. Preachers make their theological wagers far from the academy, smack in the middle of folks who have lost jobs, beaten their wives, lost children, voted for Ross Perot or Ralph Nader, and lived much of their daily lives uninformed by religious questions. Homiletic theology turns toward the audience, and like all good rhetoric, it anticipates objections, suspects distortions, and crafts persuasion. The homiletic theologian must always ask what is at stake theologically, and by what theological and rhetorical method will I persuade this particular group that it's true?

Jesus/Christ as Symbolic Center

As a symbol, Jesus/Christ is related to other symbolic acts and understandings of the faith.[12] At the theoretical level, christology is related to other theories and articulations about the faith. Christology is organic in two noticeable ways. First, in any given period, christology is horizontally related to all other contemporary thought and practice.

Christological revisions will necessarily affect those understandings; there is an organic immediacy to christology. And second, christology is always in the process of reformulating itself with regard to previous christologies; there is an organic history and future to christology. Christologies work within communities like sacred canopies; they are both theoretical and practical in their implications. Within christological systems, clusters of symbols legitimate certain values and modes of activity, they suggest virtues and virtuous individuals. As a sacred canopy, christology functions as a gestalt to indicate ideal behaviors, personality, and commitments. Christologies are organic in the sense that they organize various dimensions of belief with various dimensions of corporate activity. They synthesize worldview with practice.

We want to develop an understanding of how certain paradigms and their symbolic clusters integrate preaching, sacraments, and mission in the practice of ministry. Symbols and metaphors and narratives are not "scientific" in the sense that their meanings are obvious or objectively certifiable. Sacred canopies contain necessary ambiguities. Sometimes they work to highlight redemptive possibilities, and at other times they mistakenly lean toward demonic ones. Typing these symbolic systems helps us in interpretation and makes connections between symbolic elements. Granted, typologies can be seductively simplistic, but beginning with some basic models allows us to recognize similarities and permutations.

For the preacher, this is not just an academic enterprise. I cannot emphasize strongly enough that these christologies and soteriologies persist in local congregations. The ordinary Christian congregation operates with a hodgepodge of christologies and soteriologies. Most lay Christians are familiar with the contours of Augustinian notions of carnality, even if they couldn't locate such beliefs within the tradition. Ordinary Christian believers use Anselmian atonement theories to justify what they know as redemptive suffering and "being like Jesus." Preachers and pastors sidestep familiarity with these classical doctrines at their own homiletical and rhetorical peril and to the detriment of the communities they serve. If proclamation is an act of rhetorical theology, we must attend to the common assumptions and mindsets of those we serve. It will help us in our reflections and reformulations to understand this organic history and ongoing organic nature of christology, how it has responded to practical issues in the past, and how those ongoing shifts highlight some theological concerns while masking others. It is not enough to simply jettison resurrection without understanding how it functioned in earlier periods. And while we may well decide to relegate Anselm to the trash heap of church history, we'll be in better shape to do so if we understand how his atonement theory was trying to come to grips with the philosophical questions of theodicy and suffering. Many women theologians are uncritically appropriating incarnational christologies, wisdom theologies, and logos christologies that reinscribe two dread culprits of earlier centuries: mind/body dualism and sexist essentialism. And as Elisabeth Schüssler Fiorenza claims, much contemporary "relational" christology reinscribes individualism and limits the socio-political horizon of Christian ethics.[13] There are additional problems in the implicit anti-Judaism of the "Jesus-as-feminist" approach that still lurks in much contemporary women's theology, and there are problems with an anthropological romanticism that reinscribes the dangerous concept of "innocence" into the rhetoric of suffering. Metaphors of purity and vicarious innocence have done untold violence to the "contaminated" women of earlier eras.

So we will begin by tracing some significant christological understandings and how they shifted to accommodate new concerns or to overcome emergent practical problems. We will try to be as organic as possible in sketching out the relationships between christological reflections and parish practices. Few women theologians attend to the practical implications (beyond liberation) of local congregational life and its relationship to concepts of Jesus. Trading in an old Jesus for a new one has benefits and problems. We can be more critical and more creative if we understand the trade-offs in christological formulations.

One of the first questions to address is the undeniable christocentric starting point for an approach to practical theology. In order to avoid problems of historicity and masculinity, many women theologians want to sidestep the Jesus question altogether and speak only of God. Carter Heyward has rejected this sidestepping, claiming that abstract, ahistorical God-talk (whether of Being or life-force or essential eros) has regularly failed to account for the real problems of real humans. Heyward cautions women, and particularly lesbians, to avoid the seduction of essentialist and ontological language. Such language is part and parcel of "the liberal God of self-consciousness, [and] human potential."[14] She claims that by trying to avoid the particular and the non-neutral Jesus we have, in fact, created God in the image of an objective humanist gentleman, who is fairly neutral about any particular situation. Heyward speaks boldly of Jesus as the one who acted out and acted up on behalf of very particular people.[15]

We will assume a practical strategy: Since Jesus/Christ is the particular symbol for Christianity, christology is a practical place to begin thinking about the practices of the church. Strictly speaking, christology involves theories about the person of Christ. As a formal enterprise, christology developed through the ecumenical councils of the early church and focused on the problem of the relationship between Jesus and God. Classical christology concentrated on the metaphysics of the divine-human relationship in Jesus, but the tendency was to emphasize divinity and eclipse humanity. Theories about the person of Jesus/Christ are reflected in a variety of titles: Son of God, Lamb of God, Messiah, Savior, the Anointed One, and others.

Christology also involves theories of salvation, or soteriology, to explain how the works of Jesus/Christ could be redemptive for humanity. We are familiar with several different interpretations of the relationship between God and humanity through the death and resurrection of Jesus/Christ. Soteriology or atonement theories interpret the method of God's reconciliation with the world. Soteriologies, like christological titles, come in several varieties, but most involve some notion of sacrifice or substitution. Most traditional soteriologies are concerned with the objective "accomplishment" of Jesus/Christ in the cross and resurrection.

While systematic theologians may distinguish the study of christology from the study of soteriology, the two are never quite as clearly separated in actual practice and thought. Theories about the person of Jesus and theories about what he accomplished in his death and resurrection are inextricably tied together. For practical purposes, we won't strictly distinguish christology from its soteriological twin, but will consider them as dimensions of the same concern for interpreting Jesus who is called the Christ.

Throughout the tradition, theological shifts and practical ministry have always had a symbiotic relationship, but perhaps not exactly in the way we imagine. While we may tend to think that christological edicts are handed down from the officials for implementation, the process has probably always been messier and more communal. Christological debates probably emerge from the practical issues of parish ministry. When pastors want to know whom they may or may not baptize, what is necessary for attendance at the table, or what action to take relative to social issues, they are usually asking questions that relate to christological understandings.

The practical aspects of parish ministry have always raised questions that demand theological reflection. The liberation theologians' definition of theology as reflection upon praxis is nothing new. The church has always been involved in the circular pulse of practice and reflection. If we think of our own common experiences of invention, we realize that we develop new interpretive approaches only after we discover an ongoing need for them. We have some practical situation that demands a philosophical tool, a standard, a paradigm, a rule. As the social constructionists suggest, we are most likely in a constant process of interpreting sacred canopies to account for our activities.

What we want to explore is how and why these theoretical approaches developed, what legitimate uses might be, and what inappropriate uses of the same strategies might look like. One common strategy among women theologians has been simply to toss out those approaches that have been poorly used, without making critical decisions about their possibilities. In fact, many of our theoretical constructs have been so distorted from their original use that we may not need to abandon them so much as reclaim their earlier usefulness. Annie Dillard reminds us that we cannot address questions of Christian meaning without using its own terms, "which are symbolic at every level: cup, manger, cross, or grace, incarnation, and sacrifice…You must either learn to use these terms and like them, or relinquish this field of knowledge altogether."[16]

For some women theologians and preachers, the focus on christology is an embarrassment. The particularity of Jesus and traditional claims about his historical and ontological uniqueness have been a hindrance to interfaith dialogue. Jesus-talk raises the divinity question in ways that have traditionally been associated with exclusive claims about revelation. Many of us, particularly those of us who are liberal Protestants, have been acutely embarrassed by Jesus-talk. We are afraid that our commitments to Jesus the Christ will be offensive and will function exclusively relative to our Jewish and Hindu and Buddhist friends. We avoid Jesus-talk altogether, hiding him under a bushel that we generically call "God." Now, to be sure, our Jesus-talk is fundamentally talk about God, but our Christian God-talk is informed primarily by Jesus.

The Contemporary Inheritance

Twentieth-century Christian women have inherited a Jesus/Christ produced by centuries of kyriarchal layers.[17] The ecclesial tradition was inflexibly male, and the natural order of creation elevating human males over females was fairly intact. One of the most pervasive problems was the spirit/body dualism that emerged with the early creeds. High christologies were so stubbornly dualistic that their inherent schizophrenia plagued the church at every major turn. The social world became part of the carnal fleshly existence that was to be denied and trivialized, and ultimately redeemed through violence.

Reformation and Enlightenment thinking turned toward the inner life of the individual as the locus of spirituality and the object of salvation. The spiritualizing impulse was reinforced by much Protestant piety and by the growing emphasis on the human individual. The Protestant tradition had successfully weakened the authority of the church, but at the cost of elevating the Bible to an authoritative status. Historical criticism and Enlightenment rationality combined to give added credibility to interpretive experts; the teachers and the learners were still separated. Humanism and rationalism helped weaken ecclesiastical authority, but at the expense of replacing the theological optimism in perfectibility with a "scientific" optimism in human progress and thought. As rationalism rejected supernaturalism and the miraculous, the "problem" of divinity was solved by imagining Jesus as the ideal rational or spiritual man. Where dualistic philosophy and incarnational theology had previously rendered women inadequate, now the Bible could be used to bar women from full participation in the church.

Annie Dillard writes that "the direction of recent history is toward desacralization, *the unhinging of materials from meaning*. The function of Western knowledge is to 'de-spookify.' Christianity and early science began this process; the ideals of the Protestant Reformation and the Counter-Reformation, coupled with Enlightenment ideals of progress, human capacity, and scientific rationalism carried it still further."[18] In the short run, the trend to demystify resulted in an attempt to make sense of the "message" or "essence" of Christianity, a methodological mind/body split of separating the kernel of the gospel from its husk. Schleiermacher's Jesus was not divine in the classical sense of the word, but he was historically unique in his highly developed "God-consciousness."

American Protestant revivalism was particularly suited to these shifts. Most of the attention went to soteriology, or salvation theology. Conversion focused on the inner experience, the contrite heart of the believer. Preaching and sacraments became identified with these inner changes. Proclamation followed the sin/salvation pattern of Lutheran law/gospel sermons. The split between baptism and confirmation became even more exaggerated, with eucharist typically reserved for those who were making either rational decisions to be baptized or making informed commitments in confirmation. "The individual, with his society changing all around him, with his private prayer and reasoned vote, was the new unit of meaning."[19]

Philosophical existentialism and the therapeutic theologies of this century updated personal salvation without any fundamental changes. From the Reformation to secular existentialism was but a single, natural step. Existentialism shifted from questions of sin and salvation to questions of estrangement and self-understanding without budging the category of person as the unit of meaning. Bultmann's Jesus and the resulting salvation was as demythologized and demystified as one could hope. Elaine Pagels claims that existentialism and psychotherapeutic models of Christianity are the new gnosticism: "...a philosophy of pessimism about the world combined with an attempt at self-transcendence."[20] Bultmann's "saved" individual knew himself authentically, and Tillich's believer had "the courage to be" since acceptance by God was no longer a question. The medieval and Reformation shift to soteriology was maintained through the whole modern period, whose primary theological question for this whole era seems to be "what is *my* salvation?"

The therapeutic pastoral counseling movement in the mid-1950s simply grafted psychology onto a paradigm that was already highly personalized. Thanks to the influence of Freud, social problems were interpreted fundamentally as problems with the psyche. The therapeutic movement made existentialism a practical pastoral concern of addressing the personal needs of believers. It was a rallying cry for preaching, for church growth, and for designing Christian education programs. "Meet the felt needs of your congregation!" In the mid-'50s, Harry Emerson Fosdick developed his "project" approach to preaching, which demanded that each sermon meet a particular therapeutic need. Preaching was reduced to pastoral counseling on a group scale. It's easy to see how this fits hand-in-glove with the contemporary marketing strategies of meeting congregational needs: "Find a market niche and fill it." As Robert Bellah has pointed out, this reverses the classic pattern of ecclesiology. The mainstream church in America turned in upon itself, concerned primarily about caring for the needs of its own constituents, to the neglect of the needs of the world.

By the second half of the twentieth century, much mainline American Protestantism had come to view Jesus as either personal therapist, mystical guru, or exemplary good guy. In some circles, the Jesus who slept on street corners and made Pilate nervous has been spiritualized almost to invisibility, to a wispy Jesus of inoffensive niceness. When we consider most of the cultural images of Jesus, we are struck by the gulf that separates our contemporary symbols from the prophetic Jesus of the early narratives. As the church engaged in active public relations, the offensive nature of the gospel was toned down, so that we inherited a "lowest common denominator" savior.

Interpretive Strategies

Jacquelyn Grant has offered typologies of contemporary white feminist approaches that enable her to critique arguments at their foundational assumptions.[21] Some women appeal to the authority of scripture, some to liberation theologies, some to historical reconstructions of Jesus. Women theologians need to pay close attention to how christological arguments are supported, not only for the purposes of argument, but for the purposes of finding common ground. Before we turn to a survey of contemporary concerns, we will explore the types of warranting or supporting strategies that usually operate at hidden levels. By making these strategies explicit, we are in a better position to interpret and negotiate theological claims.

Scriptural warrants back up an argument by an appeal to the Bible, granting authority to certain positions *because they are in the Bible*. If scripture is an ultimate authority, then we will have to deal with the household codes and all the other canonical oppressions. Most women theologians who claim to take the scripture authoritatively do so according to some criterion of theological selectivity. Scriptural warrants ultimately make theological assumptions about the special nature of the Bible. The scripture must be an authority for some theological reason. If a theological reason is necessary to back up a scriptural approach, then obviously a scriptural approach is not ultimately authoritative. The Bible is important for theological reasons, usually related to a doctrine of revelation or inspiration. Scripture cannot provide its own justification as an authority.

Historical warrants back up an argument by an appeal to a historically verifiable event or saying. Historical warrants usually appeal to what Jesus said or did, either by appealing to the Bible as a historical document or to a more scientific analysis of history and culture. We see a variety of historical approaches in traditional christologies and in more contemporary christologies. One type of historical warranting is behind the red-letter versions of the New Testament, which suggest that the Bible is a historically accurate document. In contemporary scholarship, the Jesus Seminar attempts to find the most authentic parts of the New Testament, replacing the red-letter approach with a variety of colors for differing levels of authenticity. Some feminist approaches construct a system of loose historical warranting: constructing a feminist or liberationist Jesus or an original egalitarian Christian community. All historical approaches identify some event or phenomenon that is paradigmatic because it is historically verifiable, and then they measure other claims against paradigmatic historical sayings or events. Contemporary approaches include the "Jesus-was-a-feminist" or "Jesus-was-a-liberator" claims, warranting interpretations by appeal to these historical "facts." Such approaches overlook the very real possibility that the real historical Jesus was a product of his time and culture: a first-century misogynist. Or it runs the risk of reinscribing sexist behaviors, since that's the way Jesus did it. When conflict arises between approaches, the burden is to demonstrate which "fact" is most historically accurate. But an even deeper problem is that a historical approach does not indicate why Jesus is a significant figure or why some events and sayings have the authoritative status in the first place. Why does Jesus have the status to serve as a warrant? Why would the egalitarian nature of the early community be authoritative? Historical warrants, especially those related to the acts and sayings of Jesus, make theological assumptions about the exemplary character or nature of Jesus. Jesus can serve as a historical warrant only insofar as we assume a theology of incarnation or divinity.

As good twentieth-century rational positivists, we feel most comfortable when we can demonstrate that our position is more authoritative. Even those who rely on biblical authority are appealing to a kind of coherence and consistency. Our passion for rationality seeks to eliminate the subjective at every turn and to posit some objective and disinterested standard. One assumption behind biblical approaches is that an appeal to inspired scripture eliminates human subjectivity. For many biblicists this is precisely what is at stake with using theological norms to interpret the Bible. Using a standard by which to authorize biblical claims seems ultimately subjective and "irrational."

Positivism also operates among those who practice historical-critical approaches or appeals to historical events and persons. History and historical methods provide objective authority structures that function as a court of final appeal. If we can establish the historicity of an event or person ("Jesus really was a feminist..."), then our interpretation is objective and beyond reproach. We realize what is at stake if we imagine historical proof that Jesus was a sexist or that the early church was not egalitarian. If an argument ultimately relies on faith in the history, then any historical contradictions will prove devastating. Within contemporary Jesus scholarship, the historical approach surfaces in the works of John Dominic Crossan and his academic opponents who attempt to establish exactly what kind of leader Jesus was. Crossan claims that Jesus really was a peculiar kind of revolutionary Jewish peasant Cynic, as opposed to a sort of Gnostic cynic disinterested in social problems.

Again, we need to heed the warning of Schüssler Fiorenza to avoid the inherent arrogance of historical approaches. Women theologians must question the implied authority behind "'scientific quests' for the Jesus of history...[and] challenge the notion the Christian identity must remain contingent upon scientific reconstructions of the historical Jesus as founding father, feminist hero, or divine man...".[22] Authority models, whether scriptural or historical, reproduce hierarchical or kyriarchal power structures. Schüssler Fiorenza claims that we should be more concerned with issues of plausibility than with issues of proof. Historical or biblical plausibility is appropriate as a second-level strategy for exploring how well an approach "makes sense" of, or is adequate to, scripture and history. Historical and scriptural plausibility are necessary, but not absolute, dimensions of constructive christological projects.

Theological warrants back up certain interpretations and positions not because they can be scripturally or historically proven, but because they are theologically consistent with certain foundational claims about Christian faith. Liberation feminists would usually consider themselves to be in this camp, claiming that liberation and justice are ultimate norms by which to evaluate the authority of particular interpretations and doctrines. Theological warrants will frequently find scriptural and even historical support, but they do not rely on either for backing. In the most radical sense, a theological norm may be supported by the other "authorities," but it cannot prove itself by appeal to a higher authority. It is precisely this lack of proof that makes a theological approach both frightening and uncomfortable for contemporary Christians, since we run the risk of making faith claims without the "proper" authority.

Both the scriptural and historical approaches are fairly recent, derived from the Protestant elevation of the Bible and nineteenth-century historical positivism and the evolution of historical-grammatical and historical-critical approaches to texts. Most contemporary women's christologies shift back and forth between historical and scriptural approaches to reinforce each other. We have little "historical" information about Jesus or the early church outside of scripture, so such a symbiosis is understandable. However, neither approach escapes the problem of absolutizing something that is historically relative. Since both scripture and the historical context of Jesus and the early church are products of first-century culture, elevating them to a status of ultimacy provides a dangerous precedent. Faith in scripture or faith in history may finally displace faith in the God whom we know in Christ.

Many theologians mask the ultimacy of their theological commitments when they call in history or the scripture to back them up. Most women theologians want to avoid the risky situation of claiming, like one early theologian, "Even if Jesus wasn't a feminist, I am." Liberation theologians would probably be committed to liberation even if the historical Jesus was not a peasant revolutionary. Women theologians would probably be committed to a gospel of egalitarianism even if the early church was not an emancipatory community. Third World theologians would probably be committed to the poor even if the historical Jesus was a middle-class businessman.

Interpretive Strategies and Homiletic Method

These implicit assumptions function in interpretive academic practices and are appropriated by women clergy. Within the parish, unexamined theological (ideological) assumptions operate in pastoral practices of preaching, worship, and pastoral care, and they usually masquerade as either scripturally or historically justified. Congregations learn to do theology (or not to do theology) not only by *what* is preached and taught and practiced, but also by *how* the preacher's homiletical strategy offers warranting techniques. Lay believers not only learn *theological concepts* from hearing sermons, but they also learn *theological method* from hearing sermons. Preachers who make frequent use of personal illustrations imply that personal experience is a valid norm by which to adjudicate theological claims. Preachers who spend homiletical breath in detailed historical-critical exposition tend to suggest that historical research can be trusted for theological claims. Preachers who proof-text and string together Bible verses and Bible stories to support their arguments are suggesting that the Bible is its own verification. Homileticians who sprinkle sermons with references to Freud and Jung suggest to their congregations that the goal of psychological health is the ultimate criterion for Christian living.

John McClure's work on *The Four Codes of Preaching* explores the way homiletic rhetorical strategies function to teach or reinforce congregational approaches to interpreting the Christian faith. Sermons do their work in particular ways, selecting what types of material will or will not support the claims they intend to make. Preaching is not just a matter of content, but also a matter of method. Preachers make decisions about how to put their homiletic arguments together, sometimes consciously, and sometimes without the benefit of rigorous reflection. Sermons, in their use of content and strategy, actually vouch for or sponsor different ways of seeing the world, different ways of interacting with biblical texts, and different ways of valuing the tradition. Sermons encode or reinscribe theological reflection and subsequently sponsor ethical method and activity. "When people enter sanctuaries and listen to sermons, they participate in the various verbal and nonverbal codes that constitute the preaching genre of communication."[23] McClure points out that preaching is a negotiation, not only among the preacher's own commitments and interpretations, but also in regard to the assumptions of the hearers. Each congregation has already developed expectations with regard to how a sermon should be rhetorically supported, and the preacher who is not able to negotiate between personal strategies and congregational strategies will fail to make homiletic claims persuasive. If a congregation has an established "biblical" code of rhetorical strategies (or theological method) and the preacher operates with a strong "cultural" code, there may not be a productive hearing of the sermon. Biblical congregations who hear about the latest psychological findings on homosexuality will simply not be open to persuasion.

Since we are interested in practical theology and the way congregations learn theology through preaching and worship, it may be particularly helpful to examine the implicit warranting strategies behind women's christologies. Even though women theologians frequently unmask the theological and ideological assumptions behind androcentric approaches, they continue to fall prey to the same warranting structures by attempting to demonstrate that either the Bible or certain historical approaches "prove" a particular Jesus. Preachers must ask themselves, What version of Jesus is being presented and how is that presentation of Jesus backed up? Will this way of "arguing" Jesus be accessible to my local congregation? How would I have to argue this vision of Jesus in a different rhetorical strategy if I wanted the congregation to approach understanding?

A significant problem exists at the level of homiletical rhetoric when preachers abandon scriptural or historical plausibility and those warranting strategies altogether. By plausibility I mean the ability to formulate a christological approach that appreciates the witness of scripture and the historical possibilities for such an approach. Plausibility should not be confused with authoritative proof for a particular christology, but provides a helpful approach when dealing with matters of practical theology. In order to preach a gospel conversant with the tradition that includes scripture, or to interpret sacramental theologies and liturgies, christologies must be plausibly related to the language and the symbols that congregations recognize. It would be both scripturally and historically implausible to construct a christology that denied the centrality of the cross or the self-understanding of the early church as a servant community, and it would be alienating to congregations.

However, since many women theologians and preachers do not want to rhetorically reinscribe either the Bible or the tradition as ultimately authoritative, we will also have to develop strategies that rhetorically sponsor theological thinking. This is one of the most significant areas of conversation and convergence for women who do theology, and this is what makes the study of homiletics a fruitful arena. Women theologians in the academy offer theological strategies that cannot simply be "applied" in the local congregation. Women preachers have to "invent" rhetorical strategies that will honor emerging theological insights and simultaneously render them "hearable" to their local congregations. Women preachers have to find common rhetorical and theological ground with academic theologians as well as with the lay theologians they encounter on a more regular basis.

In some cases, women preachers will have a different rhetorical problem. In some congregations, or in some groups within congregations, biblical and historical warranting strategies have lost their plausibility. Within many postmodern Christian communities, appeals to biblical or historical authority are suspect. Ronald J. Allen has outlined some of the characteristics of "folk postmodernism" so that preachers can address the contemporary context in ways that demonstrate the ongoing viability of the Bible and the tradition. In these situations, the preacher's task is not so much to weaken biblical plausibility as to reinvigorate it. Among the characteristics of folk postmodernism are an uneasiness with reigning authority models, ambivalence toward scientific method, questions about the limits of diversity, increasing (and sometimes romantic) respect for the past, respect for the natural world, and a bias toward strong visual images and oral-aural modes of communication.[24] Allen argues for what he calls a constructive and revisionary type of postmodern homiletic theology that seeks to be critical both of modernity and of the Christian tradition, while maintaining or recovering positive value from both. Allen calls for a homiletical approach that follows David Griffin's commitment "to salvage a positive meaning not only for the notions of the human self, historical meaning, and truth as correspondence, which were central to modernity, but also for premodern notions of a divine reality, cosmic meaning, and an enchanted nature."[25]

The perspective of this book is the constructive postmodern stance that honors the best of the tradition and its religious insights, while opening theological reflection to the diversity and possibilities of an ever-changing world. This homiletic approach to christology must be flexible enough to entertain emerging theological strategies and still familiar enough to employ biblical/historical strategies. My method is to negotiate between (1) theological appropriateness and moral plausibility as a first priority and (2) historical/scriptural plausibility as a necessary corollary. Theological norms include the claims that God is unconditionally compassionate toward all of creation and that God is unconditionally and passionately engaged in luring the world toward justice. As part of a theological approach, I would also require that our interpretations present moral claims that are at least minimally plausible and continuous with human notions of goodness. It would be morally implausible and inconsistent to claim that God destroys life while we also claim that humans should not destroy life. God's morality must be higher than human morality, not less than or paradoxical to. Historical/scriptural plausibility does not warrant theological claims unilaterally. Our theological claims must be appropriate to claims about God's nature and morality but must also be at least coherent within what historical research and scriptural studies suggest. As we turn first to general themes and concerns and later to specific proposals, these norms of appropriateness and plausibility will generate evaluations about the fruitfulness of contemporary projects for homiletics.

Common Themes and Concerns in Women's Christologies
Suffering

One of the most common themes in women's christological reflections is the problem of oppression and injustice suffered by women. In theological language, this is the problem of theodicy, or evil. Early white feminist theologians like Rosemary Ruether and Mary Daly were quick to point out that christologies promoting the morality of suffering were powerful weapons against women. They have since been joined by a chorus of other voices who make the connection between Jesus as victim and the justification of victimizing. Joanne Carlson Brown and Rebecca Parker put it bluntly by saying that "Women are acculturated to accept abuse. We come to believe that it is our place to suffer…We have been convinced that our suffering is justified."[26]

In every context for women's theology, there are particular histories of suffering and oppression, grand-scale dramas of wholesale systemic violence against women. We're familiar with the medieval witch craze, but there are other gruesome periods of history that involve the systematic oppression of women. Katie Cannon, Jacquelyn Grant, and Delores Williams have chronicled the abuse and oppression of African American women during the centuries of institutionalized slavery in the United States and the legacy of oppression justified, in part, by Christian notions of suffering servanthood.[27] As ecumenical and interfaith groups expand to include women, there is a growing awareness of the extent to which women are marginalized everywhere.[28] Christian women in all countries join their Christian and non-Christian sisters in denouncing all forms of social, political, and economic oppression.

THE ICON OF THE BATTERED WOMAN

It may be most helpful to get at some of the pertinent issues by looking at an "ordinary" example of victimization: domestic abuse. Most local parish pastors are all too familiar with the emotional and theological terrain around incidents of domestic abuse. One battered woman coming into the pastor's study on Monday morning is sufficient to challenge all christological assumptions. The battered woman has probably internalized both the socially approved image of cultural femininity and the religiously approved image of suffering servanthood.

She has come to the pastor to find out if she should take a stand against her abuser, or if she should turn the other cheek. In some ways, her question goes even beyond the marital-role question of wifely submission and into the territory of how to be Christlike. She is not necessarily asking how to be a good wife as much as she is asking how to be a good Christian. At the heart of her dilemma is the methodological difference between Martin Luther King, Jr., and Malcolm X. Should her orientation toward her abuser be one of nonviolence (the means include the ends) or self-defense (by any means necessary)?

Now, the pastor must be careful here. At first glance we are tempted to insist on the self-defense route and encourage the woman to resist her batterer. We assure her that Jesus was a liberator and a feminist, a friend of the weak who would not tolerate abuse and violence. Since we don't want to be misunderstood to suggest that Jesus was a fighter (most women theologians reject military metaphors), we stress that Jesus was for love and harmony. However, this argument drifts dangerously close to Jesus-as-pacifist, which is exactly the position that encourages turning the other cheek.

At some point in the discussion the whole question of the cross is bound to come up. If Jesus demonstrated his radical love by dying for those who persecuted him, shouldn't a loving wife demonstrate her unconditional love for her mate by suffering at his hands? "The central image of Christ on the cross as the savior of the world communicates the message that suffering is redemptive. If the best person who ever lived gave his life for others, then, to be of value we should likewise sacrifice ourselves...Our suffering for others will save the world."[29] Without knowing it, the woman pastor and the battered woman are caught between two theories of atonement, between Anselm and a hard place. Anselm's approach was to encourage suffering as an imitation of Christ and a spiritual discipline with benefits to the believer. Luther considered Christ's suffering both redemptive and sufficient and claimed that our suffering could not reap any personal spiritual rewards. However, both Anselm and Luther leave open the possibility that our own suffering might be of service to others even if we don't get points for it. In other words, Anselm allows that personal suffering is good for the soul. Luther allows that personal suffering is good service offered to others. "Our suffering for others will save the world." And both Luther and Calvin made the disastrous turn toward the penal theory suggesting that suffering (either our own or Jesus') was justly deserved punishment. Calvin also encouraged suffering as an imitation of Christ.

Not surprisingly, many women theologians trace women's complicity in their own abuse to Anselm.[30] Brown and Parker claim that in spite of decades of theology from the underside with alternative interpretations of suffering, "this Christian theology with atonement at the center still encourages martyrdom and victimization."[31] Rita Nakashima Brock asserts that atonement theories symbolically reinforce not only domestic violence against an adult partner, but also against children. "The patriarchal father-god fosters dependence and, in his latent, punitive aspects, haunts many atonement doctrines...[t]he punishment of one perfect child has to occur before the father can forgive the rest of his children and love them."[32] And Delores Williams adds her womanist critique when she writes, "It is therefore fitting and proper for black women to ask whether the image of a surrogate-God has salvific power for black women or whether this image supports and reinforces the exploitation that has accompanied their experience with surrogacy."[33]

Clearly, Jesus as a substitute for us or as a moral exemplar who reinforces individual suffering will be insufficient to reply meaningfully to the battered woman. As we survey the contributions of several women theologians, we must keep this icon of the battered woman in view. She is a microcosm of the bigger picture of oppression that women's christologies seek to address. As African theologian Mercy Amba Oduyoye reminds us, for the gospel to be good news, it must be good news to those who are powerless and victimized.[34] It is definitely not good news when women sacrifice willingly or unwillingly to keep things the way they are.

Being in Relationship: Community

Another common theme for women theologians is the interdependence that characterizes human community. Many theologians recognize that the modern legacy of radical individualism can work against common projects and commitment to the common good. Relational approaches involve valuing the character and quality of social relationships based on mutuality. For some women theologians, this theme takes its model from the biblical image of Jesus as the community builder and obstacle breaker. For others, claims of relationality are grounded in understandings of the relational nature of the Trinity. For some, community and relationship derive from basileia values of kinship and ideal human community.

Schüssler Fiorenza is probably correct to characterize relational christologies as the most "canonical" among feminist theologians. She points to the necessary correction this alternative provides to "heroic" and "individualistic" christologies. For a number of women theologians, this shift toward the relational is a way of reclaiming the feminine dimension of theology that was eclipsed by overly masculinized approaches. Seen as either complementary characteristics or as more thoroughly holistic, relational christologies reclaim "feminine" values of support, mutuality, and friendship.

Relationality and community sometimes go beyond abstract concepts of interpersonal connections to include particular and concrete ethical situations. However, the metaphors are strained as they begin to deal with activities of justice and reconciliation. Although the intention of women theologians is clearly to use these concepts as tools for action, they are somewhat romantic and vague nouns. Relationship means to relate but doesn't necessarily indicate the content or character of that relationship. Abusive situations are, after all, relational. Schüssler Fiorenza cautions that the discourse of relationality usually operates implicitly from one of two models: either as a type of romantic love (whether opposite or same sex) or as a type of female bonding/nurturing.[35]

Her critique of relational understandings is similar to Patrick Keifert's identification of the ideology of intimacy, which operates as a strategy for turning strangers/enemies into friends. The ideology of intimacy personalizes and privatizes public social relationships that have little to do with feeling, tone, and affect. Intimacy, mutuality, and support all relate to ideas of building and maintaining a protective community within which the members are safe. Relational models trace some of their origins to the human potential movement of the 1970s and 1980s, which assume that "the purpose of human life is the fullest development of one's individual personality, which can take place only within such intimate relationships."[36] In an effort to reclaim feminine traits and strengthen theologies, many women have, in fact, projected private, familial images onto its public character. Frequently this type of relational community is indistinguishable from a support group with activities of story sharing and personal interaction. Jesus is acceptable to the extent that he embodies feminine characteristics. We have already noted that reinscribing gender dualisms or oppositions is dangerous business. As soon as we speak of "feminine" characteristics, we reinforce all the romanticism of the ladylike Jesus.

Not surprisingly, relational models of an idealized supportive community do not function well against a radical social or political horizon. Although relationship language is clearly meant to undergird interhuman respect, it typically functions to reduce conflict and to narrow horizons to those of immediate intimacy. Relational models are "nice" and reinscribe the romantic image of "ladylike" behavior at the heart of the christological crisis discussed previously. This pietistic feminization of Jesus and the church (along the lines of cultural stereotypes) limits women clergy and undermines radical political activity. It softens the prophetic edge of ministry. Jacquelyn Grant has rejected this "sweet" and "bourgeois" Jesus who reinforces costly reconciliation without suffering, claiming that a "relational" Jesus helps middle-class Christians maintain their privileged positions in church and society and leave the complaining and groaning disenfranchised out of the family.[37] Relational approaches imply a "make-nice" policy of "Can't we all just get along?" that run the risk of reducing social justice to group therapy.

Relational approches may actually oppress women more than we realize. Women already bear a disproportional burden for care and nurture. The average adult woman may have full-time professional responsibilities, full-time partnership demands, full-time parenting expectations and additional responsibilities for aging parents. These are the same women who provide most of the financing and workforce for the church. Christine Smith points out the double-bind of relationality:

> There is a myth that working women are less involved in family life today and less committed to the relational fabric of society... [The truth is] that most informal care is given by women ...We obviously live in an era when adult women are still raising children by the time their parents have become older adults. This reality makes for an incredibly complex set of familial responsibilities for women.[38]

An approach that reinforces traditional burdens of women along lines of cultural stereotypes may not serve the ultimate goals of relational approaches. Relational approaches are grounded in a critique of historical forms of relationship, particularly patriarchal and hierarchical structures of relationships. The differentiation of roles and the inequality of power that such structures presume frequently result in distorted patterns of relationship. Sometimes the relational critique focuses on types of dualism to demonstrate the inherent problems with oppositions and otherness. Relational approaches frequently reject value distinctions that subordinate one to another, arguing instead for mutual friendship, enlightened familial structures, or partnership models. If poor human relationships have been justified by hierarchical models of the divine relationship to the world, many women theologians hope to offer models of healthy human relationships as theological paradigms.

Embodiment and Experience

Closely related to relational models are embodiment theologies, somewhat more specifically related to real lived experience and embodied existence. Embodiment as a theme for women theologians is a critique of the mind/body dualism we note throughout the tradition and offers a corrective that allows women to reclaim positive value for all bodies and their natural processes. Women's approaches to embodiment begin with the assumptions that our experience is embodied and concretely real. Embodiment as a criterion for theology attempts to avoid reductionistic abstractions and to focus attention on actual experiences and events. Christine Smith suggests affirming embodiment as a non-gendered incarnation in which "God is revealed in each of us, regardless of gender, ethnicity, age, or physical condition."[39] To the extent that we associate incarnation with Jesus, he can't be an example of special incarnation, but simply a Christian metaphor of the general incarnation of God in all of creation.

Embodiment theologies are also frequently connected to ecofeminism, using the biblical image of a good creation to discuss the caring stewardship of the earth and its resources and to critique the hierarchies of the natural order theologians. By highlighting embodiment as a part of relationship, many women theologians intend to reduce the "otherness" of nonhuman life to allow for partnership with nature. Sallie McFague claims that embodiment is what we have in common with everything else on the planet and provides a web of relationship with our environment. "[B]odies are important (they are the main attraction) and we ought to honor and love them, our own and others; the body model gives us both an ecological and a justice context for theology, for it involves a planetary perspective while focusing on the most basic needs of human beings…a way of seeing our proper place as inspirited bodies within the larger body…"[40]

Embodiment is closely related to incarnational approaches that emphasize God's ongoing emergence within life. Women theologians interpret incarnation nondualistically (as McFague's language of inspirited bodies demonstrates). Spirit is not an abstract ingredient "added" to bodies. Rather, God's activity in the world is always in some particular experience or event. "Disembodied" spirit would be an oxymoron. Such an approach allows for bodied experience to be valuable precisely as concrete experience and not in spite of its enfleshment. Embodiment approaches value flesh and the material world as loci of ongoing revelation, reclaiming positive value for sexuality and sensuality. Lesbian theologians have found embodiment approaches particularly liberating, since they focus on the value of loving not only our own body-selves, but other body-selves. Embodiment and relationality together reinforce concrete relationships in ways that intend to blunt both dualism and natural order paradigms.

Probably the most daunting problem for women theologians who operate within relational approaches is that they do not always include norms for discerning what might be "right" or "appropriate" relationships. Certainly, notions of respect and justice are implied, but they are not always articulated as categories of discernment. To say that God is incarnated in all relationships and all bodies does not say anything definitive about how Godly relations might differ from un-Godly relations. Are all relationships and all bodies representative of God's life-enhancing purposes? Or do some types of relationship and incarnation reveal divine activity more than others? Without dismissing the essential value of all life, by what criteria can we be able to discuss quality of life as such discussions emerge in questions of capital punishment, physician-assisted suicide, or reproductive choice? Without dismissing the potential for divine revelation within ordinary human relationships, how can we evaluate some relationships as more life-affirming than others?

Contrary to their purposes, embodiment and relational models frequently reinscribe dualism by glorifying the inspired body and its activities, rather than appreciating the ambiguity of revelatory possibilities. Particularly within American cultural contexts, we would want to be cautious of any uncritical approach that would reinforce our preoccupations with youth and physical beauty or valorize human intimacy over social justice. The notions of dysfunction, tragedy, and evil that characterize the human condition always assume some contrast between what is and what should be and a recognition of the limits of embodied existence.[41] Incarnation may contain ongoing potential for manifesting evil and allowing corruption to emerge. Can we claim the positive value of embodied existence without overlooking the possibilities for real wickedness? Surely the ever-present possibility of corruption was what led Augustine to discuss something like original sin as a fundamental part of the human condition. One of the critical challenges for embodiment theologies is to discuss embodiment in ways that account for evil without repeating the whole entrenched classical tradition based on dualistic incarnational language.

Another challenge is to relate embodiment to christology in a way that is plausible to historical understandings (embodiment in the gospels and the early church) and to include embodiment as an incarnational theology that does not eclipse the categories of crucifixion and resurrection. Is it possible to interpret christology through embodiment categories that do not reduce the eschatological dimension to the immediate existential present? Is there some paradigm of interhuman existence that lures us *from* the future *toward* the future? Is there value both in our embodied existence and beyond it? Or are we limited to celebrating our immediate fleshly existence that we cannot keep? More pointedly, does incarnational theology ignore death, accept death, or rage against it? Or, if death is a natural part of embodiment, by what processes of discernment do we call the murder of a child "tragic" and the gentle death of an octogenarian "blessed"? If life is full of ambiguity, so is death. Contemporary incarnational and embodiment approaches are not uniformly helpful in negotiating real human ambiguity as it emerges in suffering and death.[42]

Perhaps the greatest challenge for embodiment/incarnational approaches is how they relate to the sacramental activity of the typical congregation. Certainly we can preach an embodiment cosmology and ethic and anthropology, and to do so with an eye toward the real experiences of suffering. But how do these images relate to baptism into a group of peculiar people? Baptism by whatever method and in whatever tradition almost always includes notions of a voluntary "dying and rising." Women theologians are challenged to interpret baptism's voluntary rejection of "old life" and the embrace of "new life" in ways that still affirm both the inherent goodness and the inherent possibilities for corruption. And they must do so without valorizing masochistic self-destruction.

On a similar note, if we preach and lead within average congregations, we must find ways to make sense of the whole enacted symbolism of the eucharist with its broken body and poured-out blood. We will have to discover ways of encouraging the church to be willing to offer itself to the world without encouraging individual women to mindless self-victimization. We preach within congregations whose most familiar and cherished symbols provide a common language within which we must negotiate new meanings. Part of the task for women preacher-theologians is not so much to reject symbols as it is to expand narratives and symbols beyond the straitjacket of the tradition's blunders.

Our survey of christological blunders of the tradition will attempt to walk this narrow line between wholesale rejection and blind acceptance. The theological work of the preacher is always engaged in critical appraisal. We do not just apply the doctrines or constructive theologies of others, no matter who they are or how much we appreciate their work. It is critical for women theologians and preachers to evaluate approaches based not only on their theological integrity, but on their rhetorical fit within groups of "folk postmodernists." Our hermeneutic of suspicion must extend to women's christologies as well. We cannot simply read Sophia christologies and "apply" them to all texts and situations. For that reason, my survey of women's christologies will be subject to the same questions we usually bring to the christological doctrines of the tradition. I will explore each formulation, asking questions about the nature of human sinfulness, the nature and meaning of salvation, the value of bodies, the justification of power and knowledge.

This project is concerned primarily with the particular problems that women have with the tradition and with the particular problems the tradition has had with women. The antagonism between women and the Christian tradition has been long and bloody; I do not intend to apologize for it. However, I want to avoid the posture of a growing number of women theologians who assume that the conflict is a win/lose proposition. While I want to focus on the problems of women and theology for preaching, I hope to avoid a posture that elevates gender concerns to ultimacy. While gender concerns relative to christology and preaching are existentially pertinent to women preachers and their congregations, the real issue is to engage in critical theological reflection on christologies as they inform the life and ministry of the church as a whole. The biggest problem for Christianity is not gender, but the frailty of the faith itself.

> The truth of the matter is that for the Christian, an integral part of the problem, perhaps the most problematic part, is— Christianity itself! As it has displayed itself in the New World, Christianity is the greatest barrier to its becoming a redemptive force.[43]

My greatest hope for this book is not that we will find the gospel friendly to women, or find women that are friendly to the gospel. My hope is, rather, that we will rediscover the radicality of the gospel for the church's preaching ministry.

Chapter 2

Christological Blunders of the Tradition

This is not to suggest that doctrinal development is a triumphant march of progress along a straight line from truth to truth. The historical record shows otherwise, indicating detours, U-turns, and plain forgetfulness...[1]

Theological Relativity

Our thinking about God, Christ, and the church is always in a state of change. We are sometimes tempted to insist that there is an essential Christianity that can be discerned through demythologizing strategies. We may argue that only the form of Christianity changes. Different generations may change terminology, but, we assume, the meaning of faith claims remains constant through the ages. However, it's closer to the truth to admit that faith claims, theological meanings, and the content of doctrines actually change over the course of time. Theology is not absolute, eternal, or given.

Women theologians and preachers need to keep in mind the relativity of theology, and particularly of christology, for at least two reasons. As we critique the tradition and its figures, it's helpful to remember that our predecessors were attempting to address real theological problems within real historical situations. We may decide that their achievements were flawed, problematic, or even dubious. But we should never lose sight of the fact that they were attempting to critically engage their own theological heritage to solve particular problems. It's not uncommon for feminist theologians to indict the tradition for sexism as if oppression were planned. While I would not deny the pervasive impact of sin upon theological speculation, I would hesitate to claim that misogyny has ever been a motivating factor. Recognizing the relativity of theological reflection allows us to be both critical and charitable. While pinpointing serious problems of the church fathers, we can also assume a certain goodwill toward their theological projects.

In addition to exercising retrospective charity, women theologians need to remember that they are subject to the same critical evaluations. Since all theology is relative and contextual, it is shaped by the language, concerns, motivations, and problems of particular times. Women theologians are no less context-bound than male theologians and are equally subject to error, blindness, pride, and sheer insensitivity. As one writer puts it, "even the best Christian minds can go wonky now and then."[2] Women's theologies are also provisional and subject to the same critical evaluation by other scholars, no matter what their gender, ethnicity, sexual orientation, or nationality. Invoking the "rule of experience" as a way of excluding critical discourse is ultimately a power strategy and has no place in women's studies. My own reliance on women scholars is a matter of academic focus, not privilege. I will neither exclude nor privilege majority viewpoints, but neither will I privilege women's theologies simply because they are gendered.

With these caveats in mind, the following discussion will consider some of the major blunders of the tradition. The discussion will be necessarily incomplete but will try to explore watershed figures and doctrines that have serious impact on christological thought. Some of the theories are not strictly christological or soteriological but have served to undergird and reinscribe christological blunders, sometimes invisibly. These few figures and theories must be considered in any women's constructive or revisionary approach to christology. This brief catalogue does not imply that any of the figures or their doctrines were simplistic, naïve, or fundamentally corrupt. Each doctrine or approach attempted to solve a theological problem while simultaneously creating one. This discussion will indicate problems as well as strengths, particularly as they relate to the themes and concerns of women preachers and theologians. We will focus sustained attention on mind/body or spirit/body dualism, the development of kyriarchal rationales, theologies of suffering, designations of purity and pollution, and goals for human community.

Ascending and Descending Christologies

One of the most helpful approaches for exploring christologies is a twofold typology popularized by Latin American theologian Jon Sobrino. Sobrino distinguishes between ascending and descending christologies, relative to the theoretical starting point of reflection.[3] *Ascending christologies, or christologies-from-below*, begin with the actual history of Jesus and reflect on his activities. This approach does not start with a doctrine of God and transfer it to Jesus, but works inductively from Jesus back to God. The total gestalt of Jesus' life (including teachings, parabolic acts, crucifixion, and resurrection) functions to disclose claims about God and the divine purposes.[4] The activities of Jesus among human beings become revelatory windows disclosing God. John's gospel, for all its high christology, also claims that "He who has seen me has seen the Father," suggesting that we know God through Jesus. In christology-from-below, the compassionate acts of Jesus qualified him for the "sonship" role. He acted like a son of God when he preached and enacted the reign of God. *Christologies-from-below focus attention on the relationship between Jesus and other human beings.* The foundations for christologies-from-below are the vocation and practices of Jesus/Christ. C. S. Song has characterized christology-from-below as a "people hermeneutic," an interpretive approach that serves homiletic theology admirably:

> Jesus the messiah is not made in one day. Jesus the Christ is not called into being out of the blue. Jesus comes into his own as the savior and as the Christ as he becomes more and more deeply absorbed in the impacts that men, women, and children, troubled in body and spirit, make on him.[5]

The primary symbols of christology-from-below are resurrection and the reign of God.[6] This type assumes that the crucified one reveals a compassionate God who risks death in solidarity with the brokenhearted. The risen Christ is the same as the crucified One. Resurrection signals the beginning of the new creation: a disclosure of the never-ending divine passion for a just world. This pattern of christology is fairly common to the synoptic gospels' focus on the passion story and the reign of God. And, unlike the later incarnational types, christology-from-below has strong symbolic associations with the shalom of the messianic age in the Hebrew scriptures.

Descending christologies, or *christologies-from-above,* originate from doctrinal or dogmatic claims that Jesus is the Son of God, the incarnation of divinity into human flesh. If the christologies-from-below are based on history to provide clues to God's nature, christologies-from-above are based on doxological claims that Jesus is affiliated with God prior to those historical events. The affiliation with God endows the historical acts with value. *Christologies-from-above are primarily concerned with the nature of the relationship between Jesus and God;* their starting point is the person of Jesus/Christ.

The primary symbol of christology-from-above is incarnation. Sobrino points out that in this model, "the eternal Son becomes a human nature."[7] This model claims that Jesus' acts and history are revelatory since he is, a priori, the Son of God. Christology-from-above is what we know as the classic or orthodox model. Sobrino claims that the greatest disadvantage of this model is the eclipse of the actual history of Jesus' acts and basileia theology.[8] Without the specifics of his ministry and his understandings about the basileia, the content of Jesus' character is relatively empty. Precisely what is divine about Jesus is not his ministry, but his miraculous birth, and his perfection. The actions of Jesus were not constitutive of his title, but were manifestations of it. His status as son conferred status on his ministry, life, death, and resurrection.

Christology-from-Below: Basileia and Christus Victor

The New Testament writers offer a variety of christological under-standings and titles.[9] Attempting to type christologies by titles is too reductionistic for the fluid categories these titles represent in the gospels and the epistles; the trend in New Testament scholarship is to explore clusters of meanings, overlaps, and shared characteristics. The gospel of John uses a variety of titles almost simultaneously, even though we tend to think of them as discrete categories. New Testament writers used the available categories, layering or pairing them to highlight particular theological claims.

In general, the model of christology-from-below, with its focus on passion, resurrection, and the reign-of-God teachings, dominated the earliest proclamations and the gospels. All four gospels center on a Jesus of compassion who heralds the basileia and dies in the process of his ministry. There are references in Matthew and Luke to a miraculous birth, but there is little development of an incarnational theology in either. Charles Talbert has argued that even in the Johannine gospel, incarnational thinking is associated with Jesus' ministry and not with his birth. Talbert's own reading of John is that the Word became flesh and dwelt among us *at the baptism* that inaugurated Jesus' ministry, and not at the birth of Jesus in the manger.[10] Even though the church councils later considered this "adoptionist" christology heretical, it was not problematic for the gospel writers. John's incarnation is directly related to a particular kind of salvific ministry and to the "incarnation" of God in the particular saving practices of Jesus, and not to the events of birth. Talbert suggests that the Johannine claims of a preexistent Logos have been read through the Matthean and Lucan stories to produce a tradition of incarnational christology originating in the birth of a baby.

Christology-from-below was well-suited to streams of messianic Judaism, which envisioned a prophetic-messianic figure proclaiming God's reign. The christological significance of Jesus' teachings about the rule of God was to associate Jesus with this anticipated messianic figure. Did Jesus see himself assuming the role of such a messianic prophet?[11] According to Marinus de Jonge and Jack Kingsbury, the preaching of Jesus and his self-identification as the suffering servant and Son of man were recognizable clues to his understanding of his mission.[12] Jesus fulfilled a prophetic-messianic role by calling people toward the reign of God. He shouldered the ministerial vocation of John the Baptist and could reasonably expect to die a martyr's death, which was also part of the prophetic-messianic role. Reginald Fuller has called

Jesus' own sayings about the Kingdom and his own prophetic/martyr/
messianic role in heralding the reign of God the most primitive
christology of all.[13]

> Jesus understood his mission in terms of eschatological proph-
> ecy and was confident of its vindication by the Son of man at
> the End. As eschatological prophet he was not merely announc-
> ing the future coming of salvation and judgment, but actually
> initiating it in his words and works. It is the unexpressed, im-
> plicit figure of the eschatological prophet which gives unity to
> all of Jesus' historical activity...[14]

Fuller argues that the proclamation, the teaching ministry, the
healings and exorcisms, the table fellowship, and finally the events of
Holy Week are held together as a meaningful whole only with respect to
Jesus' own self-understanding. "Take the implied self-understanding of
his role in terms of the eschatological prophet away, and the whole ministry falls into a series of unrelated, if not meaningless, fragments."[15]

Gerhard von Rad has argued that the prophetic messianic figure of
Isaiah offers strong clues to the self-understanding of Jesus and of the
early church about his vocation. Messianic work is the work of Yahweh,
and any figure who participates in those works or practices (reconciliation, establishment of justice, the reign of peace) is appropriately to be
called a Son of God, the Messiah, the Liberator, or the Anointed One.
The Anointed One is not equal to Yahweh, nor does he possess any supernatural qualities. Rather, the anointed one fulfills an office, govern-
ing and engaging in certain practices on behalf of Yahweh, but remaining
responsible to the higher authority. "When the anointed one is invested
with powers to govern in God's stead, he has also the customary throne-
names conferred upon him."[16] Since Jesus and the gospel writers make
frequent use of Isaian prophecies and images, it's not unreasonable to
attribute such theological understandings to the early followers of Jesus.[17]
The royal theology of the Psalms becomes prophetic under Isaiah, who
points to this historic period as the time for God to inaugurate the awaited
reign. The identity of the anointed one is unclear precisely because
Isaiah's hearers were breathlessly awaiting a candidate who would assume the messianic role and lead Israel into a new way of life.[18] "We
need to view Isaiah in the context of a trajectory of messianic thought
concerned with the role in the reign of God of the figure who is called
king, seed of David, servant of God, messiah, son of God."[19] The psalmic
expectations of monarchy and absolute imperial power are transformed
by Isaiah into a messianic expectation of a prince of peace, a steward of
the reign of God.

The Son of Man sayings are attributed peculiarly to Jesus.[20] Only in
Acts do we find secondary references to the Son of Man sayings.[21] Within
Palestinian Jewish apocalyptic, the Son of Man was the title of an

eschatological redeemer and not necessarily one who shared divinity with God. Scholars argue that the early church dissolved these Son of Man sayings into their emerging apocalyptic ideas about the second coming of Christ. While Jesus may have been talking about another figure and not referring to himself, the post-resurrection church with their once-removed christology began to understand the Son of Man as Christ himself. Contemporary Jesus Seminar scholarship argues that Jesus was not himself apocalyptic; however, it is understandable that his followers would tend toward the apocalyptic after his death and resurrection.[22] Jesus' followers extended the eschatological dimension of the reign of God to include the death and resurrection of Jesus. His own teachings pointed the way for their subsequent interpretations. As Paula Fredriksen puts it, "If the life and career of Jesus was the necessary but insufficient cause of Christianity, the sufficient cause was the original community's experience of his resurrection."[23] The crucifixion and resurrection narratives were central to the primitive proclamation because they indicated the interpretive strategy for the teachings of Jesus.

The earliest christology/soteriology of the church mythologized the primary salvation theory of Jesus to include crucifixion and resurrection and to point the way for the second coming. There is very little to suggest that either Jesus or the early church formed any significant incarnational theology that would have claimed divinity for Jesus. The sayings, the ministry, Jesus' own apparent understandings, and the early writings all suggest continuity with various forms of prophetic messianism or messianic prophecy.

This early christology was a form of reconciliation atonement, where the crucifixion symbolized conflict and the resurrection symbolized victory over the powers of death. This "dramatic" theory interpreted the cross as a symbol of God's engagement with the tyrants that hold humanity in bondage. The drama was resolved or reconciled with the Easter resurrection, which symbolized that God had been victorious over the powers of death. The reconciliation of the world began with this vindicating event of new life.

Gustaf Aulén refers to this primitive christus victor drama as the "classic" theory of atonement.[24] It differs from later atonement theories in that it represents the work of atonement as

> first to last a work of God Himself, a *continuous* Divine work; while according to the other view, the act of Atonement has indeed its origin in God's will, but is, in its carrying-out, an offering made to God by Christ and man on man's behalf, and may therefore be called a *discontinuous* work.[25]

As Aulén points out, this primitive christology/atonement theory is "objective" in the sense that it both enacts and discloses the real change in the whole cosmic drama. Atonement is not a change that takes place in humans individually or even between God and humanity. Atonement means that God's reconciliation of the whole world, nature, and the cosmos has begun. The early church interpreted their ministry as being part of the inaugurated reconciliation of the world; all their ministry was bracketed by God's coming in Christ and the anticipated return. The content of proclamation was the good news that Christ was risen (vindicated) and God's liberation had already begun with the disempowerment of domination.[26]

The purpose of preaching was to announce this reconciliation and to call people into a new way of being in community. The church, as the first fruits of salvation, was to be a sign of reconciliation in the world. Christians, baptized into Christ's death and resurrection, were expected to continue the practices of reconciliation and compassion (passion with) by sharing food, forgiving debts, sheltering the poor, and healing the sick. The dual reality of the cross (God's solidarity with those who suffered) and the resurrection (God's vindication of suffering) was the christological center of proclamation and mission.

Contemporary Homiletic Implications

Preachers should note that the New Testament writings, while indicating a diversity of christologies, were not significantly formed by sacrificial atonement. Early christologies assumed that God was on the side of humanity and that Jesus participated as God's earthly ambassador in proclaiming a reign of radical justice. The work of Jesus was continuous with God's intentions and was enacted on behalf of the world that God so loved. Interpreting and preaching New Testament texts or drawing eucharistic understandings with reference to sacrificial understandings is probably anachronistic to the New Testament. We will consider Anselm's atonement theory later in the chapter, but for now, we'll note that Anselm's atonement theory considered the crucifixion as a sacrifice made to God and not the symbol of solidarity and struggle against evil that the primitive christus victor theory suggests.

The christological understandings that inform the New Testament derive from available Jewish notions of the role of the eschatological prophet, the prophetic messiah, or a messianic prophet. To the extent that we know anything about Jesus' own understanding of his soteriological significance, contemporary scholars do not think that Jesus saw himself as divine, or that his work was salvific in any way other than as an announcement of God's justice. Jesus acted in faithfulness according to the pattern of a salvific leader and messianic figure. His suffering resulted from the clash of powers and was not a sacrificial offering to vindicate God's honor.

Women preachers can also avoid reinscribing "special incarnation" status to the Jesus of the New Testament writings, since Jesus' ontological status was not a primary concern of the early writers. The "Son of God" and "Son of Man" categories within the New Testament do not necessarily need to be understood as categories of special relationship, but of special vocation. The christological controversies over Jesus' special status as a divine man come early in the tradition, but not as early as the New Testament writings. O'Collins points out that the use of these titles in the New Testament writings leave the question open to interpretation. O'Collins also points out that reflections on Jesus' special or unique status derive from his vocation and his activities, not vice versa. The personal perfection of Jesus was not a central question for the New Testament writings, and his incarnational status as Son of God has less to do with his inner life than with the specifics of his ministry among the disenfranchised.

By avoiding the divinity problem, women preachers can also avoid reinscribing anti-Judaism onto Jesus. The Jesus presented in the New Testament christologies is probably thoroughly Jewish, messianic, and eschatological, although not necessarily of the apocalyptic variety. To portray Jesus as anti-Jewish or overly spiritual is not supported by the New Testament texts, nor is it theologically appropriate. Jesus is not a prophet against Judaism, but a reformer of Judaism, according to its own prophetic and messianic tradition. Women preachers should avoid the rhetorical strategy of making Judaism into an enemy of women and Jesus into a liberator of women. Likewise, preachers should avoid the rhetorical strategy of prophecy/fulfillment when it is used to discredit Judaism in favor of Christianity. Within the earliest New Testament writings (Pauline material and Mark) and certainly within the basileia teachings of Jesus, this preferential strategy is not scripturally supported. And, within the context of the basileia teachings, later Johannine anti-Judaism is revealed for the distortion it surely is.

As we move through the historical shifts, it will become increasingly apparent why this primitive understanding of the proclamation by Jesus and the meaning of crucifixion and resurrection is fruitful for preachers. This project will attempt to reclaim a demythologized version of the christus victor drama as a christological paradigm for preaching. There are several advantages, which we'll only sketch out here. First, it centers attention on the living, contextual, justice-oriented ministry of Jesus as it relates directly to his proclamation of the reign of God. However, it focuses on the ministry of Jesus in a way that makes Jesus more than just a nice guy. The New Testament writers and the early church did not have to claim Jesus' divinity to claim that he was messianic and prophetic. For the early church, Jesus was apparently something like a paradigmatic prophet, who, unlike other rabbis and prophets, continued to be in a teaching and advising relationship even after death.[27] His death and resurrection were inconsistent with certain aspects of traditional messiah paradigms, but they were consistent with Isaian messianism and necessary within an increasingly eschatologized christology. Seen in light of Isaiah's suffering servant songs, the death and resurrection of the anointed one were consistent with the canonical scriptures.[28] They signaled liberation and the ultimate reconciliation of the whole cosmic order. The fact that the early church identified Jesus so clearly with the suffering servant or servant messiah of Isaiah is a powerful clue to a more appropriate hermeneutic approach for preaching. The apocalyptic claims, demythologized faithfully, envision God's desire for a real triumph over the structures of evil, resulting in a renewed socio-historical reality. The earliest christologies were driven by a "people hermeneutic" concerned with discerning the activities of God as they were manifested in the ministry of Jesus. The vocation of Jesus among ordinary humans pointed beyond itself to its origin in God.

A word of caution is in order. A primitive approach is not authoritative simply because it is *scriptural*. An understanding of primitive understandings is helpful *hermeneutically*. We will still want to ask questions of theological appropriateness along with historical and scriptural plausibility. However, before we can reflect on the theological appropriateness of New Testament understandings of Jesus, it is critical to have some idea what they actually were. When we strip later doctrinal developments away from New Testament understandings of christology and soteriology, we find a primitive notion of prophet, messianic leader, and teacher of the basileia. Much of the contemporary trouble with Jesus derives from later doctrinal developments and not from the images of Jesus and his ministry that originate in the earliest proclamations. Women preachers who preach routinely from New Testament texts (or from Hebrew Bible texts disclosing messianic hopes) need to have a clear understanding of the images and theologies that were operative. We can reflect critically upon those understandings only to the extent that we can distinguish them from later developments.

One of the greatest dangers with any type of christus victor approach is that it can lead to an uncritical triumphalism. An uncritical use of conqueror imagery and conqueror christology can be easily literalized into a posture that justifies the use of power-over strategies within the historical church. Martin Luther argued for an emphasis on a theology of the cross to avoid any such triumphalism and to undercut notions of worldly success. Luther was probably correct in recognizing the dangers of a resurrection or victory model. Resurrection christology without the cross tends toward triumphalism. A theology of the cross without resurrection tends toward masochism. The origins of both distortions are possible given the early christus victor salvation theory of the church.

But the dual realities are also narratively held in tension with each other. Crucifixion and resurrection must be considered as a dramatic or symbolic gestalt, since overemphasis on either will lead to distortion.

The Shift to Christology-from-Above

One of the first major theological shifts within the tradition was the shift from the proclamation of Jesus to the person of Jesus himself, a shift from christology-from-below to christology-from-above. The resurrection and reign-of-God theology of the earliest communities was displaced in the first ecumenical councils as church leaders wrestled with the question of Jesus' special identity. Rosemary Radford Ruether claims that "a conflict gradually arises between the original charismatic order of Christian leadership and a developing institutional order (prophets and martyrs versus bishops)."[29] Christology-from-below was decentered from doctrinal history in favor of an incarnational emphasis. As we will trace out, the incarnational shift that began before Constantine would continue to shape christology and salvation theory. Incarnational interpretations of Jesus were grounded in early birth narratives of the gospels and were reinforced as Christianity became increasingly Hellenized. The official Christianity of the Roman Empire contextualized the crucified and risen savior to conform to the "divine man" pattern of the Caesars. The paradigm shift occurred during the first five centuries and "the Christian Church itself is transformed from a marginal sect within the messianic renewal movements of first-century Judaism into the new imperial religion of a Christian Roman Empire."[30]

One of the prevailing problems that early councils attempted to address was the question of authority for Christian beliefs. Competing interpretations of Jesus and of the faith had begun to spring up, with the result that church leaders felt compelled to define appropriate orthodox belief. The ultimate authority in any religious argument is the authority of divine mandate or approval. In the apologetic thinking of the day, Jesus had to be as authoritative as the competing prophets and gods. For the growing church, Jesus needed the authority of divine sonship to warrant the church's claims. The move to claim authority for Jesus necessitated a "chain-of command" approach, or a hierarchy of derived status. Lordship as a claim of divinity, kyriarchy as a domination strategy, and "legitimacy" as a strategy of orthodoxy all develop relative to the same metaphorical concerns for power, purity, and holiness.

The question for third- and fourth-century Christians was not the content of Jesus' message but the person of Jesus himself.

> Was he fully divine, in the precise sense of the term and therefore really akin to the Father? Or was He, after all a creature, superior no doubt to the rest of creation, even by courtesy

designated divine, but all the same separated by an unbridgeable chasm from the Godhead?[31]

The council at Nicea declared that Jesus Christ was the Son of God,
coequal, consubstantial, and coeternal with the Father, displacing the
earlier primitive creed "Jesus Christ is Lord" with a theology of processional incarnation. The Nicene formulation tried to protect the divinity
of Christ against competitive heretical theologies that over-emphasized
the humanity of Christ. Nicea bolstered the status of Jesus by including
him in the Godhead and by adding an anathema formula to rule out
approaches that might mistakenly claim Jesus as a full human
"creature."[32]

The Chalcedonian definition was a critical reformulation and one
that we will have several occasions to revisit. Chalcedon attempted to
tie up some of the loose ends from Nicea, which had introduced the
messy metaphysical notions of *persona* and *substantia*. These philosophical concepts obscured the symbolic nature of the Jesus/God relationship with the language of physical substance.[33] Following this blunder,
the Council of Chalcedon was faced with the dilemma of explaining
exactly how Jesus could literally be both divine and human. If divinity
was allowed to invade humanity, then the humanity of Jesus was not in
any way like our own. On the other hand, if full humanity was allowed,
then how could Jesus have been truly divine? Chalcedon declared that
Christ's two natures were unmixed, unchanged, undivided, and insepa-
rable. How two radically different things could be unmixed yet insepa-
rable was a problem that could never be solved logically, no matter how
hard the theologians of later generations tried.

The Chalcedonian Creed attempted to correct the theological myo-
pia of the Nicene Creed by arguing against a thoroughgoing divinity for
Christ, partly in an attempt to check the infinite regression of miraculous claims it necessitated. The questions of Mary's own ontological status and miraculous birth emerged in relation to the Chalcedonian
problem. While Chalcedon somewhat qualified the necessity for full
divinity, it didn't stop divine trickle-down. It only attempted to prevent
the positions at either extremity from becoming orthodox doctrine.[34]

Perhaps the biggest problem was the eclipse of the crucifixion and
the resurrection. Gustaf Aulén warns that isolating the incarnation and
separating it from the work of reconciliation and redemption is theologically one-sided and inconsistent with the earliest proclamations.

> The divine and loving will becomes fully "incarnate" when the
> work is finished...or in other words, Christ has brought divine
> love into the world through his life, suffering and sacrifice,
> struggle and victory...[T]he incarnation is perfected on the
> cross.[35]

This disjunction between incarnation and crucifixion/resurrection is the first critical stumble toward theological calamity, a turn away from primitive christus victor reconciliation.

Augustine

Augustine of Hippo (354–430) is a key figure in the transition between the christology of the primitive church and the growing concerns about the person of Jesus. The early church could not condone a theological position that attributed salvation to anyone but God. However, neither could they approve a theology that didn't take real flesh and blood seriously. "Without the incarnation of the *Son of God*, divine redemption would be impossible. Yet without a genuine *incarnation*, the battle against the diabolic forces of evil would not be won from the inside."[36] The shift toward the person of Jesus and his special qualifications leads to formulating questions of salvation in a problematic way. While women theologians are familiar with the emerging dualism of Augustine and the church fathers, few identify the lasting legacy of a particular pattern of formulating the christological "problem" for which incarnation was an answer. Since many contemporary women theologians use incarnational approaches in their christologies, Augustine's mistakes can be instructive.

Augustine's contribution to the salvation question (and the human question) was the doctrine of original sin. Sin and salvation paradigms always involve a problem/solution structure centering on the issue of what it is that humanity needs to be saved from. Augustine addressed the question of Christ's incarnation by discussing theological anthropology, or the nature of humanity. Jesus as Christ, as mediator, had to take on flesh precisely because flesh was the theological problem for human beings. Jesus the Christ was the savior of humanity because humans needed to be saved from their own human nature. For Augustine, sin was a biological defect, the tendency of human beings to be self-absorbed and curved in upon themselves. Since Augustine believed that the appropriate orientation of humans was to be centered on God, he understood Jesus as an answer to the question of human self-orientation. God became incarnate in Jesus/Christ to save us from something we could not save ourselves from: human fleshly attributes of self-centeredness and pride.

He offered the first psychological definition of sin and perhaps the first doctrinal interpretation of the garden of Eden as a story about "the fall," or the origin of sin.[37] But Augustine also interpreted original sin as a defect that went beyond the psychological self-absorption of humanity. He introduced the notion of sexuality and carnality as the locus of human sinfulness. His approach was certainly dualistic and based on a Platonic mind/body split, which ultimately devalued fleshly experience.

Augustine traced sin to the exercise of the human free will, which had the potential to turn away from the good intended by God. The will, exercised toward the good, would be manifest in the flesh as obedience. Exercised in opposition to the good, the will would lead the flesh into disobedience. The flesh, ever seeking its own gratification, tempts the will to turn away from goodness and becomes the ultimate benefactor of the will's exercises. It is still fair to claim that Augustine located the manifestations of sin in the flesh, even if the free will is ultimately responsible for sinning. Augustine's mind/body split strategy located the manifestations of sin in the flesh; sin was passed from generation to generation by virtue of sexual relationships. Sex, as the fleshly origin of human life, contaminated every human being and teased every will with sin.

Beyond this association with sex and flesh was a dualistic association of sin with gender. Women exemplified the loss of will and servitude to the flesh that were eternal human problems. Augustine used the allegorical device of women as "types" or symbols of the human tendency to be driven by desires of the flesh. Eve was a "type" exemplifying all that was wrong with human beings: willfulness, creaturely cravings, self-satisfaction.[38] Males, by contrast, were "types" of spirituality, representing the rational mind. Jesus was incarnated into a male body as model of appropriate human spiritual orientation. "Man alone is in the image of God."[39]

Beyond the problem of locating sin in the flesh and the concomitant problem of allegorically locating sin especially in female flesh, Augustine's most serious problem for women theologians goes beyond this. His most serious blunder was to exempt the human mind and the processes of rationality from sin. By separating the rational faculties from the body, and by locating the manifestations of sin in flesh, Augustine opened the door for intellectual pride and a tyrannical control of the production of knowledge and orthodoxy. His association of perfection with intellect and rationality and the possibility of perfect free will, a mistake that Thomas Aquinas would also make, rendered any critique on behalf of bodies theologically problematic by definition.

Augustine viewed Jesus/Christ as a mediator between humans and God. In order for Jesus as the Christ to effect our salvation, he must have been both fully human and fully divine.[40] It was precisely his non-human or superhuman perfection that gave atoning value to his death. Christ could be Mediator only by virtue of unprecedented innocence and perfection, a paradigm that necessitated a virgin birth to avoid the taint of original sin. As Augustine writes in *Enchiridion*:

> We could never have been delivered even by the one mediator
> between God and men, the man Jesus Christ, had He not been

God as well. When Adam was created, he was of course righteous, and a mediator was not needed. But when sin placed a wide gulf between mankind and God, a mediator was called for Who was unique in being born, in living and in being slain without sin, in order that we might be reconciled to God and brought by the resurrection of the flesh to eternal life.[41]

Augustine contributed several problems to the tradition: mind/body dualism, hierarchical associations with gender, the priority of rationality, and a negative attitude toward human bodies and sexuality. His more useful contributions include the claim that all humanity is subject to sin, the symbolic power of Jesus as an intermediary or locus for divine/human reconciliation, and the relationship between the self-absorbed psyche and deficiency in ethical practices.

Contemporary Homiletic Implications

Douglas Ottati notes that a radical separation between Jesus as a divine authority figure (an incarnational theology) and the reign of God as a paradigm for human community ultimately leaves us with an empty christology.[42] Without the eschatological dimension of Jesus' teachings and life practices to provide content clues, the symbol of Jesus as a static figure remains too ambiguous to be of ethical value. The creedal emphasis on his birth, death, and resurrection bypasses his entire ministry of healing and proclamation, as if redemption were a function of his birth and not related to his actual in-the-flesh ministry.

An incarnational emphasis is dualistic, since it presupposes a prior separation between spirit and body. Incarnational approaches can either undergird an overly positive theory of the flesh or an overly negative theory of the flesh. On the negative side, Christ's incarnation is a "special case" and reinforces the idea that ordinary human flesh is not a revelatory location. This negative approach is more tragic; it spiritualizes the incarnation and devalues ordinary bodies, a move that many women theologians reject.

On the positive side, we can interpret Christ's incarnation as a "general case" that reinforces the essential goodness of human experience. This general incarnational approach is more romantic, including possibilities for human perfection.[43] By this line of argument, the presence of divinity in all human experience elevates humans to candidacy for dignity. (We'll see this strategy reappropriated by incarnational and eros women theologians.) If the central identity of Jesus was the incarnation of all that is good and perfect, then ministers and the church were capable of embodying that kind of perfection. The high christology suggested by classical incarnational approaches probably leads to a comparably high doctrine of ordained ministry and ecclesiology and a very low opinion of ordinary human flesh.[44]

One of the greatest dangers of classical incarnational christology is that it can distort ministry by absolutizing the male Jesus and the hierarchical church. Incarnational thinking tends to focus on bodily activities of individuals, suggesting that it is the carnal flesh that needs redemption. This incarnational model with the procession of divinity into flesh is fundamentally dualistic and hierarchical: Ordinary human flesh and ordinary material creation is "not good" without the divine impulse of perfection that God unleashes through Christ. Mary Daly faults this hierarchical pattern, claiming that patriarchal society is inherently bound up in these mythical patterns, where "earthly processions both generate and reflect the image of procession from and return to god the father. According to christian theology, there are processions within the godhead, which is triune. The son, who is the second person, is said to proceed from the father, and the holy ghost is said to proceed from the father and the son."[45]

Women preachers need to handle incarnational christologies with care lest they reinforce dualism and biological essentialism. One common rhetorical strategy of women preachers is to align Jesus with the "feminine" side of the equation, arguing that Jesus had all the attributes of traditional femininity. In this homiletical strategy, Jesus becomes nurturing, family-oriented, spiritual, and sensitive. Jesus becomes the "relational" savior who favors authentic personal relationships of mutuality and respect. This strategy doesn't undermine the dualism, but merely shifts Jesus from one side of the gender dualism to the other. And it leads directly to the christological crisis of taming Jesus into the kind of sweet and ladylike figure that causes women preachers so much trouble in the first place.

A serious implication is the romantic notion that the rational mind is not as susceptible to sin and willfulness as the flesh. While women theologians are critical of "rationality" schemes promoted by men, they are less willing to question the theological thinking associated with other women and particularly among feminist types of christology. The idea behind this "hands-off" policy seems to be that women have an epistemological advantage derived specifically from their biology. While we wouldn't tolerate an approach whose authority was grounded on male gender, we frequently tolerate reverse sexism that justifies thought grounded on female gender. Gender loyalty is theologically misguided under any circumstances, but particularly invidious when it serves as an excuse for protecting certain types of rhetoric and discourse from critique. One-dimensional analyses, whether along the dimension of race, gender, or class, are subject to theological critique within the broader community. Women who pastor, preach, and teach must be careful not to reinscribe gender dualisms or privileged types of theological discourse, no matter how well intentioned they may be. Having female bodies does not protect us from "wonky thinking" any more than male bodies protect men. Any appeal to sex (or gender) to reject (or privilege) certain kinds of thinking (or behavior) is a surrender to Western classical dualism, and is bound to simply "reinscribe the sex/gender system in feminist terms."[46]

The Shift from Reconciliation to Retribution

Between the sixth and sixteenth centuries the dualism of incarnational christology became even more deeply inscribed. In the middle ages the church became culturally monolithic in the Western world. All the trends toward bureaucracy, orthodoxy, and masculinity continued and became culturally definitive. The gap between the clergy and the laity became an unbridgeable gulf, and the church's earlier antipathy toward heresy shifted to aggressive violence. The church and its believers turned in upon themselves, except for the times when they waged frontal assaults upon their pagan neighbors.[47]

Sociologists describe the phenomenon of the growth from sect to institution as one of increasing sedimentation and hardening. The mature institutional phase generally involves increasing role definition and stratification, the development of "experts" and specialized knowledge, and detailed attention to rules and boundaries. The medieval church fits the category of the mature institutional phase as it attends to codes of behavior, ranking of members, and the development of theological specialties. The major trinitarian and christological controversies were resolved, and the church turned to the development of eucharistic and atonement theologies. Debates over Christ's humanity and divinity waned, but only because they were thoroughly integrated into the fabric of theological reflection. As we noted in the previous section, a certain way of formulating theological questions gained priority within the church. Even though the questions about divinity and humanity had receded, future theological problems were formulated according to established categories, images, and metaphors.

Anselm

Anselm of Canterbury shaped christology more than any other figure between Augustine and the Reformation with his turn to atonement theory.[48] His treatise *Cur Deus Homo* (Why God Became Human) formulated a satisfaction theory of the cross that continues to shape christological understandings today. Anselm is a key figure for our purposes, since a majority of women theologians fault Anselm for introducing suffering as a spiritual virtue.

Anselm was particularly troubled by a theology of suffering. He found two of the most popular theories of redemption unsavory. In addition to the primitive christus victor dramatic theory, there was a ransom theory that claimed that Christ's blood was the price paid to the devil. By masquerading as fully human, Christ tricked the devil "into swallowing the hook of divinity along with the bait of flesh."[49] Anselm found it morally objectionable to speak of the devil's rights or of deception as part of the divine modus operandi. Anselm's own medieval (cultural) understanding of honor and righteousness took its primary metaphorical clues from Roman law, which demanded that violations be either punished or satisfied. Anselm was convinced that it would be dishonorable for God to simply excuse the sinfulness of humanity, and equally dishonorable to trick the devil. If God is just, honorable, and merciful, why did the innocent savior have to die? Anselm also assumed that God was omnipotent, omniscient, and immutable, so his other question is logical. If God were all-powerful, why not release Jesus from the cross? Anselm's dilemma was to figure out a theology of the cross that maintained the honor and the power of God. We must notice that Anselm didn't emphasize divine mercy apart from honor; God's mercy was within the margin allowed by the demands of honor. Anselm's God deserved payment for the sins of humanity and could not honorably rest until the balance was settled. Of course, the major problem was that imperfect humans couldn't possibly repay God for the offense, and the whole situation was a stalemate: "Only man *should*, only God *could*."

Into this theological dilemma Jesus/Christ enters as the perfect solution. Jesus/Christ, with his two natures, was in the perfect ontological position to make satisfaction. As fully human, he was in the right sacrificial category, meaning that he could meaningfully satisfy the necessity for a human sacrifice or capitulation. As fully divine, he was in the right moral category, meaning that he had the moral value to render such a worthy sacrifice. God had to become human and had to die voluntarily to pay off the debt to "himself." The death of the God-man on the cross made it "morally plausible for God to forgive."[50]

Let's notice a couple of implications. First, Anselm's theory assumes the innocence of Jesus/Christ as a starting point, shifting attention to the status of Jesus' own person. To his credit, the assumption of Jesus' moral perfection makes the ransom theory intolerable for Anselm. Moral plausibility is a good criterion, but we must always realize that it varies from era to era.[51] Second, Anselm assumes a classical doctrine of an omnipotent God, suggesting that the suffering problem is primarily a problem that calls God's justice into question. Anselm has inherited a set of doctrinal and creedal beliefs that deeply inscribe incarnational christology and particularly a two-natures christology. He upholds the Chalcedonian formula of one person with two full and unmixed natures and does not challenge either the dualisms of Augustine or the mediating christology such dualisms necessitate. Consequently, Anselm's satisfaction theory will probably not disable any of the incarnational or processional problems of attributing full divinity to Christ.

However, in spite of his concerns about moral plausibility, Anselm ties incarnation to crucifixion in a way that creates a different moral dilemma. It emphatically reinterprets suffering as something that "satisfies" God, and since it pits honor against mercy, it renders mercy meaningless. The medieval requirements of honor and satisfaction make it morally implausible for God to simply forgive sin, no matter how much it might be in the divine character. To remain honorable, God's honor must be satisfied through a willing sacrifice. Anselm has reclaimed the cross, but only at great expense to divine mercy and to human misery. Misery and suffering became honorable payments to a dishonored God. Resurrection, as the vindication of suffering, has been eclipsed. Suffering and crucifixion now stand alone as activities required to restore the divine honor.

Whereas the early church had held that God was on the side of humanity, and that Jesus was likewise on the side of humanity, the Anselmian approach assumes an adversarial relationship between God and humanity. Jesus, as the perfect meeting ground, becomes a proxy payment for God's impugned honor. In Anselm's theory, the violent nature of the cross symbolizes the catharsis of God's restitution and not a solution to injustice in the world. Justice is restored to God at the expense of human justice. Jesus reverses positions in Anselm's theory: He moves from being the target of earthly violence (in the primitive christus victor reconciliation theology) to become the target of God's right to honor, at human expense. The crucifixion of Jesus becomes an obedient act that reduces the opposition between justice and evil. Justice and evil are not antithetical to each other; rather, the evil of human suffering might somehow function to restore justice to the ontological plane.

While we can't attribute masochistic motivations to Anselm, we can easily trace out the implications of his theological reflections. Anselm did not claim that suffering placated an angry God. Rather, suffering set the balance of justice aright. Anselm's atonement theory has functioned at the practical level to rationalize suffering and to teach centuries of believers that God somehow benefits from their suffering. Feminist theologians Rita Nakashima Brock, Joanne C. Brown, and Rebecca Parker have characterized Anselmian approaches as abusive theology that justifies the misery of women and children by an appeal to divine justice. They note the deep symbolic roots of the theory in biblical images of sacrifice, which function to glorify suffering as redemptive or salvific:

> The disciple's role is to suffer in the place of others, as Jesus suffered for us all. But this glorification of suffering as salvific, held before us daily in the image of Jesus hanging from the cross, encourages women who are being abused to be more concerned about their victimizer than about themselves.[52]

Brown and Parker are correct to note that, in this model, God is estranged from humanity, cheated by human sin to such an extent that only a willing sacrifice will set things right again. The paradigm functions as a symbol of God's distance from humanity instead of God's solidarity with humanity. Jesus becomes the symbol of repentant humanity, willing to suffer indignity and death to effect justice. His holiness is constituted by willingness, obedience, and martyrdom. Therefore, to be like Jesus, believers are encouraged to "bear their crosses" in order to restore the balance of justice to the world.

The model becomes even more problematic when combined with Augustine's mind and body split and its symbolic associations with male/female oppositions. The female body, long associated with sin and the passions that must be subdued, becomes a particular focus for redemptive suffering. Jesus not only becomes a symbolic substitution on behalf of general human sinfulness, but a substitute for the distinctive offense of carnal flesh, that is, female flesh. Anselm, along with Hildegard of Bingen and Julian of Norwich, encouraged seeing Jesus as motherly in his sacrificial love.[53] It's ironic, but not surprising, that Anselm's sacrificial victim should be associated with good mothering. By this time, women ascetics and mystics were joining the ranks of monastics in their spiritual renunciation of the world. When sacrifice is the mode, associations with stereotypical female roles are not positive. Denise Carmody points out that, in the medieval development of women monastics, women were given great praise as mothers and as submissive believers but denied access to institutional power. "A few unusually strong women, such as Catherine of Siena, became reformers, wagging their fingers at sinful popes, but most saintly women bowed their heads in obedience to male authorities, who regulated their lives even in the cloister."[54]

Contemporary Homiletic Implications

Anselmian notions of the theological meaning of suffering dominate contemporary homiletical contexts. Most ordinary believers use sacrificial atonement as their primary redemptive understanding. Since preachers will invariably be preaching within situations where this understanding is dominant, familiarity with the various forms of Anselmian atonement is a rhetorical necessity for almost any contemporary preacher. Contemporary folk piety assumes that our suffering is something God requires for reasons that ordinary folks can't understand. Anselm's atonement theory operates to rationalize the suffering of apparently innocent people, and it implicates God as the one who benefits from such suffering.

Within contemporary homiletic practice, Anselmian assumptions emerge primarily with regard to tragic death funerals, to the prolonged suffering of "good" people, to the abuse of children, to violence against women, and to occasions of natural disaster. Even while our most deeply held and primitive beliefs may reject ideas of divine complicity in suffering, our public theological strategies are usually insufficient for dealing with any sustained argument against Anselm. When parishioners come to the preacher/pastor with overwhelming grief or with terrors of retribution, we may find ourselves mouthing the platitude that "God has reasons we cannot understand." The assumption that God is the beneficiary of suffering is so deeply entrenched that to deny it seems tantamount to irreverence.

Women theologians and preachers must be especially careful not to make positive associations between the sacrificial suffering of Jesus and stereotypical female behavior. Many women preachers are mistakenly encouraged by the use of feminine metaphors for God and for Jesus without noticing that they can reinscribe sacrificial suffering as a particularly feminine virtue. Emily Cheney has written extensively on reading and preaching strategies that help avoid reinforcing these mistakes. One strategy that may be particularly helpful here is what she refers to as a hypothetical reversal strategy. Women readers and preachers should ask themselves whether a particular biblical narrative (or a rhetorical approach used in preaching) serves to maintain gender subordination. If the rhetorical substitution of "men" for "women" or "fathers" for "mothers" seems to disrupt cultural stereotypes, then the original story or claim is probably sexist. For example, if Jesus' suffering on the cross is considered a perfect example of "fatherly nurturing," such an interpretation would probably be disruptive of our cultural notions; therefore, the "motherly" associations are probably gender-biased and kyriarchal. In this way, "female readers [and female preachers] can decide in what ways their identification with protagonists, both male and female protagonists, would entail the acceptance of a role that includes self-denigration."[55] We will explore possibilities for a sacrificial model in a later chapter, but for now, it's enough to note that it's inappropriate when rhetorically applied in a gendered way, in a way that maintains redemptive suffering, as a model for individual behavior, or in a way that pits God against humanity.

On the other hand, women theologians who do reject Anselm frequently make the mistake of rejecting any meaningful interpretation of the crucifixion. Women theologians and preachers need to be aware that they can preach faithfully from the scriptures, and can even preach Christ crucified, without reinscribing the disastrous sacrificial interpretations offered by Anselm. The suffering of Jesus/Christ on the cross does not have to represent God's satisfaction or Jesus' proxy sacrifice. The suffering of Jesus/Christ can be faithfully interpreted as a symbol of the world's hostility to God, and God's subsequent refusal to match violence with counter-violence. In a later chapter we will explore the special problems related to the abuse of women, misinterpretations of the cross, and appropriate feminist reclamations of a *theologia crucis*. Anselm's approach does not constitute the only option for making sense of the cross. To the extent that we worry about plausibility, Anselm's theory seems to lack consistent scriptural support.

And, as Gerald O'Collins claims, Anselm's atonement theory fails at the standard of morality.[56] Anselm's God may be honorable, but "he" certainly isn't moral by any meaningful Christian categories. Homiletical interpretations of God should never reinforce the abuse of others at the hands of the powerful, especially if that power is wielded by God. At the very least, preachers should endorse a God whose morality meets minimal standards.[57]

Thomas Aquinas

Thomas Aquinas (1224–1274), father of the Dominican school of theology, was part of an increasingly formal and scientific approach to theology that characterized the growth of universities and university-style reflection. He was part of an intellectual trend to reclaim Aristotelian philosophy as a construct for doing theology. Aquinas grafted Aristotelian biology into medieval scholasticism to provide a theological version of the "natural orders of creation." According to Aquinas, there was a hierarchy of created beings. Women were lower on the ladder of natural order, ontologically inferior to men, and less capable of resisting sin or achieving spiritual perfection. Women did not represent an inferior form of rationality, but their bodies represented a constant source of compromise for that rationality. Women, along with children, were too easily tempted by the bodily passions and for that reason had to be considered "naturally" subordinate to men. Aquinas followed Aristotle in calling women "misbegotten males" who fell short of full humanity.[58] He literalized what Augustine had claimed symbolically or analogically, arguing that women's physical generativity was the means by which human sinfulness was transmitted. According to Aquinas, gender moved beyond symbolism to became a literal and "natural" indication of a hierarchy of ideal virtues. Women not only symbolized what was wrong with humanity, but they were actually inferior to men because of their carnality. Men, both symbolizing and actualizing the higher virtue of unhindered rationality, were representatives of what humanity was called to be. Males could transcend their bodily natures by virtue of reason; females were trapped in their passionate bodies, which prevented them from exercising reason as perfectly as males. Aquinas' characterization of women as weaker vessels was a fundamental assumption justifying a male priesthood, hierarchical ecclesiology, and the fifteenth century's witch craze.

The combination of Thomist theo-biology and Anselm's Latin doctrine of atonement was disastrous. It produced a theological formulation that reversed primitive theologies of the cross (where the cross was symbolic of human evil and the resurrection symbolized victory over death) and also reinforced the authority of the church. Contemporary theologians, and particularly women theologians, make the mistake of attributing a retributive dimension to Anselm's doctrine of God. Anselm had previously rejected the punitive interpretations that Aquinas subsequently introduced, interpretations that quickly became orthodox doctrine into the Reformation period. While Anselm may have claimed that God deserved a sacrifice, Aquinas is the one who claimed that God wanted and engineered suffering as a retribution. Aquinas made the shift to what has now come to be categorized as the penal theory of atonement. In this view, "Jesus became the personal object of divine reprobation. Through his passion he suffered an abandonment by God corresponding to the lot of those condemned to hell. This suffering as a penal substitute turned away God's anger and won the divine favour for the human race."[59]

The significance of this university christology was in its articulation of the necessity for the two-natures theory of Chalcedon and in its articulation of the offices of Christ. Even though Aquinas was more concerned with the life and ministry of Jesus (which he called the "mysteries" of Christ) than his immediate predecessors or his contemporaries, he attributed their significance to the incarnation or their likeness to God's being. This reverses the more primitive pattern where Jesus was recognized as God's emissary based on his practices and not on his personality. The Thomistic understanding of the mysteries of Jesus' ministry claimed that they were meritorious decisively because of his incarnation. Incarnation, and not God's reign, was the major factor in human redemption.[60] Trickle-down christology continued to dominate medieval soteriological concerns as it had since Chalcedon.

While we may fault Aquinas for his approach, we need to notice that he had unwitting accomplices in Chalcedon, Augustine, and Anselm. Three elements came together to create the icon of the (necessarily) male savior who died for our sins: Incarnation christology made Jesus God-like, Anselm's discontinuous atonement theory made him into an obedient suffering child, and Thomist rationality codified Augustine's analogical assumptions that males were ontologically superior to women. Jesus/Christ was the God-man who suffered to please God and who became the male model for ministry. If Jesus/Christ was divine, which he must be to fulfill the sacrificial requirements, he must also be the most acceptable human sacrifice: he must be masculine. Only males were theo-morphic, in the shape of God, and only men could represent Christ as priests. The Thomistic principal of perfection pushed the notion that Christ's humanity must participate in the best of everything. This meant that in addition to his other perfections (in obedience, knowledge, morality, etc.), Christ must also be perfectly human: that is, male. Elizabeth Johnson claims that the orders of creation, theologically rationalized by Aquinas, are the foundation of the Christian structures of patriarchy.[61] As Ruether argues, this "antiwoman use of christology is argued not only on the plane of symbol but on the plane of biology."[62]

Because of the two-natures theory, Aquinas also taught that the payment rendered to God in the crucifixion was primarily the work of Christ's human nature. Because of the introduction of the punitive dimension of crucifixion, late medieval soteriology (and the eucharist) emphasized human penance and human sacrifice in the mass. The human nature of Christ (and, presumably, of the penitents) makes the offering, but the divine nature of Christ (and, presumably, of the priest) makes the offering meritorious. The divine operation involved both in crucifixion and in the mass was to bless the suffering or sacrifice of humans. According to O'Collins, Aquinas probably authored what we now know as the "classical" approach to the liturgy of the mass. "The Latin doctrine of the Atonement was completely in accord with the general nature of mediæval theology, with its typical emphasis on penance and on the Sacrifice of the Mass. The doctrine of penance emphasized the necessity of satisfaction, and the Mass was interpreted primarily as a sacrifice for sins."[63] According to Aulén, if Anselm had compromised the distinction between justice and evil, Aquinas compromised the distinction between power and love. The power of Christ's sacrifice on the cross was a function of his human nature, and was necessary but not sufficiently meritorious for salvation. Human merits were necessary for salvation.[64] So, in addition to the sacrificial interpretations of the eucharist, the medieval church also developed a system of indulgences for repentance and the remission of sins.

Contemporary Homiletic Implications

Aquinas' influence has gone far beyond the medieval church to resurface in modern Protestantism and, peculiarly, within women's own theo-biological arguments. Women theologians are correct when they identify Aquinas as the source of much antiwoman theology in the tradition. However, they don't notice the connection between this hierarchical theology and christology, or between Aquinas' hierarchical theology and the sacramental practices of the church. Aquinas, more than any of the earlier theologians, systematized the prejudices against women by appeal not only to a hierarchy of beings, but also by a particularly mean spin on the crucifixion. The two are not unrelated.

Many contemporary feminist strategies are based on the essentialist argument, assuming that women either have special needs or special gifts due to their biology. The biological argument can take the form of romanticizing or valorizing women, and the "cult of true womanhood" that emerges from time to time is just another version of the Aristotelian/Thomistic assumption. Schüssler Fiorenza and Ruether caution against any of the biological essentialist arguments that undergird contemporary women's theologies. Among them are claims of women as essentially nurturing or relational, or theories that appeal to "women's ways of knowing." Such approaches reinscribe the gender dualism inherent in Aristotelian/Thomistic biology.[65] Ruether argues that we can appreciate the particularities of the historical Jesus without idealizing them. We must, she claims, deemphasize biological particularities in favor of the message of God's reign.[66] If there is an incarnational shift, it must be toward Jesus as the incarnation of a particular message and not a particular kind of being. For women preachers concerned with sexism, this suggests that we should avoid the attempts to regender Jesus as the perfect woman or to reinscribe a hierarchy of beings where women's virtues are more Godlike or Christlike.

One of the ways this shows up most frequently in sermons is in the strategy of genderizing narratives about women in biblical texts. Claiming that female characters in biblical stories are somehow more virtuous, more open to Jesus, more Christlike in their courage or protest, is not an appropriate rhetorical strategy. On the one hand, such a homiletical strategy reinscribes a gendered (and ultimately kyriarchical) reading. Reverse sexism is not faithful proclamation. On the other hand, the strategy moves dangerously close to the heroic sacrifice model and the necessity of meritorious works for salvation. If women are somehow more symbolic of salvation because of their gendered insights and gendered activities, this runs dangerously close to a works righteousness mentality that suggests certain types of biology or behavior are necessary for salvation. Gendered homiletical strategies that elevate women and their activities are no more morally or theologically appropriate than the centuries of homiletical strategies that have operated similarly on behalf of men.

Other homiletical concerns relate to the liturgical context of preaching. We can't pursue a lengthy discussion of eucharistic theology and practices here, but women preachers need to be careful not to homiletically reinscribe any heroic notions of sacrifice, punishment, or merit related to the eucharistic celebration. One of the primary associations between communal ritual and women's theologies is the construction of the heroic, self-sacrificing individual or community. While it's not necessarily problematic to say that such rituals witness to the heroic vocation of the church, it is an easy and disastrous step to suggest that heroism is a meritorious activity *that is necessary* for celebration of the eucharist. Attributions of merit are probably too common among women preachers who want to claim that sexists should not be welcome at the table. We will probably have to examine our own prejudices against children and other "irrational" and "unworthy" types with regard to the celebration of the meal. To attach distinctions and status to any dimension of the eucharist is probably to reinscribe the orders of creation and the faulty assumptions about rationality and the necessity of merit. Since sermon illustrations frequently feature images of the community breaking bread, or theological interpretations of such activities, women preachers need to be particularly cautious to avoid reinscribing a hierarchy of believers, a meritocracy, or the subordination of children to adults.

The Reformation and Soteriology

The Protestant Reformation challenged the authority of the church, the penitential piety undergirding eucharistic practices, and continued the emphasis on salvation theories. Luther and Calvin had very little interest in the classical incarnational dilemma of Christ's divinity and humanity, at least at the theoretical level. The Reformation democratized the faith in several ways, by encouraging lay study of the scriptures, by declaring a priesthood of all believers, and by returning the eucharist to the community.[67] The Reformers and the Radical Reformers turned their christological reflections toward practical issues of Christian life and mission. Martin Luther and John Calvin were interested in christology and soteriology insofar as these theological understandings connected the person of Christ with the works of Christ for salvation and daily living. The departure from Catholicism demanded new understandings for the mediating or priestly function of Christ, new ways of structuring local congregations, and theological rationales for the eucharist. In addition to questioning the authority of the doctrinal tradition, the Reformation refocused christological and soteriological concerns on the biblical witness. As the medieval era closed, theologians and scholars came to realize how alien their speculative theologies were in relation to the charged symbols and narratives of the New Testament. With this "rediscovery" of the Bible, Luther and Calvin reoriented their christological reflections to biblical claims and interpretations.

Martin Luther

Luther was especially interested in the work of Christ for salvation, and he consequently reinterpreted Anselm's doctrine of atonement. Luther did not fundamentally challenge the Latin doctrine's theology or anthropology. God still deserved satisfaction and humans still owed it. But Luther did take issue with Anselm's interpretation of satisfaction. According to Luther, Christ not only satisfied God by his death on the cross, but did so for all time, and let humanity off the hook. Luther believed that a proper understanding of Christ's once-and-for-all sacrifice destroyed any notion of ongoing human indebtedness. Our good works might be offered to God as gifts, but they were not inducements to God's favor. No good work or accumulation of good works could secure forgiveness; Christ's death had already paid the price in full. Human merits were not necessary for salvation. Luther insisted that Christ be known as savior before he is followed as example. The work of Christ is the key to understanding the nature of his person.

There is also a significant difference between Luther and Aquinas. Luther's method emphasized the practical and experiential rather than the philosophical; he shifted attention away from strictly ontological understandings of Christ's person and the metaphysical problems of mingling natures. Luther's soteriology and christology was what one writer has called a functional approach, "...which shifts the emphasis from what happens to God [or Christ] to what happens to the believer."[68] For Luther, the important difference between his theory and the theories of Anselm and Aquinas was that Jesus functioned on the cross to reveal what God was like, self-giving, sacrificial, and radically gracious. If Aquinas and Anselm had emphasized the human dimension in Christ's atoning work, Luther shifted the emphasis to the divine dimension of the cross. We see God most clearly when we see Jesus, the mediator, dying for us. God sacrifices for us on the cross, not vice versa.

By considering the suffering of Jesus on the cross as a metaphor of divine presence, Luther was trying to resolve the perceived distance between God and the world. For those who feared God's wrath and assumed that human sacrifice was necessary, Luther offered consolation. In the cross, human suffering meets the compassion of God, and divine wrath is revealed as the "tyrant" it really is. For Luther to claim that Christ's suffering appeased God's wrath did not reject an objective claim about what really happened on the cross, but it emphasized the subjective faith perspective or "happening" in the believer. For the believer, the experience of God's wrath evaporated under the shadow of the cross. Through Christ, believers could see God differently, as one who would sacrifice the divine self for the salvation of the world. This new perspective was an epistemological shift enabling us to see God not as a powerful tyrant, but as a self-emptying servant, humiliated by our sinfulness. The image of Jesus on the cross operated as a metaphor of the reconciliation between humanity and God, with God doing the primary activity. This was why it was essential for Luther to emphasize both the human and the divine dimension of Jesus as the Christ: It was where human suffering met the compassionate suffering of God. He was unconcerned about questions of ontological status or hypostasis, but devoted to keeping the meaning of Chalcedon intact. If divinity and humanity did not meet on the cross, Luther's *theologia crucis* and its meaning for believers would have been destroyed. The body of Jesus/ Christ on the cross was where the new reconciliation was victorious. However, Luther continued to emphasize the divine presence and divine activity, precisely to guard against any notions of sacrificial imitation.

Unfortunately, Luther's epistemology of the cross was primarily an individualistic one, geared to the spiritual consolation of believers. While we may not want to fault Luther with a thoroughgoing subjectivity, the medieval trajectory of personal piety definitely breathes through Luther, later Lutheranism, and into the Radical Reformation and subsequent evangelical and existential piety.[69] And even though he rejected some elements of Thomistic rationality and christology, he did not reject the basic Thomistic assumptions about the natural order and the place of women within that order. Partly this may have been due to his twofold schema of law and gospel, which assumed that "law and order" had a divinely ordained function. For Luther, Christian vocation did not subvert the orders of creation, the mandate of government, or the responsibilities to the state. Christian vocation was exercised within these structures, and the structures themselves were part of God's plan. Men exercised their Christian vocation within the bounds of culturally defined masculinity and women did likewise. To challenge the natural orders of creation was beyond Luther's project. He retained contemporary philosophical and cultural prejudices against women, even as he rejected Mary-symbolism and Mariology along with other "papist" doctrines.[70] He defended sexual desire and married life as good gifts from God, severing the association between sin and sexuality, but his hierarchical constructs did little to allow ordinary women to benefit from this sexual emancipation. As Merry Weisner points out, this merely allowed marital obedience to replace ecclesiastical chastity.[71] We'll return to this limitation in a later chapter, when we take up a constructive women's theology of the cross.

Despite limitations, Luther's christological understandings began a shift back to the theological meanings of the dramatic *christus victor* theory. Luther's soteriology and christology outlined a form of reconciliation atonement. The crucifixion symbolized conflict between two rivals. On the one hand, there was the rivalry between God and Satan for the allegiance of humanity. And on the other hand, there were rival images of God competing in the tradition and within folk piety. Aulén notes that Luther's dramatic language and dualistic interpretations demonstrate his passion for the biblical images and metaphors. Luther started with scripture instead of traditional doctrines and then appropriated christological doctrine within biblical categories instead of philosophical categories. Perhaps his own marginal position as a dissenter led Luther to be particularly attracted to the biblical notion of powers and principalities, the captivity of humans to demonic structures, and the more apocalyptic rhetoric of the early church.

John Calvin

John Calvin's reforms were also tied to christological and soteriological interpretations. Like Luther, Calvin subordinated the incarnation to atonement. As a biblical scholar and exegete, he drew his theological understandings of Christ from the Bible, drawing attention to the distance between biblical interpretations and subsequent doctrinal developments. Whereas Luther's revisions were grounded on an understanding of Christ's work for salvation, Calvin's were driven by theological anthropology and his Augustinian understanding of human depravity. Calvin's theological anthropology was so pessimistic that he didn't think humans were much better even *before* the fall.

> Even if man had remained in his integrity, still his condition was too base for him to attain God. How much less could he have raised himself so far, after having been plunged by his ruin into death and hell, after staining himself with so many defilements, nay, even stinking in his corruption and all overwhelmed with misery?[72]

Since human beings were helpless sinners, they were also ignorant of their own good. Calvin didn't think that rationality was exempt from this perversion: Rationality was corrupt and subject to captivity. The temptation to think that rationality was untainted was in itself a manifestation of sin. Perversity and ignorance could only be overcome by God's grace, offered to us through the humility of God's taking on human flesh. Since we could not ascend to God, God would descend to humanity. Sin, then, had a double consequence: humanity became hideous to God, and God became terrifying for humanity. "Thus the man enslaved to sin cannot take up any other attitude towards God but that of escape from him, be it only by denying him…"[73]

The sacrificial act of Jesus/Christ on the cross activated both salvation and election. Jesus/Christ was fully human (except for sin), subject to passions and fears, and possessing a human soul. His voluntary abasement provided common ground bridging the chasm between God and humanity. In this way, Calvin hoped to protect the true obedience of Christ as a (human) act of free will and, therefore, a meritorious act. Calvin, unlike Luther, and like Aquinas, was more concerned to protect the humanity of Christ than the divinity of Christ. The human dimension of Christ's person was what allowed justification to be counted meritorious for humans. As humans, we are hidden (from God's sight and wrath) in Christ's humanity, partakers with him in the benefits of his sacrifice. Calvin compared the activity of humans with that of Jacob, who took on the identity of Esau to receive a blessing. "And we in like manner hide under the precious purity of our first-born brother, Christ, so that we may be attested righteous in God's sight."[74] Both Calvin and Luther claimed that the merits of Christ's sacrifice attached to humans by imputation, and not by any human merit. Luther thought the imputation was granted more through the divinity of Christ, while Calvin claimed it was through the humanity of Christ. For Calvin, the church was that gathering of the elect and a visible embodiment of God's will to save the chosen.

The unity in the two natures was still necessary to each Reformer. For Calvin, the unity of the natures was to protect against a change in divinity itself: The humility of Christ was an example for our own repentance and humility. Whereas Luther had rejected "Jesus-as-example" soteriologies, Calvin required it.

> Whence there comes to us a singular consolation, which is, that by enduring all miseries, all those things that are called adverse and evil, we share in the cross of Christ, to the end that even as he passed through an abyss of every evil to enter into celestial glory, so we also through diverse tribulations may attain thither …The more we are afflicted and endure miseries, so much the more certainly is our association with Christ confirmed.[75]

In opposition to Luther, Calvin interpreted the cross as a revelation of human sin and the necessity for human repentance and humility through suffering. One of Calvin's unique contributions to christological and soteriological thought was his own peculiar solution to the two-natures dilemma. In order to protect both God's majesty and Jesus' humanity, Calvin argued that there was a part of Jesus' humanity that was not fully "in communication" with the divine nature. It was this exemption that allowed for Christ's sacrifice to be both necessary (human) and efficacious (divine). Theologians refer to this as "extra calvinisticum," the notion that there was an extra and protected dimension of divinity that didn't communicate with the human part of Christ. This "extra" divinity was necessary for salvation.[76]

Both Luther and Calvin were captive to the notions of substitution (Anselm) and the penal theory (Aquinas). Both were quite comfortable with the language of punishment and propitiation; Christ's death on the cross was a forfeit made on behalf of humanity. Neither could break out of the theological stalemate created by the notion of a propitiation on one hand and the two-natures problem on the other. Luther and Calvin both wrote of a "war between God (the Father) and God (the Son)."[77] Luther solved the problem by a negotiation within the Godhead itself, reclaiming earlier interpretations of divine victory and reviving certain elements of the ransom theory and its notion of human bondage.[78] Calvin attempted to solve the problem without compromising God's majesty.

But note also that Calvin had his own version of the ransom theory where the "trickery" involved a negotiation between humans and the human nature of Christ. Luther protected radical grace at the expense of divine dignity, while Calvin tried to protect costly grace at the expense of divine immediacy.

Calvin's attempts to avoid cheapening grace undergird his discussion of the offices of Christ, derived primarily from Jesus' earthly ministry. The redemptive office of Christ as mediating priest (derivative of his divinity) was only one dimension of his work. Christ was also prophet and king, the teacher of the things of God. To his credit, Calvin assumed that faith included practices of grace: acts of humility and neighbor-love. While Calvin can easily be misunderstood (especially with regard to his theology of the cross) to endorse a moralistic attitude, he was always eager to avoid that misunderstanding. Neither Calvin nor Luther suggested that salvation came through human works or anything other than Christ's redemptive sacrifice. Calvin's appropriation and application of natural order and natural law was almost as thorough as Luther's. However, his doctrine of the fall and the universal depravity of human beings actually blunts any romanticism about a natural hierarchy of rationality or flesh. Calvin was much more likely than either Luther or Aquinas to be pessimistic about social structures. Calvin did not exempt social structures from critique, and thereby laid the foundation for a material analysis of social structures. As Nicholas Wolterstorff points out:

> The Calvinists knew that they ought to be exercising their obedient gratitude in their occupations and in their social roles in general, but the very Word of God which told them this also showed them that the social roles presented to them were corrupt and not fit instruments for obedience…Restless disciplined reformism, or guilt for not being restlessly reformist: these are the characteristic components of the Calvinist social piety.[79]

Calvin's insistence that Christianity be an ethical religion where Christian vocation demanded radical social neighbor-love is consistent with much contemporary liberation theology. Calvin and Luther both criticized the notions of coercive power that lay at the heart of christological rationales for social control. Luther's theology of the cross radically reconfigured power as the power of unselfish love. Calvin simply articulated it more fully and vehemently than did Luther, giving it a communal dimension of ethical unselfishness toward the rest of the world. Calvin's understanding of proper humility had as its correlate the imperative for loving others in the flesh. The right devotion to God was necessary to displace inordinate self-love so that believers could do justice to their neighbors.[80] A theology of glory is replaced by a theology of the cross, necessitating radical commitments to the less fortunate:

Christ is either neglected or given care in the person of those who need our assistance. As often as we are reluctant to help the poor let the sight of the Son of God come before our eyes, for to deny him anything is sacrilege of the deepest order.[81]

Calvin's understanding of preaching was more ecclesial than individual; preaching was to form the covenantal community in conformity with God's purposes for reconciling the world. If Luther's congregation gathered for consolation, Calvin's congregation of the elect gathered for edification, reproof, correction, and instruction. Grace might be a comfort, but it also made ethical demands. Calvin's notion of a covenant community demanded that salvation did not end with the believer's experience of grace, but resulted in a community dedicated to ethical engagement in society. Calvin's theo-ethics came from his understanding of the Law as a good gift: convicting sinners of their fallibility and forming them for social duty. Like Luther, Calvin preached exegetically, but Calvin's two-part sermons followed another familiar convention of exposition/application. He wanted to make sure that believers understood their responsibilities to reshape the world. One of his greatest concerns was the growing sectarianism of the Anabaptists and their withdrawal from the worldliness of the world. Calvin believed that the world was precisely what God wanted reformed.

Contemporary Homiletic Implications

For contemporary women preachers and pastors there is much to gain from the Reformation revisions, but there are also blunders to avoid. Luther's turn toward the human experience of redemption and the subjective appropriation of radical grace is a positive change. This shift toward the experiential attends to what we might currently recognize as a social reconstruction of God. Luther understood that persons who were terrorized by God would behave in certain competitive and self-oriented activities. He assumed that if we articulated a God who was radically gracious, even to the undeserving, we would be liberated to behave with more neighbor-love and less judgmentalism. He rejected the notion that our suffering was either necessary or meritorious, since Jesus had already resolved that issue with his own suffering. Luther's turn toward the proleptic or anticipated experiences of God's ultimate victory over Satan and demonic powers and principalities opens the door for the *basileia* rhetoric of the New Testament and the early church. Where eschatology had been eclipsed, this reclamation of the highly charged *christus victor* and ransom theory of a struggle between the powers of good and the powers of evil allowed for social engagement and critique even if he did not himself engage such analyses.

Calvin's experiential turn likewise attended to the experience of guilt, but tended to reclaim guilt (and not gratitude) as a motivation for ethical behavior. What is positive about this experiential turn with Calvin is that it shifts attention away from the inner life of Jesus to the corporate life of the community. Calvin seemed to be asking how a community's experience of ethical imperative might shape its common life in the world. His "loophole" regarding Christian vocation and the natural order allowed Christians to faithfully resist authority structures in the event that those structures were hostile to God's redemptive purposes. Even if Calvin himself did not draw out the liberating and revolutionary possibilities of this loophole, the implications nonetheless stand. Calvin's turn toward the experience and practices of ordinary Christian communities is consonant with some of the more egalitarian and radical impulses of the early church and the New Testament writings. Allegiance to God through Jesus the Christ was primary and even held priority over states and kings.

Perhaps against their own intentions, both Calvin and Luther offer strategies for challenging the power of kyriarchy. Luther's turn toward subjective experiences of mercy liberated individuals from the dynamics of guilt and shame that ultimately lead to competitive self-seeking. His theology of the cross was an epistemological strategy allowing believers to see all other individuals as those in need of mercy, and in this regard, it was radically egalitarian. If everyone is a sinner who has been forgiven, no one has the religious advantage. Calvin's turn toward communal experiences of duty turned attention to the world that God so loved. His own theological anthropology undercut notions of spiritual perfection and ontological superiority. The Christian community was an elect community, not because it was better than other communities, but because it had a mandate to serve the world responsibly.

Another advantage is that both Luther and Calvin articulated their theological projects in the language and metaphors of the biblical narratives. Both were suspicious of scholastic theology and its metaphysical underpinnings, realizing that medieval philosophical speculations had taken christology far beyond the everyday lives of ordinary believers. They were first and foremost preachers, concerned with articulating Christian claims in ordinary language accessible to their congregations and in some conformity with New Testament understandings. This return to biblical categories and theological understandings had the advantage of returning theological discernment to the common folk and their common texts; it undercut elitist theological knowledge. There are problems with the subsequent individualizing of interpretation, but they should not be sufficient reason to repeal the shift. In addition, the return to biblical categories and narratives also had the advantage of recovering the eschatological dimension of Christian faith as it related to the ethical projects of local communities. For Luther, the eschatological dimension of faith was in the personal "resurrection" of the redeemed sinner, set free for faith. For Calvin, the eschatological dimension of faith was in the corporate resurrection of the covenantal community, bent on reforming and resurrecting the world.

But there are blunders. Luther's subjective appropriation of justification through grace by faith has licensed an almost inescapable individualism. His attention to the inner life of the believer reinscribed a self-orientation not unlike medieval moralism or contemporary self-actualization schemes. This focus on the inner life almost eclipsed any sense of *common* vocation, and particularly if this common vocation involved challenging earthly authorities. In an odd split, Luther rejected the priestly authority of the Catholic church, but not the earthly authority of males! His understanding of powers and principalities did not extend to the "earthly kingdom" of social realities but seem confined to "heavenly kingdom" of spiritual powers and principalities that hold human spirits captive. His own theology of the cross could critique his truncated social vision and the natural orders of creation, requiring males to see the world in humility from the [underside] foot of the cross. For men to go through the cross, they would have to be humbled, relinquish earthly and social advantage: They would have to sacrifice their own notions of earthly power. As Karen L. Bloomquist claims, "a 'theology of the cross' (that God is revealed through suffering and weakness rather than through glory) need[s] to be applied far more directly and deeply to the heart of the current dilemma of *men* in this patriarchal society."[82] A Lutheran theology of the cross is most problematic if it is selectively applied to women and other socio-politically oppressed, but can become radically egalitarian if employed in a thoroughgoing manner. We'll pick this theme up later in a discussion of a constructive theology of the cross for women.

The most significant blunder of the Reformation theologians was in extending the development and articulation of the penal theory. A quick survey of christology and soteriology shows two major shifts: from christology-from-below to christology-from-above and from reconciliation to punishment. In some ways, the Reformation formulation is even more pernicious, since it reorients christology to the work and offices of Jesus' earthly ministry, but does so within an interpretive grid of sacrificial propitiation. Where the primitive christus victor theory was a dramatic escape from suffering, the penal atonement theories of both Luther and Calvin plunge us directly into ministries of suffering. To be sure, Luther's approach avoided works righteousness by claiming that suffering is not meritorious for salvation; however, suffering is a good gift we offer to God and to others. For Calvin, suffering was an imitation of Christ and, consequently, almost necessary for the faithful life.

Most Protestant women preachers operate within liturgical contexts dominated by either Lutheran or Calvinist understandings. Our eucharistic liturgies are profoundly shaped by sacrificial, judicial, and penal metaphors. Even those of us who preach within American free church traditions realize that most of the communion prayers and folk piety are formed by assumptions that Jesus had to die in order for us to be saved. The imaginary Rev. Ms. Jones at the beginning of this chapter is a sorry example of our own forgetfulness. We preach to people whose religious language and identity is dominated by variations on the sacrificial theme. We probably cannot afford to overlook the way these theological ideas form communities and shape their own devotional lives and their understandings of common ministry. For women preachers and pastors, the christological crisis comes precisely at this convergence of a traditional "vocation of suffering" and contemporary "vocation of resistance."

One of the other difficulties is the pastoral challenge of preaching or counseling among people who are in abusive situations. When women, children, or other disenfranchised people interpret their own suffering as divine punishment that they must endure in obedience, the "trouble with Jesus" becomes gruesomely apparent. Individuals in abusive situations internalize their abuse as something that they deserve and must endure. Sheila Redmond identifies five Christian virtues that hinder recovery from abuse, and almost all of them are intensified by Reformation theologies: the value of suffering, the virtue of forgiveness, the responsibility for chastity or sexual continence, the need for salvation, and the value of obedience to authorities.[83] Individuals who suffer in abusive relationships assume that they are guilty, that they deserve their suffering and humiliation, that their tolerance of it is a moral virtue, that they should forgive their abusers, and that they should be obedient to their abusers under any circumstances. Victims of abuse often "comply" because their understanding of virtue promotes submission to suffering as something that God desires. Their suffering is understood as redemptive. These virtues reinforce a sense of personal guilt and ongoing shame that make resistance seem unfaithful at best and impossible at worst. The paradigmatic exercise of abusive power over the powerless is constituted by theological understandings of God as the indignant male-in-power and Jesus as the obedient and submissive child. At least within the Anselmian model, God was the unmoved mover who deserved restitution but did not desire or orchestrate it. With the Reformation shift toward a penal theory and a passionate deity, the suffering of the Son becomes a divine punishment coordinated by the Father. As Rita Nakashima Brock points out:

> Such doctrines of salvation reflect and support images of benign paternalism, the neglect of children, or, at their worst, child abuse, making such behaviors acceptable as divine behavior...

[t]he father allows, or even inflicts, the death of his only son…[T]he shadow of the punitive father must always lurk behind atonement.[84]

Brock also claims that theologies whose purpose is to emphasize God's radical grace and mercy cannot do so through a narrative of abusive power. Grace and mercy cannot come through stories of punishment and violence. The experience of grace predicated by Reformation theologies is largely a sense of escape or relief from an otherwise vengeful God. Why else would we have to be "hidden in Christ" unless the punitive parent was on the prowl? Women theologians will have to find some way of making Luther's claims of grace and Calvin's claims for communal responsibility without the "motivation" of an angry God. But we will need to do so in a way that doesn't overlook the reality of human evil and the will to power.

Summary

We have traced a brief history of the major shifts and blunders in the evolution of christology and atonement theories for the purposes of identifying strengths and problems within the tradition. This survey has explored the complex accumulation of problems that are of particular interest to women preachers and pastors who hope to construct christological perspectives that do not reinforce oppressive practices against women and other disenfranchised individuals. In the next chapters, I will explore the responses of women theologians to the tradition, evaluate their strengths and weaknesses, and offer a constructive christology for preaching within the common narratives and symbols of ordinary Christian believers.

Before we turn to those concerns, it will be helpful to summarize the directions for such a constructive project. From Augustine, we want to remember that sin is a universal human reality. However, we want to avoid reducing human fragility to sexuality. Augustine's poetic device of using gender stereotypes for perfection and imperfections will have to go, along with his assumptions that human rationality is exempt from critique.

From Anselm, we want to retain the idea that our God-talk is subject to moral categories. Even if we disagree with his final analysis of what constitutes the morality and perfection of God, we want to maintain the notion that our theological reflections say something about God's own character. However, we want to reject the idea that God is unmoved, or that the balance of the cosmos will be righted by a perfect sacrifice. Substitution may not be a moral strategy in and of itself.

With Aquinas, we want to agree that the office or work of Jesus is of significance. Aquinas began the shift in the medieval period toward the ministry of Christ, even if it was a highly ecclesiastical understanding. Without Aquinas and his reclamation of Aristotle's notion of virtuous practices, we could not get to Calvin's own understanding of a communal project. However, much of Aquinas is problematic. The deep misogyny and the hierarchical pattern of the natural orders was a theological disaster. We want to stay as far from biological essentialism as possible.

From the Reformation we want to retain Luther's and Calvin's attention to the work, ministry, and practices of Christ. Their theological shift toward experience and the practices of believers is helpful. With Luther, we want to reclaim the notion that God is merciful and does not desire our misery. From Calvin we can appropriate the ethical impulse of the world-reforming community. However, we want to reject any idea of a punitive God and the ultimate worthlessness of humanity. We may also want to be cautious about Reformation notions of individual salvation.

Overall, we have sketched out a series of shifts from a christology of reconciliation that saves the world from demonic power to a christology of retribution that saves the world from divine wrath. From the primitive christus victor of the early church to the *theologia crucis* of Luther, we have marked the complexities and alliances of God and the world. As we turn to explore women's theologies, we want to keep all these precedents in mind.

Chapter 3

Women and Contemporary
Christological Options

*Few, perhaps, have really intended to do wrong; but
little do they know the embarrassment to which they
have subjected a large portion of the church of
Christ...Yes, answer, ye thousands of female disciples,
of every Christian land, whose pent-up voices have so
long, under the pressure of these man-made restraints,
been uttered in groanings before God.*[1]

Any attempt to classify women's christologies into neat categories
will be difficult and naturally reductionistic. Most of the women's
christologies surveyed here are complex and eclectic, and there are probably not many of the scholars who would consider themselves systematic theologians. Many are trained in other disciplines and come to
christological reflection for the bearing it has on ethics, ecumenism, history, or world religions. The fact that so many women are currently writing in this area attests to its centrality as an interpretive paradigm.

Still, we want to explore "family resemblances" within emerging
approaches to discover the contours of each option, what advantages
they offer, and what problems they pose for the local preacher. It's important to keep in mind that the demands of pastoral theology are different from those of other types of theology: philosophical, historical,
ethical, constructive, and sacramental. Aristotle would remind us that
theoretical proposals become wisdom only when enfleshed in practice.
We want to press toward the practical, toward wisdom, by surveying
their advantages over classical doctrines and interpretations. Preachers
and local pastors may find some new ideas intellectually satisfying and
ethically superior, but of little use within the congregational setting. One
of our guiding concerns will be whether or not certain proposed
christological understandings offer possibilities for using traditional language and symbols. So we won't consider pros and cons in a vacuum,

but within the context of congregational leadership, asking, "Is this accessible for the average believer on an average Sunday?"[2]

Sophia/Wisdom Options

We begin with contemporary Sophia/Wisdom approaches that build on theological understandings within both the Hebrew and Christian writings.[3] Within the Hebrew scriptures, Wisdom is personified as a woman in direct relationship with God and with humanity. As prophet of God, she has various roles; she's a mediating messenger to the faithful, she personifies wise counsel and the "way of the Lord," she is the gracious hostess who sets a feast for her guests. Wisdom is portrayed as a wife, sister, and friend, and sometimes as co-existent with God. But in most cases Wisdom is a narrative foil for the loose woman or harlot who leads the unsuspecting into the wrong paths. She is strong, omnipresent, righteous, and instructive: an advocate of Torah and the purposes of the Lord. She can function as a prophetic-apocalyptic figure or as a nurturing counselor. One common narrative portrays Wisdom as the prophet who came to the people, was rejected, and subsequently returned to God to wait for a better reception in the future.

The symbolic and narrative similarities to Jesus, the Holy Spirit, and Mary are apparent. As a sort of Rorschach figure, Wisdom is capable of synthesizing other mythic (and pagan) figures with radical monotheism. As a symbolic figure, Wisdom is remarkably elastic, capable of including biblical creation stories, apocalyptic restoration concepts, and the prophetic impulse. Some scholars suggest that Lady Wisdom functioned as a generic goddess figure who subsumed other goddesses within the framework of Hebraic monotheism.[4] She is a generative metaphor par excellence.

Within New Testament Christianity, the role of Wisdom/Sophia is still present, but diminished. The clearest counterpart is the role of the Holy Spirit as the ongoing contextualized voice of God to the people. Sophia/Wisdom becomes part of the Trinity as the only neuter member of trinitarian schemes. To some degree, Sophia is recast as the masculine figure of Jesus himself, the rejected messenger from God who tries to counsel followers "in the way," and she is also conflated with the virginal figure of Mary, in contrast to the whores and harlots who represent idolatry.[5]

Elisabeth Schüssler Fiorenza offers the most theologically compatible Sophia to date: a symbolic figure of Divine Wisdom who is the theological impulse behind the anti-kyriarchal Jesus basileia movement. She portrays a Jesus movement that is continuous with and sypathetic to other Jewish messianic movements and whose wisdom is that of eschatologial restoration. Divine wisdom is the "kerygma" or message of the Jesus movement and Jesus is a prophet of Sophia. Schüssler Fiorenza grounds her understanding of the Jesus movement in apocalyptic messianism, since such a movement would have been historically plausible, theologically appropriate to both Judaism and Christianity, and provides the most adequate hermeneutic approach to the eschatological dimensions of the New Testament. As long as she stresses the apocalyptic dimension of Wisdom/Sophia theology, her argument is on the best footing to provide a female figure, associated with both testaments, who promotes social and political renewal. Sophia/Wisdom is the "divine savior figure who promises universal salvation."[6]

Her appropriation of Jewish Wisdom theology offers a language world and mythological frame of reference for interpreting the attempts of the earliest Jesus movement to make sense of the ministry and death of Jesus and also suggests why later christological developments within the early church masked Sophia elements. Institutionalized Judaism and the growing institutionalization of the Christian cult demanded a rejection of anything revolutionary. And apocalyptic messianism was destabilizing to both secular powers and religious authority. "The whole tenor of apocalyptic eschatology express[es] a memory and a hope of liberation that no astute ruling foreign power could fail to perceive as threatening."[7] This prophetic/messianic impulse is integral to Schüssler Fiorenza's use of the Sophia/Wisdom figure. She argues that the kingdom language and images of both testaments can be seen as inherently political and liberating, since they relativize and displace worldly kings and kingdoms with divine sovereignty.[8] The apocalyptic dimension of Sophia theology is consistent with the messianism of the earliest proclamation:

> Jesus and his first followers, women and men, sought the emancipation and well-being of Israel as the people of G*d, a kingdom of priests and a holy nation (Exod. 19:6). They announced the basileial commonweal/empire of G*d as an alternative to that of Rome...It was also a political symbol that appealed to the oppositional imagination of people victimized by an imperial system. It envisioned an alternative world free of hunger, poverty, and domination.[9]

Schüssler Fiorenza claims that this imagined world was already partially present in the activities of the primitive Christian movement, "in the inclusive table community, in healing and liberating practices and in the domination-free kinship community."[10] And as Fredriksen points out, it's easy to see how these practices and the proclamation of messianic reversal would have been seen as politically hostile to Rome and religiously hostile to institutionalized Judaism. Such teachings radicalized the prophetic ethic at the heart of Judaism in ways that jeopardized the fragile alliance between the synagogue and the empire. Jesus, as prophet of Wisdom/Sophia, was rocking everybody's boat.[11]

Elizabeth Johnson also uses Sophia/Wisdom elements in her approach to christology. She claims that Jesus was identified in early thought as the "Sophia of God." This identification emerged because it was familiar to both the Jewish scriptures and to secular culture as "a female personification of God in outreach to the world."[12] Sophia, as co-creator of the world, protector of the poor, and teacher of mystery, is an implicit paradigm for both Paul and John. "From Paul, who calls Jesus the wisdom of God (1 Cor. 1:24), to John who models Jesus and his long discourses upon Sophia, wisdom christology offers the possibility of affirming the significance of Jesus Christ and of confessing even his divinity in a non-androcentric framework."[13] Johnson claims that reversals are at the heart of Sophia theology and that Jesus incarnates these oppositions of crucifixion and glorification, divinity and humanity.[14]

One significant problem is that the Wisdom/Sophia figure frequently symbolizes social success and respectability and is not always the subversive character that Schüssler Fiorenza and Johnson imagine. Carol Newsom argues that the Wise Woman of Proverbs 1–9 reinforces sex role stereotypes, social boundaries, and the cultural mores of the father-figure. Lady Wisdom is always contrasted to the objectified "other" or "strange" woman who represents danger (sex!) to the young man. The strange woman is off-limits, limits that are guarded by the Wise Woman to keep the young man "on the way."[15] And Cindy Nelson points out:

> In any society where women are on the boundaries, are marginalized, from the centers of social/political/economic power, they can be seen to constitute the frontier berween order and chaos. They can merge into the chaotic "outsider" world as in the case of the whore or seductress. Conversely, they can stand as the boundary markers between purity and pollution…for preaching purposes, we ought to be careful about preaching texts that portray women as the gatekeepers of a stable society.[16]

Lady Wisdom may, in fact, function more as the idealized wife and mother, who would protect Jesus from the (polluting) riff-raff whores and scoundrels he consorts with. She may not be a liberating figure at all, but a reinscription of stereotypical "motherly" attributes.[17] Certainly we would want to be careful of appropriating a Sophia figure who reinscribes female antieroticism (virginity or asceticism) or the language of sexual purity/pollution. Wisdom is socially respectable, and her followers can expect to be successful pillars of society. Jesus is not socially respectable, and his followers can expect to be quite unsuccessful, strung up.

Another disadvantage to Sophia/Wisdom approaches is the unfamiliarity of the figure in mainline Protestant congregations. Wisdom theology may be more accessible to Catholic homileticians, since a strong Mariology already offers a female figure who can be associated with both God and Jesus.[18] In fact, both Schüssler Fiorenza and Johnson recommend this association to the extent that Mary is a demythologized (de divinized) advocate of the poor and a single mother who "interrupts the kyriocentric celebration of the eternal feminine" and "subvert[s] the tales of Mariological fantasy and cultural femininity."[19] Schüssler Fiorenza opts for Mariology-from-below to coexist with a christology-from-below, which reinforces her interpretation of the Sophia symbol. Women preachers attracted to Sophia approaches will need to be careful not to reinscribe either the cultural notions of "good citizen" and social success onto Christianity or to project the stereotyped female virtues of the "good wife" and "controlling mother" onto Jesus, Sophia, or Mary. However, mother figures may be more and more accessible as christological paradigms. Almost all of the christologies under consideration have the attributes of strong women and mothers.

Another possible problem is the easy association of Sophia/Wisdom with a high Logos christology. As a symbol of spirit and mind, Sophia/Wisdom can easily play into the classical mind/body dualisms. As a variety of trickle-down christology, Sophia approaches frequently use the language of incarnation. Johnson does consider Sophia to be the wisdom of God incarnated in Jesus, an odd mind/body split that will probably reinscribe many of the problems of classical christology. Even though the female figure is personified as an embodied person, there is the risk of associating Sophia/Wisdom with the gnostic approach to right thinking and right knowledge. These are the associations most familiar to ordinary congregations and may not be the ones we want to reinforce.

Within mainline Protestantism, Sophia/Wisdom will seem most compatible with the activity of the Holy Spirit. While this continuity of the Holy Spirit with Hebrew Wisdom is a scholarly strength, it may not operate favorably within ordinary Protestantism. God's guiding presence, represented by Wisdom in the Hebrew scriptures and by the third person of the Trinity in the New Testament, bear little resemblance to each other at a practical level. Wisdom teaches ethics, good behavior, radical loyalty, and social justice, while the Holy Spirit is commonly associated within Protestantism as some amorphous inner feeling or expression of ecstasy. The activity of divine Wisdom within contemporary Protestantism (whether mainline denominations or parachurch gatherings) is interpreted as a highly individualized and internalized mystical experience. There are few norms and relatively little content for defining an encounter with this "teacher and advocate of God." Preachers may have significant obstacles to overcome if they attempt to construct

an ethical Sophia and then associate it with the Holy Spirit. The precedents for a prophetic Holy Spirit are present in the Protestant tradition,
but they don't ordinarily operate within contemporary congregations,
who prefer Holy Comforter metaphors. Sophia approaches may be particularly fruitful if handled critically by preachers. By avoiding a couple
of serious temptations (virtuous woman, individualized Holy Spirit,
gatekeeper of society) Schüssler Fiorenza's model of Sophia has integrity to the tradition and is also liberating. As the eschatological hostess,
Sophia is also compatible with eucharstic symbols and meanings.

The biggest difference between Sophia and Jesus is that she is no
tragic figure suffering on behalf of the people. The Wisdom figure of the
Hebrew Bible tradition may be rejected by people, but then she goes
home to wait it out, which could be interpreted as abandonment. Bluntly,
unless we displace a certain amount of Wisdom/Sophia symbolism, the
figure cannot be made to conform to a crucified and resurrected redeemer
figure. As far as the teaching ministry of Jesus goes, Sophia/Wisdom
may be an analogue of the parabolic or trickster prophet and an accessible figure.[20] But when we move beyond the teaching ministry into the
charged symbols of Passion Week, she probably can't be sufficiently interpreted without reversing some of the key categories.[21]

Womanist Options

African American women theologians have developed several distinctive alternatives to both classical christology and twentieth-century
white feminist christologies. Jacquelyn Grant was one of the first contemporary black female scholars to challenge the primary white feminist approaches, in *White Women's Christ, Black Women's Jesus.* Her early
critique must be set within the context of her primary white dialogue
partners: Virginia Ramey Mollenkott, Letha Scanzoni, and Nancy
Hardesty (whom she characterized as biblical feminists), Letty Russell
and Rosemary Radford Ruether (typed as liberation feminists), and Mary
Daly (as a rejectionist, or post-Christian).

One of Grant's strongest challenges to white feminists was the uni-
versalizing bias suggesting that *feminist* theology spoke to all women.
"The seriousness of the charge White feminists make regarding inappropriate male universalism is undercut by the limited perspective which
presumes the univerality of women's experience."[22] If feminists were
arguing that theology, and particularly christology, be conversant with
women's experience, how could they be so blind to the experiences of
women of color? Grant suggested that white feminist christologies were
oblivious to issues of race and class, attending only to issues of gender.
Grant argued from a christologicial assumption that since "Jesus located
the Christ with the outcast, the least, christology must emerge out of the
condition of the least."[23]

Because of her own theological starting point in the biblical narrative of Jesus' compassion/passion, Grant was suspicious of white feminist trends that weakened biblical authority or that rejected suffering as a category of theological reflection.

> Chief among [the experience of Black people] was the belief in Jesus as the divine co-sufferer, who empowers them in situations of oppression. For Christian Black women in the past, Jesus was their central frame of reference...as Jesus was persecuted and made to suffer undeservedly, so were they.[24]

We should notice that while many white feminists had rejected Anselm and "sacrificial suffering" as a total package, Grant rejects Anselm's atonement theory and reverses it to the "primitive atonement" theory. Suffering is neither God's will, nor redemptive of itself. Crucifixion is a symbol that points to the human captivity to evil power, and the crucified Jesus symbolizes God's solidarity in that suffering. Grant's rejection of Anselm is an act of solidarity with ordinary believers, for whom Jesus was a liberator and a political messiah whose mission was to free humans from bondage. As the crucified messiah, Jesus could identify with the least of these; as the risen Lord, he signified real embodied triumph over suffering.

Grant did find the feminist critique of patriarchy helpful despite its limitations. Christology must be egalitarian and not hierarchical, "the significance of Christ is not his maleness but his humanity," a theme picked up by Kelly Brown Douglas in *The Black Christ*.[25] Grant also appropriates a strategy of James Cone's by asserting that the "soteriological meaning" of the Jewishness of Jesus is important precisely because it locates salvation in the experience of socio-political marginality. In some sense, Grant argues for a continuity with the prophetic tradition of the Hebrew Bible, which puts her strategy in a better position than overt anti-Judaism, but there are still supercessionist problems behind Cone's assumption that Jesus fulfills the original intentions of God.[26] In the shift toward an "ontology of marginality," Grant aligns her christology with the positions that critique power and hierarchy of all forms and that will ultimately undercut any claims of Christian superiority. Embracing the power critique will also allow for local analyses of basic church leadership structures, which reinscribe the continuation of a privileged class.[27]

Delores Williams is another womanist theologian who uses a three-way critique of classical Christianity. Williams discusses the traditional idea of Jesus as a surrogate or substitute figure who has salvific power, but who also reinforces passivity. As a biblical theme, surrogacy is related to the suffering surrogacy of Hagar (who was a biological substitute for Sarah) and the domestic surrogacy of slaves and mammies (who were labor substitutes for white women).[28] Surrogacy has historically been a problem for African American women, who have shouldered the labor not only of white women but also of African American men. The coerced surrogacy of the antebellum period was displaced by the voluntary (but pressured) surrogacy necessitated by the unemployment or absence of black males. "In the black community black women could be pressured by social circumstances to step into the role of head of household in lieu of absent male energy and presence."[29]

With regard to christology, the problem is the place of the cross as a symbol of self-giving love: Anselm's atonement theory. "Can there be salvific power for black women in Christian images of oppression (for example, Jesus on the cross) meant to teach something about redemption?"[30] Williams concludes that nothing about God's love can be revealed in the cross and that salvific images are found in "Jesus' ministerial vision of life and not through his death. There is nothing divine in the blood of the cross."[31] Black women are encouraged to remember the cross as a symbol of human evil that should not be glorified.

Instead, Williams advocates a christology of incarnation that celebrates life, and especially the life-giving symbol of women. She admits that this will be a challenge for black male liberation theologians, who are more inclined to focus on the cross as the location of revelation. She rejects any identification or solidarity in the image of cross-bearing and redemptive suffering. God, she argues, is not disclosed in suffering, but in the promise of life revealed through the traditional image of Mary.

> The word was first made flesh in Mary's body. Incarnation, in a womanist understanding of it in the Christian testament, can be regarded as a continuum of the manifestation of divine spirit beginning with Mary, becoming an abundance in Jesus and later overflowing into the life of the church.[32]

We see in Williams' interpretation several familiar themes, including the association of spirit with a woman (similar to Sophia theology), the rejection of a crucifixion/atonement image, and the language of incarnational theology. Ethically what must be reclaimed and revalued is the role of motherhood, which does not reduce to surrogacy. Williams reclaims Mary as a central figure who displaces the Hagar and mammy figures of tradition. Liberation does not come "by any means necessary," but by the life-enhancing truth contained in images of nurturing, feeding, and caring for the least of these.

Kelly Brown Douglas rejects christologies based on liberation paradigms with their "ontology of marginality." Her major work, *The Black Christ*, explores and rejects three prevailing christological models offered by black male theologians. The christology of Albert Cleage argues for a literal identification of Jesus with blackness, claiming that Jesus was probably from one of the lost tribes of Israel and was a man of color. James Cone argues for an "ontological" if not literal blackness, claiming that Jesus was in solidarity with the oppressed. J. DeOtis Roberts offered a "universal" Christ who was both liberator and reconciler.

Douglas finds these approaches inadequate. Cleage's literal interpretation makes Christ a savior with a preferential option for blacks, Cone's Christ has a preferential option for the oppressed, and Roberts' Christ just wants us all to get along. For Douglas, the first two options allow very little internal critique for the African American community, and the last option offers little prophetic critique at all. For Douglas, a Black Christ must include an ethical commitment to the African American community, but it must go beyond that. "The Black Christ does not readily challenge Black people to free themselves from the various forms of oppression within the Black community...[C]alling Christ Black doesn't prod Black people to become a 'whole' community as it struggles for freedom."[33] For Douglas, any black Christ must be committed to the liberation of blacks from whites, to the liberation of women from patriarchy, to the liberation of gay and lesbian persons from homophobic biases, to the liberation of the poor from exploitation, and to the reconciliation of all these fragmented groups into some kind of whole community. Any analysis that privileges one kind of experience (blackness, whiteness, maleness, or oppression) distorts the fullness of Christ and the fullness of reconciliation. She wants to combine the universality of Roberts' Christ with the ethical concerns demonstrated by both Cleage and Cone.

Her womanist vision of the black Christ becomes more than an endorsement for the black community, to envision a Christ who is sustainer and liberator and reconciler. "Christ is present in the Black community working to sustain as well as to deliver it from the multidimensional oppression that besets it."[34] The black Christ is present in the black community wherever the community is engaged in struggles for human wholeness, and includes promoting life for all people both within and without the black community. Christ may be imaged as a woman, but may also be imaged as a man. Douglas holds that particular communities must contextualize Christ in their own image, so that they imagine themselves as part of the body of Christ.

With her demand that any black Christ be both contextual and open, she addresses the concerns raised by Jacquelyn Grant and Delores Williams. Where Grant wants to locate christological meanings in the experience of black women, Douglas wants to avoid any totalizing claims that black women's experience is paradigmatic. "While my womanist perspective highlights the significance of Christ found in the faces of black women in struggle, especially poor Black women, it does not eliminate the possibility of Christ's being seen in the faces of Black men who also struggle for [community wholeness]."[35] By qualifying the statement about which black men can be christological icons, Douglas avoids the temptation to valorize abusive or misogynistic men. Her criterion of radical solidarity beyond issues of race allows for internal critique of black-on-black violence and male dominance. While her black Christ can be a female, it should never be used for the purposes of valorizing women over men or for avoiding the issues of classism. The black female Christ will still be in a position to critique the economic exploitation of one female by another, since the struggle is not for individual wholeness, but for communal integrity. Such contextualizations are not ultimate or literal, but are "iconic" in their ability to address specific groups. Douglas reminds us that no one symbol or icon can be fully revelatory, but that symbols and icons need to change as the community changes.[36] Indeed, a number of iconic representations of Christ are necessary for revealing the fullness of whole community life. We must be able to see Christ in a white male, a black female, a Hispanic youth, or an Asian woman; otherwise, our community understandings will be reductionistic and distorted.

With regard to Williams' concerns about surrogacy, Douglas agrees that an Anselmian christology is problematic for black women. Coercive surrogacy and involuntary sacrifice have been part of abusive patterns for too long among African American women. "An understanding of Christ that supports surrogacy cannot be liberating or life-affirming for Black women who need to be set free from oppressive forms of surrogacy."[37] However, Douglas is not so quick to reject the tradition of the slave church, which found the crucifixion and resurrection to be symbols of radical solidarity. She contends that womanist theologians must be bilingual: accountable both to the academy and to the "ordinary" black women in the church. Womanist theologians cannot simply reject the faith understandings that have sustained women in the past. Douglas wants to construct a black Christ that is sufficiently open to the contextual demands of the day and that is also sufficiently grounded in the tradition of the black church that emerged from slavery.

In this regard, crucifixion and resurrection must remain central to theological discussions. Douglas presents slave understandings of the crucifixion that are more compatible with what we have identified as a primitive christus victor approach. "Through the cross, Jesus' suffering and the slaves' suffering became one…it forged an inextricable bond between the two."[38] It was the crucifixion of Christ, and not the incarnation, that demonstrated Christ's participation in the human condition and particularly the condition of suffering. Resurrection, argues Douglas, revealed that the death on the cross was not the last word. "The crucified one was the resurrected one—who was now acting in contemporary history" in solidarity with the slaves as they suffered and sought the vindication of liberation.[39] The vindication of Jesus from undeserved suffering and death was a paradigm of liberation.

Mujerista Options

Mujerista theology is a liberation theology grounded in Latina/Hispanic faith communities of North America. Mujerista theology seeks to articulate the theologizing of ordinary Hispanic women believers and involves ethical practice as well as theory.[40] There are similarities between mujerista theology and the liberation theology grounded in Latin American Catholic theology, but there are also significant differences. First, mujerista theology is primarily concerned with three main Hispanic communities in the United States: Mexican Americans, Puerto Ricans, and Cubans. And secondly, mujerista theology is concerned predominantly with Hispanic women, critiquing the way classism and economic oppression combine with sexism and the way that ethnic prejudice combines with sexism. Isasi-Díaz and Tarango claim that Hispanic women are not unique, but distinct, since the particular compounding of oppressions does not apply equally to Hispanic men or to other oppressed groups.[41]

Mujerista theology emerged as the limits of Anglo feminism became apparent to women of color. As Isasi-Diaz explains, "the flaws in the European American feminist movement have led grassroots Latinas to understand "feminism" as having to do with the rights of European American middle-class women, rights many times attained at the expense of Hispanic and other minority women."[42] A mujerista is committed to the communal struggle of Latina women and less concerned with individual rights. Mujerista theology is grounded in Roman Catholicism for cultural and theological reasons; Catholicism is an intrinsic part of Hispanic culture, and mujeristas find empowerment in the divine image and likeness of God made visible in Mary. As both a reflective and an ethical enterprise, mujerista theology seeks to identify structures of oppression, to name sin, and to celebrate the liberating presence of God within the community. Eschatology is central to Hispanic women's theological project, since the preferred future of God breaks in upon ordinary life, offering glimpses of liberation and redemption.

Mujerista theology takes its social location among *lo cotidiano* seriously. Isasi-Díaz identifies *mestizaje* (the mixture of white and native people) and *mulatez* (the mixture of white with black) as primary contexts for Latina theologians. These contexts are valuable because they contribute to new ways of understanding pluralism. Real pluralism, she insists, takes account of actual difference without absolutizing difference. "Our theology cannot but understand all racism and ethnic prejudice as sin and the embracing of diversity as virtue."[43] The eschatological dimension of mujerista theology envisions the coming reign of God as a coming together of peoples that is non-heriarchical and non-elitist, a *kin-dom* that neither exludes nor privileges particularity.

Lo cotidiano also takes ordinary daily experience seriously. Mujerista theology is intentionally grounded in the life struggles of ordinary women and in their approaches to faith. Grassroots ways of praying, celebrating, and honoring religious figures are not rejected, but rather appropriated as resources for reflection and practice. Jesus, Mary, the saints, and the figures of popular religion (the orishas of African religions and the deities of Amerindian religions) are all appropriated as symbolic disclosures of God's purposes. *Lo cotidiano* is a descriptive, hermeneutical, and epistemological framework. Descriptively, it is socially located among a diverse and pluralistic people. Hermeneutically, it engages interpretive possibilities provided by the indigenous religious ethos. Epistemologically, it means that Hispanic women have certain ways of interpreting reality that are grounded in family life, poverty, and *la lucha*, the struggle for freedom.

Lo cotidiano is a theological framework that Isasi-Díaz contrasts to "academic and churchly attempts to see theology as being about God instead of about what we humans know about God."[44] By locating theological claims, reflections, and activities within the particular context of Hispanic women, mujerista theology implies that revelation is ongoing, that all knowledge is contextual and provisional, and that tradition is a resource without being a tyrant. Scripture and church doctrine are subject to the living traditions of the communities. Mainline theology is subject to the subversive activity of living theological agents: the *mujeristas*.

Christology is understood primarily with reference to *la lucha*, the struggle. Suffering and the struggle to survive are the primary experiences of Hispanic women. Isasi-Díaz challenges traditional understandings that suffering is a virtue and has redemptive value. This Anselmian notion has been used, she claims, as "an ideological tool, a control mechanism used by dominant groups over the poor and the oppressed."[45] She does not want to negate the reality of suffering, but to de-romanticize the spiritual value of suffering. In a clear disregard for the Anselmian trajectory, Isasi-Díaz refuses to accept that "the God whom Jesus called Father demanded or required Jesus to suffer in order to fulfill his mission on earth."[46]

In fact, Isasi-Díaz claims that Jesus (and christology) is really not very important for mujerista theological reflection. Grassroots Hispanic women relate minimally to Jesus.[47] Understandings of divinity and divine presence are approached in other ways. A highly syncretistic adoration and emulation of Mary is more figural to ordinary faith. Tarango and Isasi-Díaz interviewed one woman who discussed God and Jesus in fairly abstract language, frequently repeating phrases from creeds and catechesis. When she began talking about Mary, though, the woman's language assumed a different intensity:

> Mary for me is just great…We have but one Mary who is the Mother of God. She is the most delicate woman, the sweetest, the one who was born without sin. She was preserved to be the mother of God, she is the biggest thing in the world. She is a model for me; but who can be like Mary?[48]

Another woman describes her understanding of Jesus as a fellow human being and equal whose suffering was an example of injustice. Even though the woman interprets Jesus' ability to endure suffering as a mark of divinity, her real identification is with Mary, the mother who suffered for her child. "As a mother," she says, "the largest portion of my suffering is because of my children."[49]

Isasi-Díaz claims that the absence of Jesus from the center of popular religion has precisely to do with issues of power and imperialism. Ordinary Hispanic faith is transmitted through popular culture and oral tradition, not through official doctrine and biblical interpretation. The history of Latin America and the imposition of "official" Christianity along with Spanish culture gave indigenous peoples little active participation in interpreting or understanding Christianity. The Bible was not taught, presumably because it did not support the kind of imperialistic faith practiced by the conquistadores. Isasi-Díaz claims that "the variety of Christianity that was planted and flourished in Latin American was a non-biblical Christianity," which was adapted into the common cultural forms available through African and Amerindian religions. The Bible and Jesus belong to the world of priests and not to the world of women. Isasi-Díaz points out that in their daily experience, Hispanic women rarely relate on an equal basis with men. How could a woman relate to a male God and a male Savior? Isasi-Díaz tells of an old woman in Texas who prayed to Our Lady of Guadalupe, the local image of Mary. When asked why she did not pray to God, she replied, "God is a man and he does not understand women's problems."[50] By contrast, folk religion has Mary and the saints at its center.

Even where Jesus is more central, it is not the same person as the biblical Jesus. It is *El Señor*, the worker of miracles, who is important for his intervention and good deeds for the people, not for what he is as God incarnate. The saints are particularly focal because the legends of the saints have not been subject to as much official church control. The saints are more adaptable, and their figures have been embellished with the qualities and functions of African and Amerindian deities, "human qualities which 'official Christianity' does not emphasize, or even recognize in the lives of Jesus, Mary, and the saints."[51]

Ivone Gebara and Maria Clara Bingemer have outlined some of the strengths of a Marian theology for Latina women in Third World countries.[52] They are part of a theological transformation that seeks to reclaim the positive aspects of Mariology. Their reformulation is more compatible with the actual living faith of Hispanic women and still in conversation with traditional symbols and images of Catholicism. Where earlier feminists (usually white European American women) had rejected Mariology as a mysogynist tool promoting perpetual virginity and submissiveness, Gebara and Bingemer have reinterpreted Mary as an independent woman who actively responds to God's call. Mary becomes a model for full womanhood, whose virginity is a symbol of autonomy from male sexual oppression and whose obedience represents freedom of religious vocation. Particularly in Latin American countries and within Hispanic communities of the United States, Mary becomes the representative of the poor and the intercessor of the oppressed. The magnificat is interpreted as a call to prophetic activity and her motherhood as giving birth to the messianic revolution. Giving birth to Jesus is an eschatological glimpse into the new order. Mary is identified with the mothers who suffer as their children are being slaughtered and with the daily struggles of the poor.

In *Mary: Mother of God, Mother of the Poor*, the authors counter classical theological anthropology with their mujerista Mariology. Male-centered anthropology, they argue, has been supported by traditional christology and has proposed an idealistic and dualistic hierarchy. Dominant groups use the ideal to trivialize the actual lived experience of those they dominate. Masculinity, disembodied spirituality, and hierarchy are supported by what Bingemer and Gebara characterize as a Platonic or idealistic anthropology, the same model we have labeled "trickle-down." They propose to correct this problem within traditional Christianity by an alternative "human-centered" anthrology, where human history and experience offer paradigms of divinity. Their approach suggests a theological anthropology from below, where the reign of God and its vision of a just human world function to critique human activities. Their Marian theology does not idealize Mary as the recipient of "trickle-down" divinity. Mary, as a fully human woman and mother, and as an advocate of the poor, functions christologically to reveal what God is really like.

> Every action of Mary, of Jesus, of the prophets, apostles, disciples, male and female, converges toward the Kingdom, toward this way of being reborn in the midst of the old human race... [People] can always generate and be generated, provided they also generate a world of justice, a world of true sisters and brothers.[53]

We notice several interesting convergences between mujerista and Latina interpretations of Marian theology and Schüssler Fiorenza's Sophia/Mary model. Along with both Schüssler Fiorenza and Elizabeth Johnson, we can only recommend a clearly articulated Mary that is a de-mythologized (de-divinized) advocate of the poor and a single mother who subverts stereotypes of passivity, sexual purity, and submission. Mariology of any variety should not be used to reinforce and reinscribe patriarchal celebrations of "the eternal feminine" or fantasies of cultural femininity and idealized womanhood. Again, Mariology-from-below must coexist and conform to a christology-from-below, which takes its ethical cues from the basileia or commonwealth of God. Within mujerista and Latina theology, Mariology-from-below must always be in conversation with Isasi-Díaz's *proyecto histórico,* which emphasizes the eschatological virtues of justice and peace. Otherwise, we run the risk of reinscribing the cultural notions of "good citizen," "good wife," and "controlling mother" onto Mary. Since mujerista theologians hope to subvert a machismo that is culturally reinscribed within Hispanic contexts, an uncritical Mariology could be disastrous for women who are oppressed.[54]

There are also convergences between mujerista/Latina theologies and womanist concerns. Jacquelyn Grant argued that since "Jesus located the Christ with the outcast, the least, christology must emerge out of the condition of the least."[55] And Delores Williams insists that God is not disclosed in suffering, but in the promise of life revealed through a revised image of Mary. Her appropriation of Mary is precisely the Mariology-from-below that rejects notions of coerced surrogacy/servanthood reinscribed by romantic traditional Mariology. What must be reclaimed is a type of mother image that displaces the surrogacy of the Hagar and mammy figures with images of caring for the least of these: Gebara and Bingemer's "mother of the poor."

Probably one of the greatest challenges for mujerista theologians would be with regard to Kelly Brown Douglas' contextual requirement that crucifixion and resurrection be held together as an eschatological paradigm. Against theologies with a strong incarnational bias, Douglas insists that it was the crucifixion of Christ, and not the incarnation, that demonstrated Christ's participation in the human condition, and particularly the condition of suffering. Resurrection, argues Douglas, revealed that the death on the cross was not the last word. Without holding the cross and the resurrection in close proximity, there is no vindication from suffering. The crucified one and the resurrected one interpret each other as a complex model of liberation.[56] Suffering on the cross is a sign of Jesus/Christ's participation in the real human situation. Resurrection is the divine "no" to such human misery.

Mujerista theologians take suffering and the real human situation seriously, and the eschatological mandate for mujerista ethics is certainly in conversation with the resurrection and new life motifs of christology-from-below. It is not as clear how Mary as the suffering mother is related to either the resurrection motif or to the eschatological horizon. One Catholic theologian has suggested that some resources may lie in reclaiming the neglected Mariological motif of the assumption. Donal Flanagan claims that there has been a historic failure to integrate the narrative of Mary's assumption into heaven with liberation eschatology. Assumption could function as a symbol of the hope of the future church, Mary as an icon of the heavenly church, the ideal state of the earthly church. Note that Flanagan's shift reflects Catholic interpretations since 1950 and emphasizes the ethical community rather than the moral perfection of the individual. Mary as icon is both a symbol of the perfect member of the heavenly church and a prototype of the earthly church. In good synchronic fashion, Mary belongs to both the heavenly church and the earthly church simultaneously; she functions heuristically as one of the saints (the cloud of witnesses), but also as the bride of Christ, the new Jerusalem, the city of God come down to earth.[57] Schüssler Fiorenza has dealt similarly with the female figures of the book of Revelation, claiming that the woman clothed with the sun (in Revelation 12) is, like Mary the Queen of Heaven, a symbolic alternative to the image of Babylon, and a prototype of the new Jerusalem. "As a heavenly and eschatological figure, the symbol 'woman' signifies not only the protection and salvation of the people of God but also the future of a renewed world."[58] This connection of Mariology, the saints, and eschatology is consonant with the ethical project of mujerista theologies and could be a fruitful enterprise. And such a connection would also integrate Mariology-from-below with christology-from-below as a way of interpreting the second coming as a symbol of God's ultimate salvation/reconcilation of the human world. Mary, as the Queen of Heaven, who has also endured suffering, would be the generative (pregnant) image of the birth of a renewed future. Such a strategy would connect suffering (symbolized christologically by the cross) with vindication (symbolized christologically by resurrection) and with eschatological hope (symbolized christologically by the "birth pangs" of the second coming) and allow Mariology to function as a thoroughgoing symbolic christology.

Incarnational and Erotic Options

We've already noted that several women theologians imply incarnational interpretive schemes when they approach christology. The strength of incarnational approaches is their intention to celebrate life and embodiment. Incarnational motifs surfaced in almost each of the approaches we've surveyed so far. Some women theologians, however, are radical incarnationalists, using that category as the primary interpretive approach for doing christology. They see Jesus as a sign of God's embodiment in human flesh, indicating that humanity, sexuality, and the earth are good. As Sallie McFague reminds us, "bodies are the main attraction." Jesus is not necessarily a case of special incarnation (that is, God was not doing something extraordinary in Jesus), but a Christian contextual symbol of God's ongoing presence in the material world. Jesus is our image of God's real and historical activity in the created world. God is incarnate in our human relationships of mutuality, creativity, and justice.

Eros, as sexual or romantic life-force, is closely associated with incarnational theologies. Eros is distinct from the familiar categories of philia (brotherly love, friendship) and agape (God's love for us). Eros embraces the notions of passion and physicality, the glory of being in bodies, and of loving our body-selves.[59] Using eros as a category allows women theologians to reimage the divine-human relationship in non-dualistic terms, avoiding the split between the mind/spirit and the body and affirming the value of embodied existence. For many women theologians, to speak of incarnation, embodiment, and eros is to de-romanticize suffering and to critique physical evil. Eros and incarnation are forces of life that confront the dominion of death with an unflinching No!

Audre Lorde, African American poet and lesbian theorist, was among the first to articulate an erotic theory. Lorde came to the attention of Christian theologians in her foundational essay "Uses of the Erotic: The Erotic as Power." According to Lorde, eros is a creative energy or life-force that is the "nurse-maid of all our deepest knowledge."[60] Several women theologians have appropriated eros to discuss the divine-human relation in terms of embodiment and incarnation. Eros is a power for good, the creative potential for life, agency that is embodied in the physicality of love relations. For these theologians, eros or erotic power is a corrective to centuries of tradition that have functioned to devalue women's bodies and bodily activities.

Erotic power is the radical power of being in the flesh, incarnate. Rather than seeing Jesus as a special incarnation, women incarnationalists see Jesus as a concrete example of the erotic power of God, which is manifested in all embodied relationships. Rita Nakashima Brock calls eros "the power of our primal interrelatedness," and Anne Gilson characterizes it as "a yearning for embodied connection with one another, a movement toward embodied justice."[61] Carter Heyward claims that erotic power is "power in right relation...foundational to both sexual pleasure and play and to justice-making."[62] Erotic power is embodied in a mutual respect for real in-the-flesh creatures. To understand divine power as erotic is to respect the fullness of being embodied, to restore our capacity for delight in ourselves, one another, and creation.

Underlying most erotic christologies is the claim that our primal sensuality yearns for mutuality in others. The claim is primarily about the human desire for mutuality, just-love, companionship, passion, persuasive touch, and affirmation.[63] As human beings, we experience such relationships as energizing and life-giving. Erotic power "heals brokenheartedness and gives courage to the fainthearted." Erotic power is an alternative to coercive or dominating power; it is the luring power that calls forth in us all that is good and delightful. We long to be in life-giving relationships, and eros is the power behind such longing.

According to incarnational theologians, the human desire for creativity and relationship is fundamental to understandings of justice. Our ignorance or denial of this erotic power leads to alienation and a drive for individuation: We strive for independence. Conversely, recognition of our radical interdependence by virtue of our embodiment should lead to sympathy and solidarity. Embodiment glories in embodiment, its own and that of others. To delight in each other demands that we develop and nurture each other toward more enrichment. To love an other is to desire and promote that person's happiness and to work toward his or her wholeness. Eros assumes mutuality and produces connectedness: Eros mandates justice.

Gilson equates eros with a "radically immanent" (incarnate) God of love.[64] Eros is a world-transforming power that is ethically associated with the idea of good. Erotic faith is inherently interconnected with justice. For Gilson, eros "works toward the eradication of violence, it is rooted in a process of overcoming alienation and disconnection. Finally, eros is the action of human beings and God together, seeking incarnations of God, of justice, of mutuality in this world."[65] Eros shatters the mold of compulsory hierarchies, violence, heterosexuality, and male supremacy.[66]

Brock claims that erotic power is the source of all other power; coercive power is erotic power that has become too possessive and distorted. Rightly understood, eros is a kind of radical vulnerability and risk, an experimental passion that appreciates embodiment, fragility, and the power of powerlessness. Eros seeks intimacy and contact and is easily identified with God's passion to create flesh-and-blood humans. Erotic power is an incarnational power, striving to become embodied. The eros of God is incarnated as creativity and openness. Jesus, as a historical incarnation of God, likewise embodies this relational power in gathering disciples, healing the sick, and creating communities of empathy and support. He is subversive, offering a kind of power that is judged as powerlessness but is, in reality, the primal power to love others into their fullest beings. For many women, the concept of relational power and interdependence is attested to by the symbol of the Trinity with its dimensions of creativity, incarnation, and presence. The symbolic interpretations of God, Jesus, and the Holy Spirit should not be literalized in such as way as to attribute "special" status to the persons. God's creative passion for relationship is manifested in all incarnations: Jesus is an example of the way God works in all events. Heyward is quick to point out that God is a spiritual force that cannot be contained in any single human life, including that of Jesus.[67] To speak of the divinity of Jesus is to speak of the way that divinity operates in all life. Jesus is not exceptional, but paradigmatic.

For Brock, all human beings are created in this divine image, "that divine power is love in its fullness, and that the community of divine power is one of justice and peace."[68] She rightly critiques the hierarchical, heroic, and patriarchal family images within christology as distortions of the erotic vision. According to her, Anselmian doctrines of atonement have reinforced Jesus as a heroic figure who willingly participates in his own victimization out of obedience to an abusive father. She critiques christologies-from-above as reinforcements for a punitive Father-God and the protection of authority.[69] However, her erotic christology demands that we reject notions of redemptive suffering in favor of erotic resistance to suffering. Brock wants to shift the focus from the "heroic" self-sacrificing Christ to the life-giving presence of Christ in the Christa/community. The heroic model of christology tends to romanticize suffering and victimhood as goods in themselves. "All such death, including the crucifixion of Jesus, is tragic and should be mourned as tragic."[70] The crucifixion becomes meaningful to the extent that it demonstrates the passionate love of God in Jesus, willing to risk everything for the world. This radical passionate love does not function to placate an angry God, but to embody a compassionate resistance to dominant power. The Christa/community takes on the vocation of Christ, displacing Jesus, and becoming the "church's imaginative witness to its experiences of brokenness and sacredness of erotic power in human existence."[71] The Christa/community is the embodiment of Jesus' healing and redemptive ministry within a brokenhearted world; the church is the incarnation of, and the eschatological longing for, mutually empowering relationships. Incarnation and crucifixion are caught up in resurrection, and with the same purpose: to pursue life in the midst of death. The Christa/community is a sign of resurrection. We are a fearful gathering, but we are lured by the erotic purposes of God's loving actions toward the world. "Our wise, willful actions carried out in the fragile, resilient relationships of the saving remnant generates the divine power that makes and sustains life."[72] Our wisdom is constituted by our recognition of death-dealing and the mature knowledge that we are "fragile."[73] We are vulnerable to all the lures toward evil and the exercise of abusive power. We are not innocent. But despite our loss of innocence, we are not hopeless. Our hope is in the loving possibilities for justice that we see (imperfectly) in our solidarity with others. Together we practice the vocation of compassionate risk that refuses to give up even in the face of disaster.

Carter Heyward is a self-identified lesbian and ordained Episcopal priest. Her work on incarnation and eros is similar to Brock's but with some significant differences, especially with her emphasis on sensuality. For Heyward, the erotic is "our desire to taste and smell and see and hear and touch one another. It's our yearning to be involved—all 'rolled up'—in each other's sounds and glances and bodies and feelings."[74] Erotic faith is that which allows us to know ourselves as holy. This knowledge attributes value to our body-selves and to the body-selves of others. Eros is the God-given foundation of our common humanity and the recognition of holiness in others. Eros grounds love and justice as manifestations of our connection. The imperative of erotic faith is mutuality, since we come to know ourselves and others as sacred manifestations of God.

God is not some abstract, spiritual essence that is added to human life, but is the "common denominator" of what is most essentially human. At the same time that God grounds our common life and provides connection, God is never just "generic," but is "immersed in our gendered and erotic particularities."[75] God is not manifested in our humanity despite our differences, but most essentially in the somewhat messy and chaotic differences of real human lives. God is neither identified with a particular gender or sexuality, nor indifferent to particularity; God is pluriform, radically immanent, embodied in particularity. Being made in the image of God means that divinity is constantly in the process of emerging in a variety of human forms, including gay men, lesbians, bisexuals, and the transgendered. To paraphrase Nancy Wilson's understanding of incarnation and revelation, "God is always coming out."[76]

For Heyward, the historical figure of Jesus/Christ is a paradigm of this general incarnational activity of God. Heyward uses the term *Jesus/Christ* to keep the humanity/divinity dimensions in proper tension and balance. She wants to re-image christology beyond the traditional pendulum swing between high christologies and low christologies and to locate christological reflection precisely within this interface of the divine/human encounter. "God rarely conforms to our expectations of what a God of power and might 'should' look like," she writes.[77] Instead, we should discern the presence of God in "the least of these," those whose power looks like no power at all. Erotic faith is humble and recognizes the common humanity (and divinity) in all people. This Christlike humility is the foundation of justice, calling us to risk losing institutional and social power.

In Jesus/Christ, "our fundamental identity is not as individuals with 'rights' but as members of One Body, interdependent and mutually

responsible for one another."[78] As the Body of Christ, the church is willing to risk its own social and institutional loss of power by standing in
solidarity with those whose lives are diminished. In this confrontation
with death-dealing power, we commit our bodily activities to resist
power with powerlessness. By risking death, we embody resurrection.
Our suffering brings life out of death. "In our vulnerability and powerlessness, as well as in the sacred power we are able to generate, we stand
together and we fall together."[79] As we offer ourselves on behalf of the
broken and broken-hearted, we embody an erotic resurrection passion
for life, committed to bringing life out of death. By imaging Jesus/Christ
as the paradigm for Christian vocation, she claims that we can maintain
a unity of purpose between God and humanity. To speak of Christ is to
claim something about our own responsibility toward the future purposes of God.[80]

The strength of incarnational or erotic christologies is precisely in
their categorical challenge to Augustine's theology of sexuality. For
Augustine, eros was fundamentally a manifestation of the human tendency to grasp and possess. Erotic behavior was enslaved to sensuality,
driven to a forgetfulness of spiritual realities. Erotic behavior or passionate yearnings were signs of the human captivity to the flesh. Women
theologians who operate from an incarnational or erotic perspective want
to reverse the categories, claiming that such other-directed passion and
desire for relationship are most definitively the character of divine power.
And correlatively, the goal of mutual relationship (that respects the integrity of created beings as subjects) is God's eschatological project.
God's purposes for the world are to gather all the constituents of creation into this divine mission and to lure them toward fulfillment that is
both pluriform and unified. Such a conception of divine power mandates just relationships and ethical commitments: Bodies *do* matter.

In this regard, incarnational and erotic christologies share concerns
and similarities with others we have surveyed. With Sophia christologies,
they offer images that are favorable and familiar to the experiences of
real women. They reduce the demand for masculinity (a problem with
classical incarnational approaches) while they maintain the importance
of being bodied as a positive value for ethical projects. Incarnational
approaches may address the tendency of Sophia/Wisdom models to
spin off into spirituality and gnosticism. With mujerista christologies,
incarnational approaches value the ordinary experiences of ordinary
women, the intimacy of mothering and nurturing displace models of
the distant and domineering Father. Like mujerista approaches,
incarnational approaches value community and solidarity with the oppressed. Brock and Heyward, while not centering their christologies on
the experience of maternal suffering, do at least allow for theological
meaning in the crucifixion. Like Sophia christologies and mujerista

Mariologies, incarnational approaches run the risk of reinscribing the traditional religious virtues of nurturing and intimacy and the cultural values of "nice" femininity. For all the incarnational demands to embody communal values of resistance and transformation, the personal virtues of mutuality and friendship may lack the prophetic edge such communities require. What sets incarnational and erotic approaches apart from Sophia and mujerista christologies is precisely the eclipse of eschatology and future. Incarnationally defined communities of solidarity and risk seem most focused on the present situation of constituting a community. While directed outward toward the world, erotic christologies have not articulated as clearly what the eschatological hope is toward which such communities point.

The future toward which incarnational approaches tend is the somewhat cozy image of intimate and sensual relationships. Interpersonal friendship and mutuality can certainly contribute to a model for the basileia, but they are hardly sufficient for the kind of radical social and political reversal envisioned in the early messianic movements.

Incarnational christologies attempt to address some of the same concerns of womanist christologies when they qualify the notions of sacrifice and servanthood with claims of respect and mutuality. Erotic incarnational christologies require the same recognition of particularity and common humanity that undergird Kelly Brown Douglas' call for an open and contextual christology that is not easily reducible to a literal icon. Incarnational christologies will be most compatible with Delores Williams' womanist christology of incarnation, which celebrates life and the generative symbol of women. Williams is more radically incarnational than either Brock or Heyward, since she rejects any identification or solidarity in the image of cross-bearing. She holds that God cannot be disclosed in suffering.

However, among other womanist theologians, there are several strong objections to an incarnational starting point. The greatest distance between incarnational christologies and many womanist christologies is precisely the primary identification with incarnation. For Jacquelyn Grant and Kelly Brown Douglas, the primary identification of Jesus with the human condition is in the crucifixion and resurrection. "Through the cross, Jesus' suffering and the slaves' suffering became one...it forged an inextricable bond between the two."[81] It was the crucifixion of Christ, and not the incarnation, that demonstrated Christ's participation in the human condition and particularly the condition of suffering. Even though Grant and Douglas would reject incarnation as a primary epistemic category, they would probably not object to either Brock's or Heyward's understanding of the crucifixion/resurrection event as paradigmatic for the church's vocational identity.

Erotic christologies are helpful correctives insofar as they restore value to physical existence. A subtle danger of romanticism runs throughout many incarnational approaches. One is at the level of romanticizing desire as a categorical good, without recognizing the ambiguities and dangers of desire. Within classical philosophy, love is generally discussed along the dimensions of agape and philia in addition to eros. Heyward and Brock tend to conflate eros with the other two categories, which necessitates their warnings about the distortions or abuses of eros; clearly they both want to distinguish "right" passions from "wrong" passions. The desire for total possession or for radical merging results in a loss of the "other" as a full subject with intrinsic value. Categories of respect and mutuality are necessary prior to discussions of eros, since the possibilities for disrespectful or abusive passion are all too real. Heyward's romantic claims that eros is *our* desire to taste and smell and see and hear and touch one another leads in the dangerous direction of defining our own desires as radically honorable and good. She tends to assume a much more romantic human anthropology than real experience warrants. If erotic faith allows us to know ourselves as holy, what allows us to know ourselves as fragile, corrupt, and imperfect? Augustine may have been wrong to see us as radically depraved in our physical desires, but incarnational theologians may be shifting in the other direction. Heyward wants to claim that the symbol of Jesus/ Christ keeps divinity and humanity in creative tension and defines the unity of purpose between God and humans. What is there in the symbol of Jesus/Christ or of the cross that points to the real tendencies of humans to engage in active, passionate wickedness?

She attempts to deal with this problem by qualifying eros in terms of respect and mutuality, in the recognition that we are all subjects with legitimate "boundaries." The personhood of persons must be allowed full integrity, lest unqualified eros smother or diminish the actual particularity of a human life. For this, though, some kind of imaginative transcendence is necessary. We can never know or taste or touch enough, since some part of the other's own subjectivity is not available. Radical intimacy is not only impossible, but unethical. We can never treat the body of another as if it were our own. Wendy Farley reminds us that human life would be impossible if we lost the capacity to transcend our own immediate experience and to recognize the other as other. "Ethical existence is based on the ability to spontaneously appreciate the humanity of another person and to desire his or her own welfare."[82] For eros to function ethically, our own desires must take a back seat to the desires of an other. Our desires may be in conflict with the desires of an immediate or distant other. This is precisely the shift that both Brock and Heyward must make in order to call for suffering solidarity. Eros, they seem to say, is the capacity to displace our own bodily desires and to give some priority to the legitimate desires of others. This sounds oddly like agape love and not like the wild chaos of eros at all. In fact, this definition of eros as a deferment of bodily desires sounds like a rejection of eros.

Brock claims to reject the image of Jesus as a tragic hero, but displaces it with a descriptive construct of a tragic heroic community. She recognizes the fragility of human existence, our tendencies toward domination, and the necessity for some exercise of spiritual discipline. She calls for us to be wise and willful in the midst of a fragile world. In an odd twist, our "wise, willful actions" generate divine power. Or, perhaps, our exercise of discipline is the source of erotic power. Are we to assume that we delight in our own sacrificial activity? She makes that shift, and in so doing, she has to qualify erotic power, suggesting that it's inadequate as a construct. Erotic faith may certainly favor life, but it must, on occasion, sacrifice desire for duty.

Finally, incarnational christologies tend to subsume the activities of mind and spirit. By what faculties do we imagine our connectedness to others? Only by the activity of imaginative transcendence are we able to temporarily ignore our own bodily desires and imagine the bodied needs of others. Being embodied is not necessarily a guarantee that we will imagine other bodies; we need to be able to transcend the immediacy of our own in-the-fleshness to notice the embodied experience of others. We are more than our bodies, and incarnational approaches do not account for the "more than" that is required for such reflective activities as theology, ethics, and politics. Sympathy and compassion for others happens precisely when we temporarily "forget" our own bodies.

Asian and African Options

One of the primary concerns of Asian and African women theologians is the contextual problem of proclaiming Christian faith in the midst of radical religious diversity. Like many mujerista theologians, Asian and African women theologians have a strong ambivalence toward the dominance of Western Christian culture. For some, being Christian involves taking a faith position that is alien to their own dominant culture and that appears to reject the native values of their birth countries. This alienation from birth cultures, the need for apologetic Christianity, and the respect for religious diversity are the primary reasons for treating so-called Third World theologians together. In Asia and Africa, women and children are the poorest of the poor, and their poverty is due in large part to Western imperialism. As Korean theologian Chung Hyun Kyung writes, "Only when we Asian women start to consider our everyday concrete life experiences as the most important source for building the religious meaning structures for ourselves shall we be free from all imposed religious authority."[83] We should be clear that this freedom does not stop at a male-dominated tradition, but expands to include a suspicion of all dominant theological options, including those of First World women and feminists. The concerns of many Asian and African women include issues of gender but move beyond them to call for the liberation of humankind. At the same time, Third World women theologians make claims for cultural specificity and respect, for recognizing different forms of marriage and different family constellations, and for honoring ancestor, clan, and tribal identifications.

Suffering emerges as a primary theological theme for Third World women who operate in contexts of extreme poverty and political oppression. Chung Hyun Kyung claims that "Asian women cannot define humanity apart from their suffering."[84] She describes the structural oppression and invisibility of women who have lost their embodied presence under "the body-killing structures of the powers and principalities of the world."[85] This "no-bodiness" is powerfully reinforced both in the culture and in religion. The systemic nature of oppression is so extreme that it leads not to anger, but to hopelessness and despair: the inability to struggle for freedom. Like any abuse victims, women in such situations internalize attitudes of self-hate, prolonged shame and guilt, and the "pseudo-safety of non-feeling."[86] Both Christiaan Beker and Wendy Farley have characterized the psychic alienation that results from suffering. Suffering individuals feel isolated from other human beings, alone in a hell that is reinforced by every social encounter and structure. Such constant and systemic oppression exhausts individuals to a numbness that kills the spirit and offers little beyond passive acceptance. They are unable to summon the strength even for anger, let alone protest. Evil seems too massive, the individual feels too powerless; survival *requires* resignation.[87]

Among Korean theologians, this sense of internalized resentment is called *han*. Reactions to *han* can involve protest or passive acceptance. Many Asian religious and cultural traditions support attitudes of passive acceptance: Hinduism and Buddhism teach that suffering is something deserved and normative. To struggle against *han* would be spiritually misguided, illusory. Therefore, the preferred orientation to the reality of *han* is live at peace with suffering, accepting it as fate. Accepting powerlessness and making peace with it allows individuals to transcend suffering as something that does not ultimately control them. Chung Hyun Kyung points out that this attitude is most accommodated by traditional Christian teachings about predestination and the cross. "To be a Christian was interpreted in such a way that women were encouraged to suffer peacefully, the way Jesus suffered on the cross, because it was God's will, predestined in eternity."[88] There was a fundamental dualism required by this attitude: Women were expected to trivialize their actual bodily experience in favor of a spiritual payoff. Traditional songs, poems, and dances by Korean women have reinforced this acceptance of suffering.

Many Korean women theologians have begun to attend to another strand of women's folk culture that supports resistance to suffering. The counter-tradition of *won-han* seeks to challenge and dismantle the structure of *han*. Through satire, folktales, and proverbs, women have called passivity into question. Many Korean feminist theologians are working to reclaim the revolutionary strand of women's folk culture and to interpret it theologically. *Minjung* theology is a grass-roots theology of the people that values life, nature, and humanity. "For the minjung women, salvation and redemption means being exorcised from their accumulated *han*, untangling of their many-layered *han*."[89]

Christology shifts from the Anselmian variety of obedient suffering to a christology where Jesus sides with the oppressed in their suffering. Jesus becomes a "priest of *han*," a suffering servant who heals, comforts, and works against futility and resignation. He is like a Korean shaman who works healing magic and exorcises evil from the possessed. If the shaman is traditionally considered "big sister" to Korean women, Jesus becomes a "big sister" redeemer, intimately involved in the daily suffering of ordinary women. Jesus as shaman is a woman and sister.

Jesus is also portrayed by many Asian women as a mother. Hong Kong theologian Kwok Pui-lan identifies Jesus as the mother who weeps for her children, noting similarities between this suffering mother image and the reality of Asian mothers' fear and suffering for their children. This image of Jesus as mother is similar to mujerista approaches for christology. Chung Hyun Kyung also explores the meaning of Mary for Asian women, centering the approach in Mary's suffering and in her autonomous discipleship. Mary's virginity is not interpreted as literal chastity, but as sexual autonomy. For Asian women who are forced into lives of prostitution, this image is liberating. "The virgin birth, then, means the end of the patriarchal order...[and] shows women that salvation is sufficient without men."[90] The suffering of Mary for her crucified son is a Christlike compassion, a sorrowing so deep that female experience becomes a metaphor for Jesus' own sorrow for humanity.[91]

> It is the very person on the cross that suffers like us, was rendered a nobody, who illuminates our tragic human existence and speaks to countless women in Asia. We are not looking to Jesus as a mere example to follow, neither shall we try to idolize him. We see Jesus as the God who takes human form and suffers and weeps with us.[92]

Lee Oo Chung compares Jesus' suffering with the sorrows of women and especially of mothers. Writing about the woman who anoints Jesus, she subverts typical First World homiletical approaches by claiming that the woman identified with Jesus not because they were both boundary-breakers, but because they were both familiar with suffering.

African feminist theologians operate from similar concerns. Desperate poverty, hunger, and thirst are daily realities. Women are marginalized by many dimensions of local culture and indigenous religions, and many of the worst abuses have been reinforced by traditional Christian interpretations about women. One writer explores the devastating effects of Christian teachings about marriage that have, in fact, reversed cultural protections of women. The traditional African practice of polygamy allowed women culturally approved strategies for economic survival and the protection of their children. While we tend to think of polygamy as a type of "gross ownership" of many women by one husband, our focus on "possession" masks some of the benefits of polygamy. If we look beyond the benefits to the husband, we can also see that polygamy assumed a sort of communal solidarity and accountability for protecting the vulnerable. Wives shared child-rearing and domestic chores communally, and they were the domestic religious practitioners in charge of healing practices and performance of special rituals. Tribal elders and elder councils had provisions for protecting women from cruelty and often "met to settle serious cases of incompatibility in marriage."[93]

Women were still second-class citizens. The status of women was derived from their husbands and their children. A single woman or a childless woman was a social failure. A married woman with children was in a slightly better position, even though her success reflected favorably on the husband and failure reflected unfavorably on her. To be sure, women probably did not ever enjoy what we would call "public" honor, but she and her children were considered valuable to the whole community. To be a wife and mother was at least instrumentally important to the well-being of the whole community and a distinct advantage over being either a single childless woman or an unwed mother. Marriage was the best that many African societies could offer a woman, and polygamy ensured that every woman could find protection in marriage.[94]

Christianity, with its implications for submissive wives and monogamous marriage, displaced the tribal marriage system that had functioned, at least minimally, to protect women from poverty, ostracism, and abuse. Husbands were advised to send away their wives, relegating wives to the status of concubines and children to the status of bastards. The "lucky" women who were still wives were divested of their social protection and religious function. They could no longer practice tribal healing arts, and they were expected to be subservient. Their husbands could assume authority as heads of the household, a position previously reserved for wives. The unchecked authority of husbands allowed escalating patterns of abuse and tyranny.

Many African women theologians appropriate a liberation christology very similar to that of early white feminism. Jesus is the liberator, the paradigmatic feminist who spoke out against the sexist practices of Judaism. Grace Eneme, a Presbyterian from Cameroon, claims that "Christ was the only rabbi who did not discriminate against the women of his time."[95] Jesus was for gender equality, and we see this demonstrated in his acts of healing and acceptance of women. Jesus evidently knew that women had special spiritual gifts, "the gift of intuition and the capacity for prompt action," and he purposely chose women as witnesses to the resurrection.[96] A similar theme surfaces in Elizabeth Amoah's essay on the healing of the woman with the flow of blood. Amoah blends the model of Jesus as liberator with the model of Jesus as healer to reclaim (with a radical political twist) women's traditional rights of healing. The woman is valorized because she decided to break the rules. It is her courage to challenge the rules that leads to Jesus' recognition and healing. "True salvation," writes Amoah, "always challenges existing laws."[97] The twin themes of Jesus as liberator and as healer characterize many of the theological projects of contemporary African women.

Musimbi R. A. Kanyoro claims that these concepts from Western Christian feminists are a great gift to the church, and particularly to African women, who were typically instructed in the most evangelical and socially conservative traditions of Christianity. Rather than challenge Western feminism as elitist, many African women have adapted it to their own immediate contexts, in spite of charges by male church officials that they were being brainwashed by the West. Kanyoro is thankful to Western feminists for revealing the extent of patriarchal practices within the tradition, but she cautions, "gender alone cannot define the injustices that women experience globally."[98] She wants to tread softly to name oppressions within African culture and religions without rejecting them wholesale. "For generations, telling these stories of dehumanizing cultural practices was taboo."[99] She wants to encourage women to tell the narratives of genital mutilation, child betrothals, and the devastation of HIV/AIDS without making them feel they must stop being culturally African to do so.

For many African theologians, this reclaiming of women's religious roles as healers and bearers of (a silenced) oral tradition is indeed prophetic; by reappropriating African cultural roles for women they can critique the "rules" of patriarchal Christianity as well as the cultural oppression of women. Anne Nasimiyu-Wasike claims that of all the various christologies available to African women, the image of Jesus as healer is the most accessible.[100] As healer, Jesus cared about physical and spiritual healing as well as the healing of the earth. Our spirits, our bodies, and even nature have been captive to the sins of humanity. Jesus as healer/reconciler is the paradigmatic exorcist who casts out demonic manifestations to restore all of creation to wholeness. Such a model is in direct contrast to the hierarchical model of Jesus as "chief," one of the common male-generated christologies.[101] Chiefs are male, healers are female.

Mercy Amba Oduyoye is perhaps the "mother" of African woman theologians. As Oduyoye writes, "Finding myself in the camp of liberation theologians and Christian feminists was as natural to me as claiming the priesthood of Okomfo Anokye, the self-determination of his sisters, and the coordinating ability of Abena Gyata. This woman could not have been a leader if she had not been perceptive and compassionate, bold, persistent, and accountable to the group for its well-being."[102] For Oduyoye, since the blood of these two leaders continued to flow in her veins, she was both empowered by and accountable to their vision. One of the common themes in Third World women's theologies is remembering the ancestors, particularly strong mothers and sisters. Remembrance serves to invoke the sense of their ongoing presence in the struggle, and serves to strengthen and expand the community. Through memory, the ancestors maintain a living presence within the community. Oduyoye claims that this sense of community presence and accountability is what constitutes the essence of being human. To be human is to be in responsible relationship.

It is from this perspective that Oduyoye challenges the concept of sacrifice. Her understanding of human community assumes an eschatological dimension when she speaks of the christological mission of the church. The purpose of the church is to declare "the rule of God in the world."[103] This declaration happens through proclamation and service, but also through its ability to "represent the shape of a human community when it is fully submitted to the will of God."[104] The church incarnates the God we know in Christ as it attempts to be the first fruits of the kingdom, both a sign and a sacrament of the new humanity. We are both Christlike and Mary-like when we bear the signs of hope in the "womb of the church."[105]

Oduyoye demands that the manner of embodying the mission cannot be separated from the mission itself. And it is this specific understanding of embodying the mission of the church that allows her to approach the concept of sacrifice. "It is in this respect that I wish to situate the Christian's call to self-denial, forgoing privilege and embracing a simplicity of life whose wealth is not only in being poor-in-spirit but in being a church of the poor for the sake of the kingdom."[106] Sacrifice is not so much an individual spiritual discipline as it is the communal orientation of the church toward the world. Sacrifice is strictly delimited to corporate acts that embody the church's solidarity with the poor and oppressed. The church that risks its own corporate survival to minister to the last and the least, that forgoes social status to serve those on the bottom, that repudiates institutional wealth and the accumulation of property is like a "bride" of Christ who serves to build a household of integrity and mutual service.

The most dramatic difference between these notions of sacrifice surfaces when we consider sacrifice within the proleptic mission of the church. The wifely model of individual sacrifice serves to reinforce the power and authority of the husband and reduce conflict. It is not exercised for the purpose of freeing the oppressed from their bondage. The purpose of individual sacrifice is to keep the weak in her place of powerlessness. "It seems to me that the expected kenosis of women and their compliance have enabled men to be the chief architects of history."[107] The wifely model of community sacrifice is essentially opposed to the maintenance of power structures, committed to dismantling power-over schemes and in radical solidarity with those who need liberation. The community in submission to the head of the household always acts on behalf of the powerless to empower them, "only insofar as it promotes the values and life-style of the kingdom of God, and insofar as it is enjoined by both churchwomen and churchmen alike."[108] And it does so without regard for its own self-preservation. The church is called to pour itself out for the world.

Oduyoye's reinterpretation of sacrifice not only radically reverses our traditional (and Anselmian) notions of Christian service, but also corresponds to an African cultural reality. Tribal practices of sacrifice are generally understood as communal practices enacted on behalf of a person or persons in distress. Because the whole notion of community is endangered when one person is in trouble, the community restores balance by offering sacrifices on his or her behalf. So far, there is a strong correspondence to the communal sacrifice that Christian faith requires. But, like the Christian model, this indigenous model is subject to distortions in the same direction. Since women are the domestic stabilizers in African culture, the women naturally become those most accountable for making the sacrifice. Sometimes the sacrifice requires donating goods and services, sometimes it involves donating an animal, sometimes it involves donating the self. In a similar shift, women are the ones with the most to lose from instability and the ones to whom the sacrificial responsibilities fall. As a communal notion, sacrifice for the protection and restoration of the weaker members corresponds to the kingdom model of a sacrificial community. When sacrifice is individualized or assigned according to gender stereotypes, it is subject to the same distortions and inequities that we see within Anselmian versions of Christian atonement.

The church's mission, demands Oduyoye, is to expand the expectations of sacrifice beyond gender stereotypes and individual responsibility. We are not called to reject sacrifice, but to radicalize it as a communal ethic undertaken for the protection and restoration of the powerless. The church's mission would be better promoted "if *all*, not just women, learn to operate in the spirit of *self*-denial."[109] She reclaims the traditional model of the strong African mother and a communal understanding of sacrifice to reorient the sacrificial mission of the church toward one that will not reinforce oppression and sexism. "Be a woman," she writes, "and Africa will be strong."[110]

One of the strengths of the Third World theologies we've surveyed is that they easily contextualize Jesus into their contemporary situation with very little loss of integrity to the primary symbols and images of the tradition. Whether imagining Jesus as healer or big sister or guru, these approaches operate within traditional christological categories, and primarily that of crucifixion. None of the women surveyed appeal to an Anselmian interpretation of cross and salvation. Rather, they all seem to gravitate either toward a liberation model or an eschatological reversal model. The liberation models are the familiar Jesus-as-liberator or Jesus-as-feminist models that operate in early white feminist work. The eschatological reversal model is the more primitive christus victor model of the earliest church. In that model, Jesus is the cosufferer with the world, in solidarity with the weak and poor.[111]

Like the Sophia and mujerista christologies, many of the Third World women identify Jesus with a female figure, whether Mary, tribal mothers, big sisters, or healers. Again, we notice one of two patterns. Either the female figures are interpreted according to romantic (heroic) notions of "the strong woman" or according to suffering solidarity notions, where females are cosufferers with Jesus and in solidarity with the poor. These female figures embody a kind of nurturing wisdom that has strength without authoritarian power and are easily projected as paradigms for community. Most of these women reject any romantic or derivative role of mothering and don't want to limit women to nurturing roles. They all work hard to avoid reinscribing "feminine" virtues of passivity and individual self-sacrifice. There are still some places where romanticism and biological essentialism surface. We should probably remember Schüssler Fiorenza's caveat to de-divinize any Mary figure and to operate with a Mariology-from-below. Otherwise we do run the risk of reinforcing stereotypical behavior in a gender-selective way. Even without reinforcing standard feminine virtues, the approach that reinforces the essential strength and heroic qualities of women is hardly to be preferred. This is precisely the stereotype that Delores Williams and several womanist theologians reject, since it supported the notion that women could withstand suffering (i.e., suffering is not a problem for women). And with regard to Mary's virginity, we'll have to be careful to avoid either a self-righteous celibacy or a moral purity. Sexual autonomy is not anti-eroticism.

With the exception of Oduyoye, there is minimal attention to eschatological images of future community. Several of the Asian and African theologians write within contexts where cyclical nature cosmologies imagine a restoration of the natural world but do not project into a distant future. And it's also fair to assume that eschatology is as problematic for Third World women as it is for many First World theologians. Crucifixion can be reclaimed as an interpretive category, since it was historical. However, there is certainly a cross-cultural bias against resurrection and eschatology regardless of cultural context. The supernatural character of the images leads to their rejection as fantastic and intellectually questionable. Virginia Fabella, from the Philippines, breaks this pattern by demanding that the crucifixion and resurrection be treated as a symbolic whole, calling the cross without the resurrection a "dead-end theology."[112] I would expect that further ecumenical dialogue between Catholic and Protestant women in the Third World would be particularly fruitful in the development of eschatological visions. A focus on the eschatological dimensions of Mariology would be the natural location for such a conversation.

Another problem that lurks in many of the Third World theologies is the anti-Judaism behind the traditional Jesus-was-a-feminist approach.[113] Several of the theologians reinscribe an unfortunate supersessionist christology that is probably a theological disservice to the faith. Within radically pluralistic contexts, the assumed superiority of Christianity over Judaism or any other faith tradition is probably disastrous. I think the truncated eschatological vision may be part of the problem, since many of the formulations stop short of projecting what an ideal human community might look like. Contextualizing Jesus won't solve the problem as long as the reinterpreted Jesus is still the best lord in town. However, because of the radical religious diversity within Asia and Africa, perhaps some of our most creative interfaith visions will yet emerge from those women theologians. Within both contexts, the common ground that I would identify for such conversations would focus on indigenous understandings of the ancestors as those who have eternal life through the community. The ancestors can be imagined as an invisible community that accompanies us into the future.

Summary

We will turn next to a constructive proposal, one that takes seriously the challenges and strengths of the various options. Through this survey, we've noted several recurring themes and problems, but we've also noticed that each option raises its own particular insights and contributions. All of the options surveyed reject Anselmian interpretations of the cross and salvation. All of them value contextual experience and the particularities of being embodied as women. Even though Schüssler Fiorenza claims that the relational incarnation theologies are the most canonical, that phenomenon is probably limited to North American feminists. We've seen less evidence of incarnational approaches outside the

First World context. Almost all of the non-Western options center on the themes of suffering and community. With the exception of Delores Williams, all find some meaning in the symbol of the cross.

We have taken seriously the charge that white feminist theologians have not always taken the experiences of other women into consideration. At least here, we have tried to honor other perspectives. Even though no one woman theologian can presume to speak for other women theologians, each does her work in the presence of other women theologians. How can we learn from these different approaches? And how can we begin to develop a working christology that operates from a consistent core of theological meanings?

We'll have to keep several parameters in mind. We must develop a christology that takes human suffering seriously, but without glorifying suffering. We must develop a christology that takes bodies seriously, but without glorifying embodiment. We must develop a christology that nurtures life, but is not afraid of death. We must develop a christology that envisions the future, but doesn't trivialize the present. We want to use images of women that respect sensuality, motherhood, and female experiences. But we don't want to romanticize or essentialize anything like "true femininity" or "universal female experience." But most critically, how can we incorporate these different perspectives into a supple christology that has intellectual, ecumenical, and local integrity? We're accountable to a number of constituencies, but our primary audience is still the local congregation. We can't use a Sophia christology one week, an erotic christology the next, and a Jesus-as-feminist christology another time. How can we think globally and preach locally, especially in the First World context of corporate greed, national imperialism, and the Christian right? We need to negotiate these claims in the language of ordinary believers. And we need to avoid, as much as possible, reinscribing the blunders of the tradition.

Chapter 4

A Metaphorical Christology of Salvage

> *Each time we speak of "Christ," we are saying some-*
> *thing about ourselves, about all women and men and*
> *our capacity to act in unity with the purpose of God...*
> *Certainly every theological examination of Christian*
> *ministers should be designed to elicit critical reflection*
> *upon the intellectual framework of such faith.*[1]

Having sketched out vulnerabilities within the historical tradition and having considered the concerns of several different women theologians, I will turn in this chapter toward gathering and integrating their strengths, particularly as they relate to preaching. This constructive homiletic christology is a proposal for women preachers and theologians concerned with the task of presenting a contemporary and transformative christology by way of the tradition's most familiar stories and symbols. This proposal is designed primarily for women who are preaching within the North American context, but always with sensitivities to the diverse perspectives within women's theological discourse. It will probably be most accessible to Protestant mainline preachers, but it's intended to be flexible enough for adaptation within a number of Christian contexts. This working christology does not pretend to be a universal women's christology, but an elastic christology that allows for different approaches to be highlighted and explored within the language and symbols of ordinary Christian believers. It is a christology whose primary purpose is to be contextualized through the vulnerability of metaphor, to produce homiletic reflection grounded in familiar terms but open to new levels of meaning.

Guidelines for a Constructive Homiletic Christology

Since this is a homiletic christology, it must make use of familiar biblical symbols and ideas, ordinary cultural understandings, and the experiential reality of the world we actually inhabit. Because of the rhetorical setting within more or less ordinary communities, our language cannot be too technical, nor can our concepts be overtly philosophical. While we may use biblical language and ideas, we want to be careful not to reinscribe them as insider jargon or religious technical language. This is particularly important when we consider traditional theological categories like salvation, redemption, grace, and faith. Thomas Thangaraj offers the following definition of christology that will be helpful as we work toward a constructive model:

> Christology is the critical and constructive task of imaging the significance of Christ, that is, the events surrounding and including Jesus of Nazareth, for providing a normative vision of God, world, and human existence, and a transformative orientation for human living.[2]

Thangaraj argues that while multiple christologies may be appropriate, not all contextual christologies are fully adequate to the task of preaching within a pluralistic world. All christologies are subject, he claims, to certain norms or criteria. Minimally, christology must be significant at a theoretical level, making some argument about the *indicative* situation or the state of things in a general way (sin, sovereignty, bondage, etc.) and some argument about the practical or *imperative* situation of human ethical behavior. Homiletic christologies must be able to name the situation we are in as well as the vision toward which we yearn. Thangaraj offers a list of guiding questions for developing local christologies that have global sensitivities, which is the kind of contextual christology I'm advocating.

Is the image intelligible? Christology is an imaging or image-building activity and must be judged on the basis of its intelligibility and communicative ability. This is the rhetorical concern toward which this whole project is directed. Can this christology be preached to ordinary congregations familiar with traditional narratives and symbols? Thangaraj is quite emphatic that this question can be answered only in relation to the audience of the christologian. Intelligibility, the first and perhaps most critical norm, rests primarily with the audience. I would also add that the criterion of intelligibility demands that we avoid the loophole of theological paradox or mystery. And, since christology is frequently the center of folk theology, I would also require that christological images have internal coherence with other theological claims.

Does this image enable transformative praxis? Thangaraj uses Leonardo Boff's discussion of orthopraxy (right practice) as an alternative to questions about orthodoxy (right belief). I have intentionally shifted my discussions toward communal practices instead of communal identity. Questions of identity almost always devolve into questions of right thought or right doctrine. With Thangaraj, I want to keep the questions centered on the explicit programs and practices of local congregations. This attention to practices raises questions about privilege and benefit (which usually emerge as identity questions). We should always ask who or what cause is served by a given christology? What interests does it represent and what concrete projects does it support?[3] This is the hermeneutic of suspicion that all the women theologians have asked relative to power and kyriarchy. In many theological projects these questions emerge relative to gender, race, and class discussions. I would also want to add the categories of children, gay and lesbian individuals, and the nonhuman world.

Is this image disciplined by historical data? To some degree, I think Thangaraj is asking Elisabeth Schüssler Fiorenza's question about plausibility and how well a particular christology is supported by all historical data. Thangaraj is worried about more than historical plausibility, since he considers historical warranting to be necessary but not absolute. Theological claims must be grounded in actual events, but their historicity alone does not constitute status as eternal truths. I think one of his subtle warnings here is to avoid grounding christological claims on "myth" or mystery.

Does this image affirm plurality? The image of Christ cannot claim finality and exclusiveness or fail to accommodate new possibilities. This is particularly important for women theologians who are concerned not to reinscribe exclusivism as a theological blunder. I think it relates more specifically to Christian preachers who are concerned not to reinscribe anti-Judaism or other claims of uniqueness into their christologies. Thangaraj claims any christological image must be flexible and open-ended without being radically "protean" or cave in to utter relativity. Within traditional christologies these exclusive tendencies show up predominantly in purity and pollution metaphors, in election language, heaven and hell images, or relative to the orders of creation. We'll consider the challenges of Christian preaching and pluralism in the next chapter.

Does this image enhance the community's worshipful devotion? Thangaraj discusses this in terms of possibilities for personal and communal relationship and commitment, but I would also want to consider sacramental understandings that have some consistency with the tradition. Can we practice eucharist that still equates the elements with the symbolic blood and body of Christ? Can we still practice baptism, using water and the language of death/rebirth? Although this may seem to be begging a ritual question, this is precisely the kind of dilemma that faces women preachers. Community practices and the discussion of community worship are integrally related to each other and directly related to the christological images in use. We will look at in-house practices and other-directed practices in the last chapter.

Does this image maintain the priority of God? This criterion is primarily a demand for humility and the recognition of human finitude, but it also suggests a concern for avoiding docetic claims about Jesus' divinity.

Thangaraj demands a christology that promotes monotheism, and particularly a monotheism that maintains the unconditional love and compassion of God and the universal imperfection of humanity. One of Thangaraj's concerns is to avoid absolutizing humanity, Jesus, or the church into idols.

I would add three more questions to the list.

Does this image trivialize or romanticize suffering? We have seen that christologies that do either are inadequate to the experiential questions raised by women and by other disenfranchised groups. Since the demands of plausibility and rhetorical context require us to wrestle with theologies of the cross, we will not be able to escape the suffering problem by avoiding the cross. We will have to construct a theology of the cross that honors the traditional narratives and the facts of history without reinscribing claims of satisfaction, substitution, or penalty.

All of the women theologians we've considered are united in their rejection of Anselmian trajectories of atonement theory. They reject any notions of a christology driven by the claim that God somehow desires or deserves our suffering. There is also significant uniformity in their concern for the real suffering of real women. Yet, there is a tension, because several of the christological approaches also envision an ethical community that is willing to suffer and take risks on behalf of the oppressed. Clearly, we must make some distinction between kinds of suffering and the purposes of suffering. As Wendy Farley claims, we must imagine a christological approach that "struggles against the evil from both directions," empowering victims at the same time we engage oppressive practices.[4]

Does this image support any type of mind/body dualism? This concern should be operative at all implied levels of a christology. If Jesus/Christ is a metaphor of the human/divine relationship, any dualism is bound to be reinscribed either in our notions of God or notions of human beings. Christological dualism that favors the consciousness of Jesus, or his inner states, or his perfect mind, will also tend to favor the reason or intellect of God and the reason or intellect or attitudes of humans. Christologies that emphasize the bodily or enfleshed perfection of Jesus/Christ will have similar lack of balance when we engage in either God-talk or in reflections about the nature of humans. Incarnational language, as a favorite of women theologians, must never valorize flesh over mind, nor can its claims move toward any biological essentialism.

Does this image project a vision of the community's shared commitment toward the world that God so loves? We must also make our christological claims in such a way that there is a unity of purpose between the acts and sayings of Jesus and God's aims for the world. Our preaching *about* Christ must have integrity with what we claim Jesus/Christ himself preached. To preach the gospel is to preach toward the future of God's purposes: a world of reconciliation and justice. To continue the preaching and the ministry of Christ, we move beyond making isolated claims about his nature or the personal morality of specific acts; we must continue to preach the good news of a reconciling God whom we know in Christ.

Elisabeth Schüssler Fiorenza makes a similar claim, arguing for what I would call a "basileia bias," which privileges those interpretations grounded in visions of the socio-political restoration of the world.[5] Her approach is only penultimately concerned about historical proofs of what the early Jesus movement was really like. She is primarily concerned with interpretive approaches that articulate a liberating vision for women. I would not limit these interpretations to those that liberate women, but rather would explicitly include the liberation of women along with liberation for all disenfranchised groups and individuals.

Jesus/Christ as Metaphor: Chalcedon Revisited

Simply put, we must imagine Jesus as a sign-act or metaphor for the relationship between God and the world. We will develop a functional christology, bracketing out questions of ontology or the relationship between Jesus and God. As a symbol or metaphor highlighting God's nature, we consider Jesus/Christ as a disclosure of God's orientation and activities toward the world. To say that we know God through the acts and sayings of Jesus is not to make ontological claims about Jesus' own person, but to say something definitive about God. This metaphorical or functional christology allows us to project Godlikeness onto the actions of Jesus/Christ without attributing a special category of divinity to the man himself. For Christians, Jesus *functions* as God, representing or making God present to us.

As a metaphor, the image of Jesus/Christ is like God in some ways and unlike God in others. Metaphors use one reality to disclose another; they use a familiar term to uncover or reveal something unfamiliar. Sallie McFague's discussion of metaphorical language draws on the work of Paul Ricoeur to remind us that metaphor is more than a poetic ornament for illustration or flair; metaphorical language is fundamental to our human way of making meaning. Language is essentially metaphorical, "seeing one thing as something else, pretending 'this' is 'that' because we do not know how to think or talk about 'this,' so we use 'that' as a way of saying something about it...spotting a thread of similarity between two dissimilar objects, events, or whatever..."[6] When we say that love is a rose, we are not making a category mistake, but are claiming that there is something about love that is rose-like, with its blossom, its thorniness, and its ultimate withering. Metaphor is not ornamental and dispensable, but is ordinary language. "It is the *way* we think."[7]

With regard to Jesus, we use the familiar concept of human flesh and human activities to interpret the unfamiliar concept of God's activities and purposes in the world. We do not need to literalize this understanding and reduce either Jesus or God to each other. Metaphor contains both "is" and "is not," and is never a full fit. Metaphorical theology and particularly metaphorical christology must always guard against this tendency toward unpoetic literalism. While we may find metaphorical similarities helpful for understanding, we must also remember the implicit "and it is not," that resides within metaphorical language. God is both revealed and veiled in our metaphorical language. Some dimensions of divinity are disclosed by christological metaphors and some dimensions are hidden by metaphor. Nonetheless, our starting point for developing a metaphorical christology is to notice the similarities.

Through a metaphorical strategy, we can reclaim the *religious meaning* (if not the metaphysical meaning) of the Chalcedonian claim that Jesus was both human and divine. We do not have to accept the metaphysics of the creed in terms of literal substance and person. Again, McFague points out that metaphors are intended to be symbolic and not literal. Metaphors that are reduced to a literal meaning become idolatrous, as our survey of the tradition has demonstrated. We can claim that Jesus functions metaphorically to disclose two dissimilar concepts to us: God's mode of acting and human modes of acting. As Carter Heyward suggests, Jesus is what God would act like if God were to become a real human being. Human activities are *not* divine in a literal sense, but they are, in terms of similarity, consistent with divine purposes. We may reasonably classify human activities as holy or righteous or divine when they act in concert with God's purposes for salvaging the world. Our own human activities are Godlike when they simulate the Godlike activities of Jesus: feeding the hungry, healing the sick, caring for the lost. God's own self is revealed to the world when we embody an extraordinary purpose through ordinary acts. As one womanist scholar puts it, "God is as Christ does."[8] Jesus is divine metaphorically and by analogy when he engages in practices of radical compassion. This is a helpful qualification to the vagueness of some eros and incarnational christologies, which tend to attribute divinity to all embodiment.[9] Certainly we can claim that God is immanent in all dimensions of creation, but we would hardly want to claim that God's redemptive purposes are being revealed in every case. God's love is more than the desire to be connected and in relationship, "all rolled up in each other." God's redemptive purposes are served not primarily by intimacy, but by particular practices of justice and compassion.

If the practices of Jesus are consistent with God's purposes, they are also consistent with ordinary human possibilities. Jesus reveals divine aims through ordinary human activities. He eats meals with ordinary people. He touches the sick in order to make them well. He challenges the practices of his own religious community and the political power structures. He does human things. He teaches, argues, comforts, eats, talks, weeps. He gets tired and needs to get away from time to time. Ordinary human activities can reveal divine purposes. The advantage of understanding Jesus as fully human is that we can claim ongoing revelation, through fully human agents, into the present and toward the future. God's purpose for a renewed world is revealed in the ordinary compassionate activities of ordinary human creatures. We don't have to talk in tongues or halt hurricanes over the East Coast. We reveal God when we do ordinary things for extraordinary purposes: when we lobby for welfare reform, when we forgive the wrongs that others have done, when we share a common meal with folks who are not like us. Each ordinary act *can* become a sacramental moment in which God's purposes are embodied and revealed. But not every human act or practice is equally revelatory or disclosive. Our activities are revelatory of God only to the extent that they conform to God's redemptive purposes for the world.

Basileia Practices and Community Vocation

As a metaphor of the intersection between God's purposes and human activity, this christology is first and foremost a christology-from-below. To claim this is to claim that our christology emerges from the actual lived reality of the social world. The starting point for such a christology is not an a priori doctrine of God that we project onto Christ, but a starting point in human experience. "It begins its thinking on earth with the gospel memory of the life of Jesus, and finds there the basis for the discernment of how the risen Christ is operative in the world today. The paradigmatic role of Jesus on earth becomes a source of light and energy fueling the church's own mission in the world."[10]

C. S. Song calls this starting point a "people hermeneutic," grounded in the experiences of the poor, the marginalized, and the suffering. The preaching, the parables, and the activities of Jesus all take their shape relative to the kingdom of God, the *basileia tou theo*. Jesus preached and taught about the reign of God, his parables pointed to the upside-down reversals of social reality, and his miraculous activities of healing and exorcism were all signs pointing to the goal of God's reign on earth. The cross and resurrection as a metaphorical "gestalt" embrace the reversal of suffering toward new life. Jesus' own resurrection becomes a metaphor for new life and the new world. The implicit assumptions of social renewal disclosed in all the women's christologies correspond with the tradition's primary symbols of resurrection and the reign of God. Both are easily interpreted as social realities grounded in a "paradigm shift" of the community's self-understanding. Resurrection and the reign of

God are metaphors of the new life already experienced by a community of believers and that hints of redemptive future. Christ, as the ongoing spirit of redemption and new life, is present to the community when they share the feast and tell the stories. And the redemptive work of God in Christ continues, not exclusively but recognizably, in certain compassionate practices performed by the community of believers.

Notice the shift in our interpretations of the reign of God. Many of us learned a highly individualized and spiritualized interpretation of the reign of God: "The reign of God is within you." This standard interpretation suggests that the inner experience of the solitary individual is the location for the kingdom, that God's reign is within *you*, the singular person. The shift in perspective that I'm suggesting assumes that God's reign is located among the people, within the lived reality of a community. God's reign is among *you all*, or as folks in the American South might say, among y'all. God's reign is a communal and relational reality that takes shape socially as people begin to live in ways of justice and compassion. In Christ, we have been grafted onto, adopted into, God's plan for redeeming the world.

Community and the Reign of God

For preaching, this suggests that we speak not to solitary individuals, but to a community. We preach to the collective identity of the gathered believers. Within the community, where two or three are gathered, the living spirit of the God we know in Christ takes its shape and does its work. Preaching evokes or names the presence of God within the community and the vision of God for creation. Naming God's redemptive presence forms the community for its mission in the world. In the same way a grandmother might tell stories of ancestors to impart a sense of generational continuity, the preacher tells the stories of the faith to shape a peculiar community for its shared life together. Preaching binds the community to a shared vision and a shared common project: acting redemptively in the world.

The community operates within the world that God so loves, to name and project the shape of God's reign. The community is a sign to the world, in its mutuality and its work for justice, that God is still alive and reconciling. The reign of God is not the church's identity, but its visionary goal. The new age of God is the dawning of a just world, the faint glimmers of a better common life. In the Hebrew Bible, this vision was identified as the promised land, the New Jerusalem (God's peace), the jubilee, the day of the Lord. This eschatological vision of a just world was not heavenly escapism but a down-to-earth picture of what God intended from creation. The Hebrew scriptures trace out a world where violence has ended, where the predator and the prey are no longer enemies, where widows and orphans are cared for by society, where no one is hungry, and where death has disappeared. The land flows with abundance, the vines produce good wine, and the fields overflow with bounty. There is neither scarcity, bloodshed, nor power structure. God's future reverses the ravages of history and renews it with the vision of a just world. And notice that the future is not just for believers, but for all of creation. God's future is the future where all of humanity and the natural world live together in increasing productivity and equity.

The community's vocation is continuous with Jesus/Christ's vocation and with God's vision for a redeemed world. *Christian congregations have as their primary vocation the reconciliation of a disrupted social and natural world.* We become messianic and prophetic in the general understanding: We assume leadership in righting wrongs, establishing justice, practicing peace, healing the sick, feeding the hungry. Our vocation is continuous with the vocation of the biblical Israelites: to love mercy, do justice, and walk humbly with God.

In order to protect ourselves against grandiose notions of election, we should understand election not as special status, but as special responsibility, making the same "functional" shift in our Christian self-understandings that we continue to sketch out for Jesus/Christ. As the church, we are not elect in terms of divine preference (we are not special people), but elect in terms of special vocation (we have a special task to perform). We understand that our prophetic vocation sets us apart from those who operate with different agendas, marks us as a people called to be distinct (but never separate) from the business-as-usual world. The Christian community, like Jesus/Christ, is not holy by virtue of its own perfection, but holy insofar as it practices the acts of compassion that are consistent with God's purposes. The church, made up of ordinary human beings doing ordinary tasks for extraordinary purposes, is as fallible as ordinary humanity.

The biblical witness addresses this shared vocation of the people of God. The scripture is a witness to communities of faith for their constitution in the world. Our post-Enlightenment habit of reading the Bible in solitary could lead us to believe that the mandates and revelations are directed to individuals for their spiritual edification. However, the oral tradition undergirding the scriptures is addressed not to ordinary individuals, but to faith communities. This double-mindedness, being in the world but not of the world, is what makes the biblical witness peculiar. When we preach to congregations, we should preach to the collective vocational identity of believers and not just to the inner anxieties of solitary individuals.

This understanding of the scriptural and homiletical "target audience" is a significant shift from the revivalist and existentialist assumptions that have dominated much of this century. This approach does not ask "Who am I in relation to God?" or "Who am I in relation to the world?" as if the Bible is an answer to generic questions of personal meaning. Rather, this approach asks, "Who are we, the church, in relation to God?" and "Who are we, the church, in relation to the world?" In relation to God, the church is that group that confesses its corporate sinfulness and lives in corporate mercy, what David Buttrick has called "a being-saved community." In relation to the world, the church is that group that organizes its communal activities to heal and restore the world, not to convert everyone to Jesus. This hermeneutical strategy reorients the meaning of the self beyond its own identity, to a shared identity and vocation. This social interpretation provides personal meaning that transcends individualism, a sense of belonging that transcends alienation, and a projected future that transcends the immediate brokenness of the world. The being-saved community offers a proleptic participation in the basileia.

A Social-Metaphorical Hermeneutic

So far, I have distinguished between metaphorical and literal interpretive approaches and between individual and social (communal) interpretive approaches. It may be helpful to clarify the way these different approaches function homiletically. Since most of the New Testament christologies, from which most preachers routinely preach, are at least marginally apocalyptic and supernatural, some type of demythologizing is necessary when we present the theological meanings or concepts that are carried in those metaphors. Since I am working primarily within the primitive christus victor theory, let's explore how different interpretive strategies highlight different dimensions of meaning.

The primitive christus victor theory interpreted the death and resurrection of Jesus/Christ as a drama of the conflict between God and Satan. Satan had, through the "powers and principalities," taken humanity captive. This captivity to evil, experienced at the socio-historical level as violence and power-mongering, was wrecking God's plans for abundant life. The ultimate sign of evil was the actual captivity and execution of Jesus. His betrayal by a friend, his abandonment by his disciples, his delivery by the crowd to execution, were all understood as confirmation that the world was in a horrible state of sin. The crucifixion of Jesus for crimes of compassion was *not* something that God deserved, desired, or orchestrated, but was an example of the depths of human captivity to Satan. When Jesus died, God resurrected him, reversing the power of the so-called powers and principalities and vindicating Jesus' ministry. Christus victor, or the victorious Christ, was not a title of political or social status as much as it was a statement about the legitimacy of his practices. The same way we might say, "Dietrich Bonhoeffer: Acquitted by God," the early church referred to the risen Jesus/Christ as "King," "Lord," and "Victor."

A literal and individualistic interpretation of this dramatic narrative might suggest that Jesus is victorious in saving the individual from hell. This evangelistic and revivalistic interpretation assumes that the object of salvation or redemption is the human individual before God and that the vindication involves a release from the consequences of sin. Such an interpretation considers Jesus/Christ to be the winner of souls, the lord of the heart, and victorious over a personal captivity to sin. In this scenario, Jesus/Christ literally saves the soul from eternal damnation.

An expanded literal interpretation involves the protection and elevation of a particular social group. In this reading, Jesus/Christ displaces other kings and lords by becoming the power-mongering kyriarch over all others. Jesus/Christ becomes the symbol rationalizing all imperialism and conquest. As we've already traced out, this shift in the christus victor model developed under Constantine and continued through the medieval period to justify the actual power and hierarchy of the church and theocracy. Such a reading is also common in the history of modern Western Christianity, where Christ as a militant conqueror has been a justification for extreme imperialism and violent missionary activity. More recently, under the Reagan administration, an apocalyptic literalism functioned to fuel American patriotic hostilities toward Russia ("the evil empire") and other non-Western nations.

When we shift from literal interpretations to metaphorical interpretations, the same individual and social readings emerge. I would place existentialist demythologizing in the category of metaphorical individualism, where the victorious Christ saves the alienated individual from meaninglessness. The conquest is won in the battle between the paralyzing fear of nonbeing and the faithful courage to be authentically related to God and the world. Certainly, Bultmann's strategy to salvage apocalyptic symbols and eschatological metaphors for modern communities was to address the life situation of the isolated individual in an increasingly fragmented world. Close to the existentialist approach was the development of a therapeutic approach, grounded in the psychological language of personal wholeness and self-actualization. Variations of this existentialist-therapeutic strategy dominate contemporary mainline homiletics in the United States.

Finally, the interpretive strategy that I'm suggesting is a metaphorical social approach to demythologizing dramatic or apocalyptic elements within biblical and traditional christologies. In this metaphorical social approach, Jesus/Christ is the symbol of God's purposes manifested through the church as a sign of life in the world. The conquest is not the individual soul, not the Christian world against the non-Christian world, nor the struggle for self-identity. The conquest is the subtle, persuasive ultimacy of love over power. Conquest and victory are redefined through the transformative rhetoric of folly to suggest that real victory is the kenosis of domination. The rhetoric of folly is the Pauline strategy of reversal, where real power appears to be weakness, where real victory looks like defeat, and where the sovereign appears to be a nobody. The church is the community whose vocation is to "conquer" the kingdom of death through practicing the stewardship of life.

A Metaphorical Theology of Salvage

The meanings of theological terms change over time. In the previous section, I alluded to theological shifts in the meaning of salvation or redemption. Even as we use the language of sin and salvation, the metaphors for these related concepts change. Sin and salvation have been interpreted through the paired metaphors of dirt and cleanliness, sickness and health, pollution and purity, brokenness and wholeness, and a number of other similar pairings. Paul Ricoeur has explored the evolution of the symbolism of evil to argue that our ways of talking about evil become interiorized as sin when they are expressed in the consciousness of the presence of God. Ricoeur focuses on primary biblical myths and narratives to investigate human awareness at the most elemental levels through symbols of stain, blot, blemish, illness, and guilt.[11]

Many of our inherited metaphors have become rigid and no longer offer the hermeneutical resilience necessary for adaptation. We have difficulty hearing of stain and cleanliness without immediately interpreting it within a given framework of personal failure and perfection. We hear of disobedience and immediately conjure up memories of the Adamic myth. Women theologians attend to issues of language and metaphor, not only to open up new meanings, but also to develop new modes of talking about old meanings. "Because every age experiences sin and salvation differently, new metaphors must be generated."[12] New metaphors are not just invented, but are developed with respect to their metaphorical fit, the image systems they generate, and their overall adequacy to traditional narratives and symbols. "What preachers can do is to unpack traditional metaphors to see what kinds of experiences they once conveyed and, thus informed, seek contemporary images to conjoin the *now* of our lives to the *then* of the cross."[13] Notice that I am not suggesting we eliminate the primary symbols, nor that we invent new ones, but that we develop new metaphorical and rhetorical strategies for conveying understandings.

The metaphor that I am suggesting here is similar to the root meaning of salvation, the Latin *salvare*. Salvare means to save, to deliver from sin, to protect or maintain. It also has medical connotations involving soothing or remedial agents for healing. Both metaphorical trajectories, deliverance and healing, have strong associations with the tradition.

Deliverance can be developed primarily as a spiritual or epistemological category as freedom from old ways of thinking, old status orientations, or faulty beliefs. Deliverance can also be developed as a social or political liberation from practices of domination. Healing has similar possibilities for either spiritual or embodied meanings. Healing as a metaphor for spiritual renewal usually involves eliminating spiritual illness through the application of some spiritual cure. As a metaphor for social restoration, healing remedies the brokenness of human relationships or the divisions within the "body politic." Healing and liberation are popular metaphors among women theologians, but they are also somewhat ambiguous given their relative familiarity within the tradition. When women theologians speak of healing or liberation, these terms are frequently heard in the more traditional ways: Healing is a miraculous activity done by Jesus, or deliverance is a change in spiritual status.

The metaphor of salvage has the same linguistic source as salvation but offers a more immediate physical image. Salvage as a primary metaphor allows us to bracket ontological differences and traditional explanations in order to allow for a continuity of expressions, whether we are discussing the practices of God, of Jesus/Christ, or of the church. Salvage sounds enough like salvation to offer metaphorical familiarity, yet it is odd enough to generate new thought. I hope to demonstrate how shifting to the metaphor of salvage opens up new meanings when we discuss God's basileia purposes for creation, the meaning of Jesus/Christ's life and ministry, the identity of the local congregation, and the purpose of the church in the world. Since metaphors cannot be pressed too literally into service, I will also try to indicate the limits of its usefulness.

Salvage and Contemporary Apocalyptic

My reflections on salvage as a Christian metaphor come from a recent novel by Paul Auster, *In the Country of Last Things*. Auster does not pretend to be writing from a religious perspective, nor does anything in the interplay of characters and plot necessarily suggest Christian interpretations. Rather, he deals with the themes of classic tragedy: chaos, honor, responsibility, destiny, and human freedom. His characters are multidimensional and complex: a strange combination of predictable habit and spontaneous adaptation. His storylines are both bizarre and familiar, involving extraordinary coincidences as well as moments of sheer novelty. Auster's narrative style and character development are suited to my particular appropriations because of the theological claims this reflection promotes. Human experience is fragile, frequently tragic, and on occasion, surprisingly providential. Human beings, as creatures of habit, structure their own lives as predictably as possible but have no ultimate control over their own future. They inherit the accumulation of past events and must always operate within those limits, but somehow the future is unpredictably open.

The style of *In the Country of Last Things* is grim and apocalyptic, an urban nightmare where anything resembling an ordered social or political life has collapsed. It is set in the immediate future in a country very like the United States. Our heroine, Anna Blume, has left her home on the other side of the water to come to this place in search of her brother. She is shocked almost to numbness. In this "country of last things," over half the population is homeless, and even those who have housing can expect it to be taken by force any day or night. Streets and buildings disappear without notice, here today and gone tomorrow; the landscape is littered with trash, architectural debris, and bodies. Theft is so common it's no longer illegal. Starvation and illness are rampant. There are two basic vocations in the country of last things: being part of the death industry or being part of the salvage operations. The death business is highly organized, as the primary function of the remnant of government. But the private death industry is also successful. People who have lost their hope will do almost anything to die, and the market offers them death by assassination, special suicidal jumping platforms, programs of physical exhaustion, and the more pleasant euthanasia centers.

For those who are not committed to dying or killing, some form of scavenger life becomes necessary. Some scavengers collect waste materials to sell for fuel. Others salvage bits and pieces of broken objects to repair and sell. Anna Blume becomes a scavenger of objects.

> As an object hunter, you must rescue things before they reach this state of absolute decay. You can never expect to find something whole—for that is an accident, a mistake on the part of the person who lost it…What another has seen fit to throw away, you must examine…and bring back to life…Everything falls apart, but not every part of every thing, at least not at the same time. The job is to zero in on these little islands of intactness, to imagine them joined to other such islands, and those islands to still others, and thus to create new archipelagoes of matter.[14]

Salvaging is the daily vocation of Anna Blume, but it is also the primary social vocation of those who befriend her in the country of last things. She has a shifting constellation of acquaintances, a hodgepodge assortment of people who rescue her from time to time, and in whose company she resides toward the end of the story.

Through a series of mishaps, Anna finds herself in the Woburn House, a provisional homeless shelter/first aid center/soup kitchen. Woburn House had originally been the private residence of a wealthy doctor but had been transformed into a kind of halfway house for the homeless when the social fabric began to disintegrate. Dr. Woburn had given up his private practice to raise funds and public awareness for the homeless, but the work was always difficult and gruelling. However, even in the face of an increasing homeless population, Dr. Woburn and his followers continued to offer help everywhere they could. Anna, having suffered a tragic miscarriage, came to the house just shortly after Dr. Woburn's death. The other workers were astonished at her recovery, since no other guests had been able to survive without the doctor's professional care. Anna explains:

> …I served to justify their determination to keep Woburn House open. I was their success story, the shining example of what they were still able to accomplish…Mr. Frick believed that I had actually risen from the dead. "You was already in the other world. I seed it with my own eyes. You was dead, and then you come back to life."[15]

The dilemma of the Woburn House was that it was only able to offer finite relief. Only the workers and the very worst of the homeless could stay. As soon as guests were healed or renewed, they were sent back out to the streets. The Woburn House was not "heaven on earth" as some had come to imagine, but a completely ordinary house where the food was adequate, the beds were clean, and there was some relative safety. For the visitors, it was a brief and modest sanctuary. For the workers, it was a place of demanding round-the-clock labor.

Auster paints a realistic and unromantic portrait in this terminal land. We don't know what happens to our heroine, only that she has left her epistolary reflections behind for an unnamed recipient. She and her partner leave the anonymous city for the "north country" to pass through the Millennial Gate, the dangerous threshold to a purportedly safer territory.[16] We never know if they make it. There are, in Auster's work, no unambiguous characters, no comic endings. The "resurrection" of Anna is only witnessed by the illiterate driver for the Woburn House. The hope for a better future or a better place drives all the characters, but none of them ever have confirmation of it beyond rumor and unfounded hope.

One of the best dimensions of this work is the picture of "success" that the author projects. The richest and most feared people in the book are those who control the death industry, and particularly the governmental hegemony over dead bodies. The Woburn House closes primarily due to a funeral violation, the unlawful burying of a body. Success, for Auster's last country, is the resistance to death and its enterprise. The characters we grow to admire are ordinary folks who refuse to cooperate with the "kingdom of death" in any of its manifestations. They band together to devise strategies of resistance and subterfuge, refusing to grant death and its lackeys any satisfaction. Even the final death in the narrative is fraught with gospel reverberations. Those who have gathered to witness the illegal funeral subsequently deny it in the presence of the authorities. Anna climbs into the grave to look for something that has vanished. This particular death is the final straw for the workers at the Woburn House. After it, they disband.

I won't push allegorical interpretations upon the story. I don't want to equate any particular character with Jesus or a particular disciple, since almost all of the characters suffer, salvage, and survive. The Woburn House is a metaphor of the church, but only insofar as it attempts to salvage the homeless. There is a trickster element in the Woburn House and its personnel, a way of cheating death that, pursued literally or allegorically, would be unethical. Pushing the recovering homeless victims back out on the street is probably too heartless an image, even though it would be an improvement over many urban ministries. And Anna's vocation of salvage is directed toward inanimate objects for the purpose of her own survival. We should be careful to avoid the obvious temptation to objectify those needing salvage or to engage in salvage activity for our own immediate benefit.

However, some general contours do emerge. The vocation of Anna, the vocation of Victoria (her lover), and the mission of the Woburn House are all consistently (if not perfectly) allied in their goal to alleviate physical misery. Intense physical attraction (eros) is consistent with this ministry, but so is intense physical labor and selflessness: Eros is a product but never a goal of the house. The workers labor hard to salvage what they can. Their work is humiliating. They must touch and be in constant contact with the losers of the country of last things. They risk exposure to the bizarre weather elements and to the medieval hegemony of the government.[17]

Their work is intensely spiritual as well as physical, for Auster will brook no separation between the state of the body and the state of the imagination. The imagination plays tricks on the body, and the body plays tricks on the imagination. The ambiguity of the mind/body problem is key to Auster's narrative world. "Faced with the most ordinary occurrence, you no longer know how to act, and because you cannot act, you find yourself unable to think. The brain is in a muddle. All around you one change follows another, each day produces a new upheaval, the old assumptions are so much air and emptiness."[18] The body and the mind are unified phenomena; without thought, the body is unable to act; yet without familiar bodily experiences, the mind is unable to operate. We are not reducible to either body (eros) or mind (logos); rather, we are a union of the body and the mind.

Salvage in the Kingdom of Death: Christus Victor Revisited
Powers and Principalities

As an apocalyptic urban nightmare, *In the Country of Last Things* opens up possibilities for a socially transformative interpretation of the apocalyptic christology of the early church. As Aulén and others have pointed out, the apocalyptic understanding of the early church and its narratives was a decidedly socio-political interpretation. Using the language of demonic possession, powers and principalities, kings and kingdoms, the early church claimed that the whole world of human interactions was dominated by evil and power schemes.

If we bracket any literal interpretation of supernatural demonic forces, we can easily agree with the apocalyptic assumption that the whole human world suffers from evil that takes shape in our very human structures of power and politics. Theologian Douglas John Hall uses Auster-like language and images to describe our collective captivity to the industry of death:

> What better way to describe the situation of the nations of earth in the last quarter of the twentieth century than to say that they have made a covenant with death? There has been a tacit agreement among the powers that be that life, if it is to endure, can only be guaranteed by a dangerous pact with death...With the kind of fervor usually reserved for fanatic forms of religion, the empires pile up the weapons of megadeath.[19]

In the mythic religious language of the early preaching, humanity is enslaved to evil powers and dominations. We do not have to reject notions of individual sin or of the social reality of power. The Augustinian claim about original sin carries the same philosophical assumption: Human beings are inescapably subject to the power of sin. We don't have to reduce sinfulness to the activities of individual flesh or to bad thoughts or to "evil demons out there." The metaphorical and social interpretation of the mythic narrative allows us to claim that, since the day of creation, we have been involved in human experiences that are inescapably subject to the temptation of evil. This is the theological anthropology and theological sociology of the early church, it's what Augustine, Luther, and Calvin sought to retain: Humanity is universally subject to the power of evil. When we deny that we are captive, we conjure notions of social progress, romantic optimism, manifest destiny, all forms of human pride that overlook our eternal human fragility. On the other extreme, we can capitulate to a tragic and doomed outlook on life. We lose hope. Giving in to captivity has the social character of apathy, temporary gratification, and, ultimately, despair. Hall characterizes these social manifestations of despair as the sin of sloth:

Because we cannot achieve our superhuman ambitions, we seek compensation in the frenetic pursuit of subhuman pleasures (and pains!). We have sensed at some deep level of knowing that the vaunted modern dream of human lordship, including that special version dubbed "the American Dream," has been wrecked… we are sinking into a corporate depression. At the rhetorical level we continue halfheartedly to mouth the language of official optimism; but in fact we are losing the very capacity to hope.[20]

Here is the classical theological dilemma: We cannot save ourselves from our own human condition. All of our schemes end in distortions of power, either taking too much or taking too little. We do not see any alternatives between taking control and losing control. The human situation is a history littered with the destructive fallout of the battle between the powermongers and the powerless. Again, we recall Wendy Farley's claims that an appropriate theology in the face of human fragility "struggles against the evil from both directions," empowering victims at the same time we engage oppressive practices.

The Foolish Power of God: Cross and Resurrection

What kind of power does God disclose through Jesus/Christ that liberates victims from domination and at the same time calls into question the practices of domination? Our metaphorical christology must somehow image the power of God in ways that offer continuity for the ethical practices of congregations. Bluntly, if the power of God disclosed in Jesus/Christ is that of a submissive victim, then our congregational practices will encourage passivity and submission. If the power of God disclosed in Jesus/Christ is the power to kill powerless victims, then we likewise justify the use of coercive force to terrorize. The tradition has made both mistakes, occasionally and disastrously; these blunders have been committed simultaneously to reinforce the image of a helpless victimized humanity at the hands of a power-hungry God.

Sally Purvis claims that our understanding and experience of power will be shaped to a large extent by our place in the social order. She identifies two faces of power: coercive power and power as life. Coercive power, which has characterized our theologizing about God, is the power of control. Power, in and of itself, is a neutral commodity: It can be used for good or for ill. Negative power is power-as-control and contains both the notions of domination over and manipulation. Power-as-control is inherently unjust and oppressive, since it is based on inequality that values some persons and their practices less than the personhood and practices of others. When inequality is reinforced theologically, or when one person or group is granted dominant power, the shape of relationship that is generated is nonreciprocal and controlling.

Power-as-control has several features. First, it is propagandistic: it controls ideas, concepts, and thought. It exercises the power to interpret and define reality. One of the primary exercises of *conceptual control* comes in the definitions of what is orthodox or heretical. These religious categories control what may be considered to be knowledge and what is accepted as truth. Power as *behavioral control* determines what practices are and are not allowed. Purvis explores the historic examples of witches and herbal arts, contemporary women and birth control, women and ordination. This kind of power operates by evaluating, depending upon who practices them. Certain practices are legitimate if men practice them but are not legitimate if women practice those same activities.

Power-as-control is also exercised over personal activities. Beyond the restriction of certain activities, personal control actually restricts the life-experiences of certain persons, regardless of their practices. Personal control is most frequently exercised as the anathematizing of groups of people, restriction of their movement, and ultimately, violence. Power as *relational control* attempts to manipulate relationships. Beyond the obvious danger of associating with a "wrong" person, which certainly discourages many, there is also the attempt to regulate the ways that people may relate to one another. Examples include the control of marriages between blacks and whites, women teaching men, gay and lesbian relationships.[21]

Power as life or power-for-life is the paradoxical power to resist death and control through the vulnerability, fragility, and apparent insignificance of life-power. Power-as-life reverses all the power-as-control strategies and operates persuasively to open up conceptual, behavioral, existential, and social freedom. The kind of power that God exercises is seen decisively in the narrative event of the cross and resurrection. The cross and resurrection represent "the astonishing reality that God's power is not controlling, but is the power for life."[22] The cross operates as a critique of power-as-control and crucifies our notions of dominant power. Purvis even goes so far as to claim that the "re-socializing" knowledge at the center of crucifixion is the image of a male who acts contrary to notions of masculine power. Jesus, as male, rejects the privileges of kyriarchy and patriarchy that have traditionally been attached to the masculinity of God. Virginia Fabella claims that by being male, "Jesus could repudiate more effectively the male definition of humanity and show the way to a right and just male-female relationship."[23] The cross stands as a witness that God's power is not coercive, controlling, or manipulative; it is a power that looks weak to those who regularly practice domination.

Is the alternative to coercive power really life-giving? According to Purvis, the only alternative to coercive power is the power toward life. Purvis probably does not distinguish between the crucifixion and the resurrection as much as would be helpful, but seems to collapse the two into the cross. However, I will follow Purvis' implicit theology of resurrection as the power for life. As a whole gestalt, the cross and resurrection function to encompass the whole reality of human life as the struggle to live freely in the face of death. Wendy Farley concurs with this interpretation of the cross and resurrection when she claims, "If the cross represents the incarnation of divine compassion [passion with] in the midst of rupture, the resurrection suggests that evil is not absolute; signs of the kingdom, memories of justice and mercy break into the very midst of history."[24] Farley interprets the incarnation, the cross, and the resurrection as a narrative whole, suggesting that evil is real but not ultimate, and that God's compassion is the power to resist. The redemptive presence of God does not in fact defeat evil, even though the eradication of evil is its proleptic purpose. Nonetheless, God's radical presence has its real victories. Farley claims that "compassion remains the ground and power of resistance, of hope, of a transformation of the future and a recovery of the past: fragments of liberation and a return to the center."[25]

The resurrection is God's non-violent, cruciform resistance to the powers of death, a refusal to allow death to have the final word. Death, and especially death on the cross, is against God's purposes. The divine vision of a just world is in opposition to the death-forces that dominate human existence, and the resurrection is a metaphor of God's power to reverse the dynamics of death. Properly understood, claims Purvis, the "power of the cross" subverts its own nature as harmful and oppressive and becomes instead an intellectual, spiritual, and communal resource for radical change."[26]

This new construal of power is the only kind of power that will liberate, build communities, and offer hope for life. Purvis refuses to reduce this power-for-life to eros. Eros as an alternative power-for-life doesn't account for our real situation of powermongering, nor does it offer a genuine critique of the kingdom of death. Eros, as an ongoing generative capacity, creates life from life but cannot create life from death. In an erotic theology, death is the ultimate end of eros. For Purvis and other women theologians of the cross, eros as a solitary concept does not offer the radical hope and reversal generated by the resurrection out of death.

Purvis claims, against Brown and Parker, that this understanding does not trivialize suffering, but rather critiques it mightily. The communal requirement to build one another up is life-enhancing but not individualistic. It does not oppose the needs of one individual to another. The power of the cross is that it demonstrates the power of God embodied in a community that does not value controlling power as an interhuman strategy. As a primary organizing scheme, the cross and resurrection resocialize communities away from the hegemony of control-oriented schemes. The power of the cross enables life-enhancing practices of love in concrete ways, taking account of the actual needs of the other and the actual needs of oneself. The paradoxical power of God in the cross and resurrection communicates a genuine redemptive power, since it embraces life while rejecting domination at the same time, working against oppression from both directions. We've already noted that while most eros theologies do offer strong vision of power-as-life and power-for-life, notions of resistance, critique, or dangerous vulnerability are implied rather than explicated by the metaphor of generativity. Salvage, as an explicitly remedial work, is metaphorically more honest that something has gone wrong and intentional action will be necessary for productivity.

Resurrection is an image for salvaging from the most ultimate dislocation and dismemberment: death. If the image were of a lesser violence or a lesser humiliation, the reversal would not be as radical. Weakening the scandal of the cross would concomitantly weaken God's redemptive power. If God is not in the business of healing and overcoming the most devastating obstacles to life, then God's power is too limited to be radically liberating. God's power as creator (eros) is perfected in the divine power to redeem what has been destroyed. As Aulén claims, "The cross and resurrection represent the work of atonement as first to last a work of God Himself, a *continuous* Divine work..."[27] Just as the creation story creates life out of the chaos of nonlife, the resurrection symbolizes the salvage operation to bring life, once again, from nonbeing.

Demythologizing the primitive christus victor christology along these lines helps women preachers appreciate the cosmic language and drama of biblical apocalyptic in a way that is accessible and ethically relevant to contemporary congregations. The early church certainly understood its ministry as embodying the crucified and risen Jesus/Christ. They understood the radicality of this vision as a subversive alternative to the dominant powermongering of imperialism. This "dangerous memory" can become a communal strategy that takes suffering and violence seriously and understands that the only alternative is a rejection of power-as-control schemes.

Taken together, the cross and resurrection disclose God's presence to those who suffer, God's alternative to abusive power, and the transformative hope of renewed life. Taken together, the cross and resurrection provide a balanced alternative to the masochism of submissive suffering or to the pride of unchecked triumphalism. The hope of resurrection provides a resistive strategy to death-dealing, while the reality of the cross humbles our own pretensions that human nature is loving and essentially good. Neither romanticism nor pessimism have a place in Christian theology.

Wisdom and Folly

If the cross and resurrection reverse our notions of power, they also reverse our notions of wisdom and folly. Rather than individual rebirth or new beginning, the church becomes the community that is already beginning to live in the world according to a new construal of power. Jesus/Christ as an image of wisdom reverses our traditional notions of wisdom as a way of ensuring social success and acclaim. God nullifies the "somebody" powers and structures of a theology of glory toward the "nobody" powers of a theology of salvage. The language of reversal and subversion offers a model of faithfulness whose "power" is the apparent weakness of compassion and whose "wisdom" is the foolishness of refusing to play the power game. The purpose of this "rhetoric of folly" is to trivialize the worldly power structures by not giving them the honor and acclaim typically accorded to them.

Rodney Kennedy has written extensively on the rhetoric of folly as it functions in Pauline rhetoric and as it can function to subvert notions of worldly success (power).[28] For preachers, and particularly for women preachers who operate within Sophia christologies, understanding the rhetoric of folly is essential if we want to avoid reinscribing cultural values of domination and control. Within a rhetoric of folly, vulnerability is strength, love is power, social failure is religious success. The rhetoric of folly points to the church that is gutting its budget to feed the hungry and proclaims this as a great success! The rhetoric of folly reverses notions of power and wisdom to *subvert the social control these notions have over people's lives.* If seeking status is a "sinful" human value, then the rhetoric of folly claims that losing status is a virtue. This is not an exercise in wishful thinking, but an exercise in reeducating communities to operate by different value systems.

When we reconsider Sophia/Wisdom christologies, we must remember to do so from the underside; such christologies can reinscribe dangerous cultural values. We noted earlier that traditional uses for the Wisdom character functioned to reinforce socially acceptable roles for women. Wisdom was a narrative foil set in opposition to the loose woman or the whore who tempted young men to foolish behavior. However, in primitive christologies, wisdom language was set in clear opposition to the power structures. Jesus as Wisdom or Sophia was a subverter of popular "logic" who offered an alternative wisdom to his followers. In conformity with the Hebrew scriptures and with the New Testament, Jesus is a prophet that the people rejected, the same way that those in power typically reject subverters of the social structure.

To the extent that we can reclaim Wisdom or Sophia as an interpretive category, it must be within the assumption that Jesus/Christ is anti-kyriarchal and sympathetic to a different power strategy. The wisdom of Jesus/Christ and of an appropriate Sophia model will subvert domination strategies and cast a suspicion on rigid ways of knowing. The eschatological and even apocalyptic thrust of early subversive wisdom christologies must be maintained in women's theologies. Lady Wisdom can be a subversive christological figure only to the extent that the future orientation persists. "The whole tenor of apocalyptic eschatology express[es] a memory and a hope of liberation that no astute ruling foreign power could fail to perceive as threatening."[29]

Both Schüssler Fiorenza and Elizabeth Johnson lean toward this subversive reading. Johnson claims that reversals are at the heart of Sophia theology and that Jesus incarnates these oppositions of crucifixion and glorification, divinity, and humanity. To the extent that Wisdom/Sophia is a demythologized advocate of the underside of social structures, the connections are appropriate. But Sophia christologies must be extremely careful to promote social critique and transformation rather than the conventional wisdom of social conformity and control. Sophia/Wisdom can very easily be coopted as a "logical" support for those in power: gatekeepers of the social order.

In her work on the Lutheran theology of the cross, Mary Solberg explores the cross as an epistemological strategy for this realistic religious understanding that avoids imperialism of any kind. Solberg contrasts the theology of the cross with the theology of glory. We noted earlier that one of the greatest dangers of a resurrection theology is its tendency toward a theology of glory (the same problem emerges with incarnational theologies). The theology of glory, against which Luther contended so vehemently, has functioned to justify power-over schemes as signs of God's victory over the powers of evil. To be sure, theologies of glory do identify God with the those who fight against evil. Unfortunately, triumphal theologies have usually been little more than a matter of putting someone else in power. Triumphalist christologies do not operate with any intrinsic critique of power itself, but seem to assume that the problem is one of displacing one dominant power with another. The theology of glory generates human pride and creates followers who prefer "works to suffering, glory to the cross, strength to weakness, wisdom to folly… "[30] The theology of glory emerges in nationalistic, ethnic, or religious justifications to power that suggest the power-holders have God on their side.

Solberg critiques the theology of glory by suggesting that a theology of the cross humbles human pretensions, questioning "legitimacy of the powerful as knowers" and "how knowledge is produced under conditions shaped and maintained by power-over."[31] The epistomology of the cross is fundamentally suspicious of power and always favors a perspective sympathetic with those "relegated to the margins or backwoods of the dominant meaning-system."[32] A theology that keeps the cross and the resurrection in tension recognizes the ambiguities of human fallibility; otherwise this construal of alternative power can easily evolve into romantic ideas of the possibilities of human progress. While resurrection as a category honors the embodiment commitments of eros and incarnational theologians, its partner category, the crucifixion, stands as a critique of power and a reminder of human fragility. Human beings are probably not universally predisposed to be loving, generous, kind, and engaged in mutuality. Human nature is fully ambiguous, embodying both good and evil tendencies. The cross critiques evil while the resurrection promotes a genuine hope in the face of that fragility.

The cross and resurrection, taken as a narrative and metaphorical gestalt, is a christological metaphor of God's passion to salvage the world. Together, they take evil and suffering seriously, they identify human complicity and captivity in power structures, they offer a subversive alternative to power-as-control, and they offer a vision of renewed life as a result of rejecting coercive power. They do not separate the mind from the body, since there is no epistemological or political advantage granted by the cross and resurrection. In the resurrection, the body/mind reality is reunited under a different power construct. The Pauline letters call for a transformation of mind and body, claiming that in the resurrection we become some strange entities: spiritual bodies that are not reducible to either spirit or flesh. As dualistic as Pauline theology can be, this understanding of the reunion of spirit and flesh, under the compelling knowledge of alternative power, stands as a beacon of hope to our own theological dilemmas. In Christ, we become unified selves again, to work for the wholeness of the world.

The power of God, disclosed through the event of Jesus/Christ's crucifixion and resurrection, is that of the noncoercive power of being in genuine caring human relationships with each other and with the world that God so loves. This alternative kind of power allows us to see ourselves and others for the fragile human creatures that we are. But beyond this, the power of God in Jesus/Christ is the power to tenderly salvage what is salvageable, the power to be in solidarity with those who suffer, and the power to proclaim and to practice life in the midst of death. As Anna Blume reminds us, we never expect to find anything whole. Nevertheless, we find whatever little bits and pieces there are that allow for the salvage operation to commence. "Everything falls apart, but not every part of every thing, at least not at the same time. The job is to zero in on these little islands of intactness, to imagine them joined to other such islands, and those islands to still others, and thus to create new archipelagoes of matter."[33]

God's power is the power of salvaging the mess that all of creation is in. Jesus/Christ, as a metaphor of the agency of salvage, presents this truth to us in a way that critiques suffering, offers renewed personal understanding, and suggests a vision of the new heaven and new earth where power-as-control does not reign supreme. Where Jesus/Christ is understood as the primary model for the church's ministries, it is this crucified and risen salvager who suggests communal strategies for living proleptically "in the kingdom of God." The cross and resurrection tell us about the nature of God, the nature of humanity, and the proper God/human relationship. In continuity with God's divine project for a just world, we become agents of salvage in the ruptured world.

Incarnation of God's Purposes

Much of what we have already discussed relative to the resurrection image corresponds to concerns raised by women theologians who prefer the category of incarnation for christology. Resurrection, as a metaphor of reembodiment, values the embodiedness of all creation and offers an image that reverses the ravages of death and decay. Within the salvage model, resurrection claims that life is to be cherished, salvaged, and restored to a unity that includes the dimensions of mind and body. This double focus has the advantage of avoiding mind/body dualisms involved in classical or contemporary formulations that tend to favor one dimension over the other. Resurrection as salvage can include an individual restoration of the mind to the body, an individual restoration of the body to the mind, a communal reintegration of spirituality with ethics, or a social "repair" that unites.

Gustaf Aulén has claimed that "the incarnation is perfected on the cross. Here divine love appears in its unfathomableness and inexhaustible power. This becomes evident when the light from the resurrection illuminates the completed work of his ministry."[34] I would want to agree with Aulén's basic assumption but rephrase it slightly. The incarnation of God's salvage operation is disclosed in the basileia teachings and acts of Jesus/Christ. God lives in these acts and teachings, God's vitality is apparent in the death-to-life power disclosed in the cross and resurrection. God lives in the apparent foolishness of cruciform rejections of the power game. God is alive in every disclosure that power-as-control leads to death and that power-as-life is the only alternative.

What kind of God was incarnate in Jesus/Christ? The God we meet in the life, death, and resurrection is one who will risk everything to salvage the death-bent world. The God incarnate in Jesus/Christ takes shape in the ordinary activities of feeding the starving, forgiving the unforgivable, offering hospitality to losers, touching the contaminated, befriending scoundrels, and doing all variety of things that the world associates with foolishness and foulness. The God disclosed in the fleshly practices of Jesus/Christ renews the world in apparent powerlessness: refusing honor, refusing power, wasting money, consorting with undesirables, and helping hopeless causes. The God disclosed in the fleshly practices of Jesus/Christ will stop at nothing to salvage the world. The *threat* of death does not terminate the salvage operation, and *death itself* is powerless to stop the ministry of salvage. The God we meet in the fleshly practices of Jesus/Christ pours the divine self into the world without hesitation.

Since resurrection always presumes some form of death or nonbeing, it offers either radical critique of the "old body" (particularly helpful when social or political bodies need new life) or a radical hope that even the most hopeless situation can be salvaged. Many women theologians will object to this movement from death to life because it has been construed as a necessary movement requiring suffering and death to precede new life. I'm not suggesting the kind of necessary relationship that would rationalize suffering or death as a prelude to renewed being. It would be dangerous to suggest that individuals must "go through the cross" to get to resurrection. To posit these two stages as necessary would be to separate them metaphorically and to focus on one dimension in isolation from the other. However, the movement from death to life is a more apt description of the actual experiences of most humanity and the movement that most fully encompasses the kind of radical reversals sought by women theologians. Resurrection as an incarnational or eros category recognizes the threat of real death, real suffering, and real finitude that marks the created world. Resurrection as incarnation does not devalue life or function as an escape from life, but honors the yearning for fulness of life in continuity with God's purposes.

To speak of the incarnation of God in Jesus/Christ in this way is to make claims that honor the historicity of the prophet from Galilee without claiming radical uniqueness. To say that Jesus/Christ was a particular incarnation of Godly practices avoids metaphysical problems while maintaining the centrality of the basileia teachings and acts to provide content to the category of incarnation. This strategy has the advantages of continuity with prophetic messianic understandings of the pre-Jesus movement, without the disadvantages of anti-Judaism or other forms of Christian superiority. Jesus/Christ was an incarnation of God's messianic purposes only relative to his message, his works of compassion, and his practice of power-in-love. Jesus/Christ assumed the prophetic messianic role projected by the history of Israel in continuity with God's purposes for the world. Jesus/Christ was not, in his inner life, any special form of divinity, yet his practices and his teachings disclose the unique nature of God's purposes in a way that undercuts pretensions to special power, special status, or special wisdom. To articulate Jesus/Christ as the incarnation of God in this way has plausibility with regard to whatever minimal claims we can make about his own self-understanding, without stretching the claim to retroject feminism, Marxism, or other ideologies onto Jesus/Christ.

In addition, this claim about the resurrection-as-incarnation of God in Jesus/Christ closes the gap between the "crucifixionists" and "incarnationalists" without trivializing either position. The divide between white feminist incarnational christologies and many womanist crucifixion/resurrection christologies finds common ground with an approach that resolves the tension between incarnation and resurrection. We noted in the last chapter that Jacquelyn Grant's earlier work on christologies charged that white feminists paid too little attention to the most meaningful symbols within the African American tradition: crucifixion and resurrection. Grant rejected Anselmian atonement to reclaim a more primitive christus victor approach, arguing that suffering is neither God's will, nor redemptive of itself. The cross symbolized the human captivity to evil power, and the crucified Jesus symbolized God's solidarity in that suffering. Jesus was a "political" messiah in the poetic sense of the term. His rejection of dominant power, his support for the disenfranchised, and his subversive worldview could only make the powerful nervous. Jesus offered a rhetorical and metaphorical argument for a different reality, a different conceptual scheme that involved different kinds of power and different kinds of benefits. As the crucified messiah, Jesus could identify with the least of these; as the risen Lord, he signified real embodied triumph over suffering and the domination of power.

This synthesis of incarnation and resurrection may also meet some of the objections of womanist Delores Williams, whose primary objection to the cross was in its surrogacy. Williams rejected any redemptive content for the cross, claiming that salvific images are found in Jesus' ministerial vision of life and not through his death. If God is primarily disclosed through images of life, perhaps the vocation of the living Jesus and the risen Christ can answer her objections to the isolated meaning of the cross.

This proposal for synthesizing incarnation with resurrection speaks most directly to Kelly Brown Douglas' demands for a christology that is prophetic and transformative without resting on ontological claims of marginality. Recall that she had rejected Cone and Cleage for their racial imperative, and she rejected Roberts for his nonprophetic universal Christ. She calls for a prophetic Jesus/Christ who is not reduced to any particular image (black, female, white, male) but is elastic enough to embrace numerous images while maintaining a prophetic critique. It was the crucifixion of Christ, and not the incarnation, that demonstrated Christ's participation in the human condition and particularly the condition of suffering. Resurrection, argues Douglas, revealed that the death on the cross was not the last word. "The crucified one was the resurrected one—who was now acting in contemporary history" in solidarity with the slaves as they suffered and sought the vindication of liberation.[35] The vindication of Jesus from undeserved suffering and death was a paradigm of liberation. Douglas demands that the liberating message of Jesus/Christ be the principle by which christologies are legitimated, but not any ontological claims about his marginality, his race, or his gender.

Rearticulating incarnation as part of the crucifixion/resurrection salvage operation has the advantage of including the mujerista and non-Western concerns for locating God's solidarity in the experience of suffering. To assume that the cross has no positive theological meaning (as Williams claims), or to subsume its meaning under the category of incarnation (as Brock and Heyward do), is to trivialize the theological reflection of mujerista and non-Western women. Mujerista women, along with Asian and African women, locate their epistemological starting point not in the experiences of essential interrelatedness, but in the experiences of extreme physical suffering and nobody-ness. Mujerista theologians critique suffering from the eschatological vision of a pluralistic community in solidarity. Asian and African women (with the exception of Oduyoye) critique suffering from the Jesus-exemplar model of liberation and healing. One of the problems we noted in the last chapter was that mujerista Mariologies lacked an eschatological dimension, that most of the Asian and African healer/shaman/sister christologies lacked an eschatological dimension, and that incarnational and eros christologies lacked a clear eschatological dimension.

By articulating incarnational claims within a crucifixion/resurrection paradigm, it is possible to project an eschatological future where death is reversed, suffering is transformed to new life, hunger is met, and power-as-domination collapses toward power-as-life. The eschatological vision, cast in the Jesus sayings as the reign or basileia of God, becomes Isasi-Díaz's *proyecto histórico* against which our captivities are critiqued and then subverted. Resurrection as the future social incarnation of God's purposes can function as a communal vision, not just for the church, but for the whole creation. This rearticulation allows us to graft several concerns together into an overall pattern. This approach projects an ideal future (mujerista), critiques the present situation (all options), takes suffering and death seriously (womanist, African, Asian), rejects the domination that kills (eros and incarnational), revives what has been lost or almost lost (African, womanist, and maybe eros/incarnational), and reverses the death spiral toward an abundant future (Sophia).

The Salvage Operation in Community: Suffering, Sacrifice, Servanthood, and Surrogacy

For the early church, the language of resurrection provided ways for the community to speak about the ongoing presence of Jesus/Christ within the community. The theological claim of "the resurrection of the dead" operated as a consolation that those who died in Christ would continue to live and be related to the community. The belief in some kind of relationship that continued beyond death allowed the early believers to subdue the fear of death that tempted them to inactivity. Belief in the resurrection allowed the communities to continue practicing the basileia in the face of death-threats, to continue proclaiming justice and caring for the disenfranchised. The belief in the risen Christ and in the general resurrection of the dead functioned to keep the community bound together for support and bound together for their justice-making. For us to say that we believe in the resurrection is a way of associating our own corporate mission with the living presence of the God we know in Jesus/Christ, to associate it with other believers, and to understand our corporate mission as a "resurrection business" that salvages others from death.

Mercy Amba Oduyoye has described this as the christological vocation of the church in the world. She claims an eschatological "mission" for the church when she declares that its purpose is to incarnate "the rule of God in the world."[36] This happens through proclamation and service, but also through its ability to "represent the shape of a human community when it is fully submitted to the will of God."[37] Submission to God's will is a problem when God is a tyrant who demands and justifies suffering. Submission to God's will is liberating when God is involved in salvaging the world from power-as-domination tyrants. Here is precisely where we should engage Thangaraj's demand for radical monotheism and Calvin's "loophole" for institutional critique. Thangaraj's demand for radical monotheism can interpret Oduyoye's call for submission, since the call for radical monotheism demands rejecting idols, whether they take the form of masculine power, national loyalty, gender allegiance, class devotion, racial commitments, or sexual orientation resolutions. In other words, Oduyoye's understanding of submission to God's will is an informed submission, or a submission through suspicion. Submission to another is not threatening when that Other reliably and eternally rejects domination. The crucifixion "epistemology" reveals that any commitment that finds itself in competition with the *kenosis* of power is suspect. The cross calls all our ways of knowing into question, asking "for whom?" and "for what?" These diverse commitments are not inappropriate, but when they become ultimate (idolatrous), they are suspect. Attempts by various groups to get their share of the power are subject to scrutiny from within and from without that community of identity. This is the same claim for radical transformation that Kelly Brown Douglas calls for when she rejects christologies based on "ontological marginality" or what other scholars call "identity" or "essentialist" arguments. Any analysis that privileges one kind of experience (blackness, whiteness, maleness, or oppression) distorts the fullness of Christ and the fullness of reconciliation.

Calvin's loophole, to which we referred earlier, requires that Christians exercise suspicion toward earthly collectivities and institutions to discern their compatibility with God's purposes for transforming the world. This is one of the only formal instances in classical Western theology where the right to protest and resist assumes a theological mandate. Calvin's anthropology was diametrically opposed to a radical sanctioning of hierarchical orders, primarily because Calvin assumed that our minds were as subject to deception as our bodies were to temptation. Calvin's epistemological orientation was one of profound suspicion regarding humanity's ability to reason.[38] Calvin is, in this regard, the author of the hermeneutic of suspicion, not just at the individual level, but explicitly at the level of institutional power and privilege. Calvin (along with Luther) would have rejected any notion of "the essential goodness" of human nature, or the fundamental human desire for mutuality. Calvin assumed that part of the teaching vocation of the church was this constant reminder that faith in human beings was always misguided. He was no romantic when it came to discussions of desire, rationality, or goodwill.

For Oduyoye, our submission to God is an informed submission, requiring us to ask the hard questions. What kind of power? For whose benefit? And at whose direction? For Oduyoye the church incarnates the God we know in Christ as it attempts to be the first fruits of the kingdom, a sign pointing to the shape of God's eschatological world of justice. If the church is called to be this kind of sign in the world, the bearer of salvage, this doesn't prevent other salvage operations from being Christlike. We will turn to that discussion in the next chapter, but for now it's necessary to note that the peculiar identity of the church as the bearer of salvage doesn't mean that the church is the only bearer of new life. We are both Christlike and Mary-like when we bear the signs of hope in the body of the church. We are also shaman-like, sister-like, and healer-like when we practice the in-the-world vocation of reversing death and suffering.

Oduyoye demands that the manner of embodying the mission cannot be separated from the mission itself. And it is this specific understanding of embodying the mission of the church that allows her to approach the concept of sacrifice. "It is in this respect that I wish to situate the Christian's call to self-denial, forgoing privilege and embracing a simplicity of life whose wealth is not only in being poor-in-spirit but in being a church of the poor for the sake of the kingdom."[39] Sacrifice is not primarily an individual spiritual discipline, but it is the communal orientation of the church toward the world. Sacrifice is strictly delimited to corporate acts that embody the church's solidarity with those whose lives need salvage. The church that risks its own corporate survival to minister to the last and the least, that forgoes social status to serve those on the bottom, the church that repudiates institutional wealth and the accumulation of property is Christlike, acting to salvage the world that God so loved.

Notice the different purposes for which Oduyoye suggests sacrifice and suffering. These virtues are not required for individual submission to another individual, nor are they required to placate God or secure our own salvation. They are practical virtues, necessary for discipleship in the world. Jacquelyn Grant, womanist theologian, reframes servanthood in the language of discipleship. She rejects servant language for the reasons that it has been abused in the past, selectively imposed on those who are at the bottom of every social hierarchy. Servanthood has been reversed to reinscribe the powerlessness of the powerless and the captivity of the captive. Rather, the language and rhetoric of servanthood should be directed toward the category of discipleship, where it can undercut the rhetoric of domination/submission "to foster a more inclusive discipleship. The kind of wholism [*sic*] sought in womanist theology requires that justice be an integral part of our quest for unity and community."[40] Grant goes on to argue for a model of discipleship that avoids the gender requirements traditionally associated with that calling.

Grant's need to qualify what she means by discipleship is no more than the qualification Oduyoye seeks for servanthood or sacrifice. None of the biblical metaphors for community identity and action are exempt from distortion. Even the metaphor of discipleship carries the implied corollary activity of "cross-bearing." We can only reorient the notions of suffering servanthood or sacrifice in terms of somewhat explicit conditions and purposes. Suffering can only be a legitimate ethical posture if it is a suffering with those who need to be salvaged, and a suffering that resists power-as-domination. The notions of suffering-with or cosuffering as a compassionate act of consolation are not inappropriate, but they are inadequate. Christologies that focus only on the cross and interpret it as a sign of either emotional or embodied solidarity stop short of the full radicality that includes resistance and reversal. Suffering or servility should never be promoted as alternatives to resistance, but only as strategies of resistance. Suffering on behalf of the reign of God will involve a subversive strategy of destabilizing power structures and resisting abuse. Suffering whose primary goal is to maintain power-as-domination schemes is neither redemptive nor faithful, but may in fact be capitulating to powers and principalities. With Isasi-Díaz, we should challenge traditional understandings that suffering has redemptive value in and of itself. Notions of heroic suffering have been used, she claims, as "an ideological tool, a control mechanism used by dominant groups over the poor and the oppressed."[41] With her and other women theologians, we do not want to negate the reality of suffering, but to de-romanticize the spiritual value of suffering as an end in itself.

Carter Heyward claims that in Jesus/Christ, "our fundamental identity is not as individuals with 'rights' but as members of One Body, interdependent and mutually responsible for one another."[42] As the body of Christ, the church must be willing to risk its own social and institutional loss of power by standing in solidarity with those whose lives are diminished. In this confrontation with death-dealing power, we commit our bodily activities to resist power with powerlessness. By risking death, we embody resurrection. Our suffering brings life out of death. "In our vulnerability and powerlessness, as well as in the sacred power we are able to generate, we stand together and we fall together."[43] As we offer ourselves on behalf of the broken and brokenhearted, we embody an erotic resurrection passion for life, committed to bringing life out of death. By imaging Jesus/Christ as the paradigm for Christian vocation, she claims that we can maintain a unity of purpose between God and humanity. To speak of Christ is to claim something about our own responsibility toward the future purposes of God.[44] Heyward calls for a "spirituality for suffering that is steeped in solidarity."[45] This spirituality requires communities to take a voluntary stand with those who suffer and to be present with them, "offering ourselves to one another." Heyward, using the traditional language of suffering servanthood, reorients the purpose of suffering toward the vision of righteousness and justice. Suffering is not a passive spiritual virtue exercised by an individual in order to tolerate injustice, but a corporate activity exercised in order to subvert injustice. "The root-source of our vocational purpose as Christians is to create life in the midst of death and despair."[46]

The image of the cross and suffering solidarity is at the center of this communal vocation. Theologian Harvey Cox made use of this cruciform understanding of vocation when he addressed a group of young adults. After his lecture, Cox responded to a question from a self-proclaimed Generation Xer. The young woman claimed that for Jesus to be relevant to her peers, he can't be a hero, but he must be human, flaws and failings and all. Cox responded by referring to a comment by John Dominic Crossan. According to Cox, Crossan claimed that if he were making a movie of the crucifixion scene, he would begin with a tight shot of the cross in all its gruesome reality. Then he would have the camera pull back to show a landscape plentiful with crosses. Jesus was not a solitary heroic figure, but part of a whole class of victimized people.[47] So, we can imagine that a true image of divinity is one who is in solidarity with the suffering, in league with them and sharing the same suffering they endure.

Rita Nakashima Brock makes similar claims for the risky communal vocation of the Christa/Community. We noted in the previous chapter that even though Brock wants to reject the image of Jesus as a tragic hero, she displaces it with an image of the community willing to risk suffering in the pursuit of justice. She recognizes the fragility of human existence, our tendencies toward domination, and the necessity for some exercise of spiritual discipline. The only suffering or servanthood that is legitimate is suffering that pursues justice, suffering that is in solidarity with the disenfranchised, and suffering that willingly risks safety to enhance life. Suffering is neither redemptive nor is it necessary for salvage. However, a vocational identity that pursues justice can assume that some type of suffering is inevitable if real powers are being confronted. With Heyward, we can commit to a deromanticized view of suffering, "offering them no pretense of magical solutions, no theological rationale for suffering, no feigned light-heartedness or denial of pain and fear."[48] And, with C. S. Song, we can claim our vocation in the world by realizing that "Jesus *is* the crucified people."[49]

The vocation of serving the world toward justice involves notions of humility, risk, but above all, action. Roberta Bondi reminds us of the biblical mandate to resist evil in an active way. "It is useful to speculate on what would have happened to their friendship with Jesus if they [Mary and Martha] had simply responded to Lazarus's death by saying, "We must be quiet and accept it as the Lord's will."[50] Action is a more complicated reality than simply what one does. Hannah Arendt claims that, unlike mere labor or work, action makes known the mystery of the who above the what. Action reveals both the sort of person one is (the kind of community one joins and that one projects) and the mode of life one inhabits. Arendt claims that action is the stuff of which narratives are made. Because it arises within a complex network of influence and counterinfluence, action is more complex than the outdated Enlightenment portrait of autonomous agency. Action is fragile; to act is to undertake a risk, for action by its very nature depends upon others for its nurture and accomplishment, occurring as it does within an intricate "web of relationships." Action is always interaction; it is relational, interdependent, and profoundly communal.[51] And according to William James, the difference between imaginary drama and real drama is that real drama has real winners and real losers, real consequences of real deeds performed in real freedom against real odds of success or failure.[52]

Kathleen Talvacchia makes helpful connections between solidarity, vocation, action, and real deeds. She outlines two goals for the ministry of compassion. First is the understanding that compassion is not mere sympathy, but a "willingness to suffer with others in the cause of justice-making." Suffering with does not imply a necessary or automatic participation in that suffering, since "the very fact that we are choosing such a stance is evidence of our inability to experience what they experience." Rather she advocates an understanding of suffering solidarity as a community's willingness to "give up our privileged state in regard to a specific issue in order to stand with others who are experiencing injustice, working with them to resist it, and to transform the situation." The second goal follows from this first one and involves a shift from an attitude of solidarity to practices of committed behavior and activity. "This involves the concrete actions to bring about justice for a disempowered group. It seeks to change structures of privilege and domination into genuinely inclusive structures of just relations."[53]

Talvacchia's two moments of the suffering solidarity phenomena conform to the dual tension I have claimed within the crucifixion and the resurrection gestalt. The first moment involves a rejection of worldly power, the kenosis of power-as-domination, where the Christian community relinquishes its own claims to social power in order to stand with a whole group of victimized people. Within contemporary Christian congregations, this means that local communities must expect public misunderstanding and censure if they opt to stand in solidarity with any disenfranchised group. There is enough social backlash within local communities and within denominational structures for local congregations to expect ostracism, threats of financial withholding, or the rescinsion of ministerial authority. Local congregations, and their clergy, can expect social pressure ranging from the rhetorical to the political if they take a public stand with those that local convention considers unworthy. The second moment is perhaps more threatening to local communities: a position of active nonviolent resistance that challenges specific rules and structures in order to change them. Action is always interaction, and real drama involves real winners and real losers, real consequences of real deeds performed in real freedom against real odds of success or failure.

We do, then, move away from notions of salvation as purification or some nostalgic return to primal perfection. Salvage work is messy, risky, and subject to failure. Salvage work necessitates coming into contact with what is corrupt, touching the unclean, risking contamination. The rhetoric of folly operates at this level, to reverse the purity and pollution oppositions in favor of the messier option. To say that Christians are involved in salvaging is to understand our own character as a being-salvaged community committed to the salvage of the world. We are not somehow above the debris, but are part of the material being salvaged. We join God in the ongoing salvage of the world. To salvage involves getting dirty, taking risks, courting failure and social rejection. Salvage work is the opposite of redeeming the world through purification.

Salvage work involves the lovely embodied image of intimacy and touch, but not for our immediate pleasure. Salvage requires us to touch what the world has seen fit to throw away.

Salvage and the Icon of the Battered Woman

This theology of salvage, as a communal vocation centered on the cross and resurrection, produces a distinctly different understanding and posture toward those who are victims of suffering. If we return to our earlier pastoral situation, the specific incident involving a battered woman, we can explore how the rhetoric of folly and a communal ethic of salvage transforms traditional pastoral and homiletic approaches to questions of domestic violence. I will, for the purposes of clarity, walk through the theological claims and the pastoral/communal actions consistent with a theology of salvage. I intend to avoid reinscribing a mind/body dualism, a romanticizing of victimization, a christology of lady-like virtues, or a christology where Jesus is either a feminist or a revolutionary.

There are two dimensions of the problem. First, there is a pastoral dimension of counseling and nurturing the individual woman toward a vision of liberation from violence. Second, there is an ethical dimension of the community's solidarity and intervention in the situation of violence. These must be theologically related and coherent: presumably a pastor/preacher will have already established through preaching and other teaching strategies what the vocation of the congregation is. These two strategies, involving nurture and intervention, are part of one unified understanding of a christology of salvage, and it's advisable not to truncate ministry by engaging only one strategy.

At the level of nurture, the pastor/preacher will need to make some clear theological claims to the woman who seeks help. Let me be clear that I'm not suggesting a pastor sit down with a checklist and subject the woman in crisis to a barrage of theological claims. I am suggesting that if pastors understand what is at stake theologically, they may be better prepared to deal on the spot with women in crisis and to interpret what theological concerns underlie certain questions and comments.

Among the theological "truths" that a pastor must present to a victim of familial violence, the first and most critical is the assurance that God does not desire her suffering and is not punishing her. A pastor can appeal to the whole spectrum of biblical images that involve just relationships, narratives that envision a world of peace and nonviolence, or the prophetic appeals to care for the oppressed. But among the most important claims that a pastor can make to the woman in crisis is that she is not a victim of *God's* wrath or punishment. Her suffering is not something that pleases God. Victims almost always internalize violence as personal guilt. Without arguing either about her *particular* innocence or guilt, a pastor can assure the woman that God deals with guilt by forgiving it and not by punishing it. Another popular religious notion undergirding abuse is the idea that faithfulness demands obedience to authority. This will raise the whole question of her abuser's right to lord it over her and the spiritual requirement to "sacrifice her body" to him. The theological counter to this assumption is the claim of radical monotheism that calls us all children of God, and that there are no earthly "fathers" to whom we owe obedience.

When an abused woman asks if she should just "forgive him and turn the other cheek," the pastor should be prepared to be an advocate for forgiveness, but without placing this burden on the individual woman. The strongest advantage of the approach I've been advocating with regard to subverting the cycle of violence is to reimage the traditional Christian responses from problems of individual moral agency to communal moral agency. By shifting the burden of forgiveness from the woman to the congregation, several problems are solved at once. First, it releases the woman from ongoing internalized blame and feelings of shame. Forgiving an abuser is difficult at any point, but it is particularly difficult at the time of immediate crisis. While forgiveness is certainly a Christian virtue, and while the woman may ultimately need to forgive her abuser as part of her own healing, it is morally suspect for a pastor to put the burden of reconciliation on the victim. Darby Ray discusses the hardship this places on a debilitated victim. When forgiveness becomes the primary action, and it must be granted by the victim in order to secure her own and her abuser's salvation, the woman assumes the entire responsibility and guilt for any failure to resolve the problem. As a primary strategy, forgiveness alone does nothing to end the violence, but subtly enlists the victim in her own continuing victimization.[54]

It is the vocation of the community to stand with the woman and to act as an agent of forgiveness and intervention on her behalf. We have argued all along that the ethical mandates within the biblical tradition are primarily mandates for communities as they organize their corporate life in the world. The "you" of "you should forgive and turn the other cheek" should never be directed at a solitary member of a community to the exclusion of the other members. One of the most peculiar, yet traditional sacramental gifts of the church has been the intercessory ability to offer and proclaim forgiveness on behalf of God. One of the most dramatic acts the church can initiate is to forgive the sins of the abuser. As a fragile human community, we may not find such forgiveness easy to proclaim, but it's more appropriate and more charitable than expecting the abused woman to bear the spiritual burden of forgiving her abuser. The church's forgiveness of the offender may, in fact, model forgiveness to her and for her. The woman in crisis might ultimately find resources within the church that enable her to experience mercy and to extend mercy. Every action, including the extension of mercy, is fragile, and by its nature depends upon others for its nurture and accomplishment. As an agent of salvage in the world, the Christian community can proclaim God's radical forgiveness of the abuser without putting this initial burden on the victim.

"Turning the other cheek," is a biblical phrase that has lost almost all its potential for radical resistance, since it has been construed as a method of "making nice." When we compare turning the other cheek to the other two alternatives, the potential for resistance becomes clearer. When someone slaps us on the cheek, we tend to have one of two reactions. The first and most human reaction is to slap back. The second reaction is to abandon the situation and flee. To stand toe-to-toe with an abuser is to refuse either violence or immediate escape. To turn the other cheek is a refusal to submit, a refusal to fight, and a refusal to abandon justice. Turning the other cheek is not an invitation to violence, but a resistance to violence.

More importantly, though, turning the other cheek is not the task of the solitary victim. For the victim to turn the other cheek, she will need the immediate physical support and presence of the community. Turning the other cheek is the strategy that should be assumed, in surrogacy, by the community in solidarity with the woman. The body of Christ is not wholly located in the solitary body of the individual abused woman. The body of Christ is present in the community that stands in suffering solidarity with the woman in crisis. We make a serious mistake when we place communal responsibilities for reconciliation on the victimized individual. Turning the other cheek can be a dramatic intervention if the woman presents herself to the abuser in the presence of her advocates, who will be willing to absorb threats on her behalf. As an intervention strategy, turning the other cheek can operate as a nonviolent confrontation wherein the community refuses to run away from the abuser and refuses to engage in counterviolence. As a first step in the intervention process, turning the other cheek might be an occasion for the members of the community to tell the abuser that he must stop, that they will continue to intervene, and to help the woman gather her belongings in preparation to leave. If there are children involved, this intervention should be done in their presence, as a form of proclamation and of solidarity with them. Children in any abusive situation need to know that there are strong advocates who will stand up to abusers.

The riskiest and most dangerous time for a woman in an abusive domestic situation is that moment when she subverts the power of the abuser by leaving or threatening to leave. Most of the murdered victims of domestic violence are killed in their efforts to detach from the abuser, since this autonomy directly threatens his exercise of power-as-domination. It is at this moment of heightened vulnerability that a congregation must exercise radical and ongoing advocacy for the woman. The Christian community does, in a sense, become the surrogate victim, willing to face the wrath of the abuser *in her place* and willing to salvage her from violence. Radically committed Christian communities will assume the risk and the burden of protecting the woman, ensuring her physical safety in a shelter or in their own homes, providing for her financially, and bringing her abuser to a nonviolent moment of intervention. We will risk ourselves, on her behalf, in the service of justice-making.

At the second level of solidarity, communities will become politically involved, in secular politics and in denominational politics, to change whatever structures of violence assist the perpetuation of abuse. The best use of human resources would be for several local congregations or several denominational bodies to sort out different facets of domestic violence for the purposes of specializing in particular problems. One church might explore the establishment of safe shelters, or a system of safe houses; another might get involved in legislative changes required to offer protection to women; another might work within school systems to teach children about nonviolence; one might develop lay counseling services or support groups for victims.

Pastors typically recommend forgiveness and cheek-turning as faithful responses of an individual. Such recommendations do nothing to subvert power, do nothing to salvage those in crisis, and do nothing to risk their own well-being. But Christian action is fragile action. Acting on behalf of another is to undertake a risk, since action depends upon others for its nurture and accomplishment. Action is always interaction, and profoundly communal. This particular action, of salvaging those who suffer, makes the redemptive presence of God in Christ immediate and embodied, "it makes known the who above the what." Sacrificial suffering, on behalf of the weak, makes known the God we know in Jesus/Christ. Our communal vocation of bringing life out of death discloses the God of the cross and resurrection.

Preaching, Resistance, and Dangerous Memories

One of the responsibilities of an ethical community is to keep alive what Johann Metz has called the "dangerous memories" of dignity and mutuality, victory, and strategies of resistance.[55] These dangerous memories echo throughout a community's specific historical past, their shared narratives, the stories of their predecessors and ancestors, and their own fragile victories. Such memories can continue to fund hope, project a better future, and empower communities to work for justice.

Sharon Welch, along with others, claims that one of the enemies of justice-making is the death of the imagination, which gives rise to a culture of despair and a posture of resignation. "The death of compassion follows the death of the imagination" and leads to the inability to act or envision any better future.[56] Welch traces the function of dangerous memories within the novels of several African American women to claim them as powerful narrative sources for transformation. "The responsibility of remembering the past and seeing the horrors of the present is not borne lightly. Nor is it a responsibility that is borne alone." Welch explores the way such communal memory is reenacted in Paule Marshall's *The Chosen Place, The Timeless People*. The characters of Bourne Island perform a masque every year during Carnival, recreating a slave revolt led by Cuffee Ned. According to Welch, Marshall's characters bear their dangerous memory of enslavement and freedom as a legacy for the future:

> Through the masque, the people of Bourne Island relive their past and remember what is required for freedom. They remember a time of overturning the power relations that still imprison them and experience again the joy that comes with freedom, the dignity and well-being, the delight of "being a people," of working together for justice.[57]

Wendy Farley calls on Welch's category of "dangerous memory" to discuss the Christian tradition and the task of pastoral ministry. Scripture, church, the sacraments, and the tradition are all mediators of "dangerous memory," which can continue to mediate power to resist suffering and evil in the present. Farley claims that even "for all their ambiguity, the church and scripture also can mediate the compassionate power of God in history."[58] She cites the witness of the prophetic voices, the images of the promised land, the parables of the kingdom, and the Pauline house churches as a record that "reminds human beings of the possibility and reality of divine compassion active in history." [59] The church, in all its ministries, mediates two distinct but related realities: the vision of a redeemed world and the power through which redemption arises. Such a witness to the "nonfinality of evil" includes an imaginative vision that functions as an alternative to the powers and principalities. This vision should not be an ahistorical escape, but a future historical hope. The table fellowship of Jesus, the strange assemblage that followed him from town to town, and even the odd parables of the messianic banquet provide a dangerous memory of fellowship whose power can continue to bring new life.[60]

At the very least, preaching can sketch out the contours of this alternative future and keep dangerous memory alive. Even though we will regularly preach about specific social issues, the more enduring strategy is to offer the communal imagination a shared future toward which they yearn. This is much more than simple narrative theology or narrative homiletics, for telling the stories alone is not sufficient. The task of preaching is to tell the stories, reinterpret the symbols and metaphors, to re-rejuvenate the vision of faith as it relates to specific times and tasks. Preaching is more than retrieval and more than the didactic task of "opening the scriptures." Preaching, as a rhetorical activity, offers a persuasive vision of the future God intends, the past and its resources, and the present with all its ambiguities.

We will have to move beyond telling our own personal anecdotes and using illustrations of individual sports heroes and suffering individuals. We will have to think, imagine, and discern more communally. We will develop the rhetorical strategies to speak of group experiences and group activities: We will have to use illustrations that conjure images of community activity and not just that of lone individuals. We can also learn from womanist theologians, mujerista theologians, Asian and African theologians how stories (images and illustrations) of the ancestors function to "resocialize" communities into their identities and vocations. With Korean women theologians, we can look for counter-narratives and stories of *won-han*, or resistance to the resignation that suffering begets, reclaiming not only stories of our mothers and grandmothers, but appropriating any counter-narratives of group resistance. African women theologians already have a religious tradition that includes the ancestors, providing them with a strategy for constructing an imaginatively shared community that stretches back into the past, but forward into an eternal community of saints. The mujerista strategy of integrating the local piety venerating the saints is another example of a homiletical strategy that projects a communal vocation. Within the narrative and metaphorical fluidity of shared legends, communities can project their own understanding of a broad community of justice, advocates of the "nonfinality of evil" who surround the contemporary community to nurture their resistance. In this way, homiletical method supports a homiletical theology of community.

Ordinary Christians learn a significant amount of their theology at church. James Harris has argued that most of the theology internalized by Christian communities comes to them homiletically and through the worship event.[61] In addition, the largest gathering of the congregation occurs for the worship event. There is no other occasion within contemporary religious life that simultaneously reaches the community to provide interpretive perspectives and offers a vision of redemption relative to their peculiar context. Harris also claims that the sermon, as an oral form, is easily replicated to those who didn't hear it. Sermons are frequently carried home to other family members, to work for repetition among colleagues, and even in bars and restaurants. "Moreover, because there are hundreds of churches in every city, the voice of the preacher is heard from every corner of the community, and this voice affects the beliefs and practices of an inordinate number of people."[62] Televangelism, for all its hype and its scope, is strangely decontextualized and impotent, and does not construct a face-to-face religious community engaged in shared projects. We speak to a collective identity about their collective purpose, offering them a shared vision of communities empowered to act together for God's purposes.

Offering an alternative vision is probably the most significant work a pastor can undertake if she intends to nurture her community toward salvage. As humble and ordinary as preaching is, as fragile and empty as language can seem, it may be the single most effective resource the average pastor has for addressing theological issues and presenting dangerous memories. We assume, along with most women theologians, that the control over language and the resulting thought patterns are central aspects of changing or reinforcing behavior. We have considered the escalating patterns of control suggested in Sally Purvis' discussion to note that power-as-control is legitimated and maintained by language and modes of thought. Conceptual control is the propagandistic control of ideas, concepts, and thought. Power-as-control mediated through language exercises the power to interpret and define reality, to determine what is considered to be knowledge and what is accepted as truth.

In order to subvert power-as-control at its origin, we must be prepared to offer another vision of reality, a vision that is mediated through language. This subversion will be most dramatic if we can, indeed, subvert the primary symbols and narratives from oppressive interpretations to transformative ones. Elisabeth Schüssler Fiorenza and Alexandra Brown have made similar arguments regarding the use of traditional symbols and metaphors, claiming that we should "convert" the symbols and metaphors rather than abandon them. Brown explores the use of Pauline rhetoric in First Corinthians to demonstrate the writer's stages of rhetorical subversion that result in a reversal of the meaning of the word *wisdom*. Schüssler Fiorenza makes a similar argument relative to the imperial warfare language of Revelation, claiming that through repetitive rhetorical strategies, the meaning of King, Conqueror, throne, and glory are all reversed according to what we've identified as the rhetoric of folly.

Preaching is an oral activity that constructs the symbolic universe of a local congregation. As oral/aural language, preaching has an immediacy for a community of believers, making present to them their own past, their own present, and their participation in the future. Through the use of imaginative language and illustrations, preaching has the power to make present to hearers what had previously been distant or absent. As Mary Catherine Hilkert argues, preaching is an act of the sacramental imagination, which, through naming, invokes the immediacy of grace and the presence of Christ.[63] Preaching "echoes the future" of God's promises by naming them in the present. As Dietrich

Bonhoeffer likewise claimed, preaching is a sacramental activity that makes Christ present to the community.

> The proclaimed word is the incarnate Christ himself…both the Historical One and the Present One. He is the access to the historical Jesus. Therefore the proclaimed word is not a medium of expression for something else, something that lies behind it, but rather it is the Christ himself walking through his congregation as the Word…In the sermon the foundation for a new world is laid.[64]

Preaching is nothing more and nothing less than the invocation of the dangerous memory, the subversive presence, and the transformed future of the God we know in Jesus/Christ.

Chapter 5

Visions of the Basileia:
Practicing What We Preach

> *Rituals are not merely another form of art or play, al-*
> *though they are surely artful and playful. Rituals are*
> *perhaps the oldest, they are in many ways the oddest,*
> *members of the performance family. Their business in*
> *society is to effect transformations that cannot other-*
> *wise be brought about.*[1]

From the very beginning we've acknowledged that liturgical practices present a special problem for women preachers. Liturgies are frequently the most fixed and traditional parts of any regular Sunday service
and consequently can prove to be the most resistant to change. Even
where women preachers have successfully proclaimed an emancipatory
gospel, they are frequently undone by the eucharistic liturgy that does
little more than reinscribe exactly the bad theology the preachers were
trying to eliminate. Sacramental life, and particularly eucharistic practice, is an immediate practical problem for many women ministers simply because it exists in the same space and time with the proclamation.
Calls to worship, creeds, confessions, and eucharistic liturgies cannot be
bracketed out; they are immediate "data" for the congregation and for
the minister. Besides this practical problem, there is also a theological
problem. Even if preaching and liturgy did not happen at the same time,
they share the same theological dimensions, symbols, narratives, and
metaphors. Preaching and liturgical practices flow from the same fount
of stories and claims. They are theologically related at their source: the
Jesus tradition.

And because liturgical practices involve bodies and actions, they
are among the most rudimentary and routine behaviors that congregations enact as a unified community. Ritual behavior, as it is interpreted
and as it is practiced, is implicitly related to the way congregations imagine themselves acting together and toward each other. We may not always

reflect on such dimensions of our liturgical behavior, but our understandings of power, community, generosity, and other-directedness are informed by the routine ways we interact with each other within the worship context. Even when we don't reflect on our ritual practices, they inform our understandings of ethical activity, interhuman relationships, friendly and aggressive contact, and the sharing of resources. Ritual behavior implies a congregation's orientation toward each other and toward the rest of the world. There is no "mereness" to ritual life.

These two dimensions of Christian practice are practically and theologically related to the homiletical christology of salvage outlined in the last chapter. These two dimensions are the in-house practices of ritual behavior that we traditionally call sacraments and the less formal (but no less critical) world-oriented practices of compassionate contact. I use the word *contact* most intentionally, since I will claim that both our insider practices and our world-oriented practices involve the notion of physicality and touch. Sacraments or sacramental acts are always connected to real physical elements (bread, wine, water, oil) and real physical activities (eating, drinking, immersing, sprinkling). And our world-oriented practices involve no less physicality: They involve physical acts of touching, feeding, and healing. Both our insider practices and our world-oriented practices reveal what Augustine referred to as "invisible grace made visible."

Our insider sacramental practices and our world-oriented contacts are fundamentally related in ways that most Christian communities not only ignore but rigorously undermine. By sketching out a metaphorical relationship that plays on the ambiguities of the words *practice, act,* and *perform,* I intend to argue for an interpretive approach to sacramental symbols and forms that undergirds our acts of compassionate contact in the world.

Ritual Practices and Rehearsing the Ideal Future

Ritual theorists are fairly united in arguing that ritual behavior constructs an imaginary world where certain behaviors are constitutive of that projected world. Ritual involves "the integration of thought and action categories," wherein certain types of behavior are codified and practiced by a group.[2] Mary Douglas, an anthropologist who specializes in ritual behavior, claims that our ritual behaviors synthesize what we believe about the world and how we are to act in that world. According to Douglas, rituals structure social relations, frame experience, and regulate interactive possibilities. Ritual is also creative and can "mysteriously help" interpretation and action. Ritual suggests what is orderly relationship, meaning, and action.[3] These theatrical or dramatic behaviors imitate or anticipate desired behaviors in the envisioned world.

Tom Driver explores the relationship between pretend behaviors and real behaviors by considering the ambiguities in the language. This ambiguity, he claims, "shows us what kind of actors human beings are."[4] We use the notions of "act" both in the dramatic sense of pretense, as well as in the sense of effecting real deeds. The same ambiguity resides in the uses of the word *practice*. I can easily say that my son is outside practicing his skateboarding in preparation for a contest. If so, you understand that his current activity of practicing is not the "real" event; it is somehow preparation for that event. When stage actors practice their lines, they are readying for the real event. In this sense, practice is a prelude to real activity. However, if I say that my neighbor practices internal medicine, you know that I do not mean to suggest he is less than fully prepared. This use of "practice" connotes the real activity itself and not an imitative prelude. The same ambiguity shows up in our notions of performance. I can say that my husband performed *King Lear* or that my neighbor performed stomach surgery, and you will understand that my husband did not really become King Lear, while my neighbor was not just pretending to cut someone open.

What ritual studies help us understand is that the pretend or imaginary aspect of ritual behavior is not necessarily disassociated from the "really real" and efficacious nature of ritual behavior. Seen from one perspective, these behaviors might be understood primarily as the theatrical acting out of a myth or narrative. This is what people mean when they scorn ritual behavior as "mere" ritual or pretend. Of course, ritual behaviors gradually do take on mythical interpretations over time. However, rituals actually seem to develop the other way, as desired social behaviors (those contributing positively to the envisioned future world) become dramatically codified, practiced, and elaborated through mythical rationalizations. The behaviors seem to come first, and the myths emerge from the dramatic "practicing" of them that accumulates over time.[5] As dramatic behaviors, they suggest which kinds of real in-the-world actions are valued by the religious community. Ritual is not the expression of deep feelings and motivations, but rather the "laying out of ways to act, prompted by felt needs, fears, joys, and aspirations."[6]

Douglas argues that one of the primary ritual constructs operates along the axis of what we consider to be dirty (undesirable) or clean (desirable). Behaviors are classified as dirty; people are considered contaminated; places are ruled unclean or dangerous. These symbolic or metaphoric oppositions are precisely the ones we've explored informally throughout: sin and salvation, sickness and health, purity and pollution. Douglas claims that pollution ideas are concerned with maintaining order. Through symbolic patterns, purification behavior expresses an understanding of the universe and establishes and enforces social behavior. "Reflection on dirt involves reflection on the relation of order to disorder, being to non-being, form to formlessness, life to death. Wherever ideas of dirt are highly structured their analysis discloses a play upon such profound themes."[7] Purity and innocence are concepts that almost always function within religious discourse as strategies for the exclusion of "contamination." Mary Douglas has argued rightly that where there is the language of purity and contamination there is an underlying ethical impulse. "Where there is dirt, there is a system."[8] Along with Mary Douglas, Annie Dillard argues that ideas of purity tend to be manifested in practices of exclusion. "Purity seeks to eliminate. Its worshipers from the right or the left wage war with swords."[9]

Therefore, if ritual theorists are correct, a study of ritual behavior will disclose the persons, activities, and relationships that are considered desirable and those that are to be rejected. Or, to put it another way, ritual behavior acts at the most elemental level as a tool of conceptual control, then as a tool of behavioral control. It is a propagandistic effort to control what kind of thinking is appropriate and what counts as reality, and to associate that orthodoxy with orthopraxis. Ritual exercises the power to interpret and define reality, what may be considered to be knowledge and what is accepted as truth. As Douglas writes, "Dirt is matter out of place. Dirt is never a unique, isolated event…Uncleanness or dirt is that which must not be included if a pattern is to be maintained."[10] Notions of dirt imply ethical behaviors, group dynamics, and categories of people and behaviors that should be considered dangerous:

> The ritual creates harmonious worlds with ordered populations playing their appointed parts. So far from being meaningless, it is primitive magic which gives meaning to existence…The prohibitions trace the cosmic outlines and the ideal social order.[11]

Christian Rituals: Purity/Pollution Patterns

To translate this into interpretations of Christian ritual would suggest that our sacramental activities originated as imitations or rehearsals of activities that would not only hint at the basileia, but that would actively promote it and effect it. In addition to certain desired behaviors, Christian rituals would also indicate what kinds of persons and relationships were appropriate to the realization of the reign of God. Women theologians have long realized that our sacramental practices have promoted and reinscribed certain prejudices against women and other disenfranchised people.

Following is a quick survey of sacramental theology that will sketch out the shifts by which the ritual activities of the early church were transformed into models of individual purity. Activities that were essential to the early church became anathematized or made dirty by subsequent generations. This purity and pollution opposition is a critical part of our understanding of world-oriented activities. If we are to subvert the abusive practices (whether within sacramental rituals or world-oriented practices) associated with the symbols of purity and contamination, we will have to reverse them at the level of the symbols and the symbolic rituals themselves. Through a rhetoric of folly, we will have to make contamination attractive and purity unbecoming. Readers may want to skip back and forth between this section and the summary section at the end of chapter 2.

The *primitive sacraments* of baptism and eucharist attended much more to the contours of God's reign than the contours of individual worthiness. Liturgical practices developed from the centrality of the cross and resurrection. Early Christians broke bread together to remember the crucified and risen Christ, but also to continue the dramatic example of his table fellowship. The supper "made Jesus present" to them by extending the experience of table fellowship. They also broke bread together to proclaim the vision of a whole world gathered at a common table, a foretaste of the messianic banquet. The inclusion of social outsiders was a common theme in the gospel miracle stories of the loaves and fishes and in the parables of the messianic banquet or wedding feast. Preaching and the supper went together, because they projected the same eschatological hope.

At baptism, these early Christians "put on Christ." They were sealed in his death and resurrection. Baptism symbolized not only a shedding of sin and of an old way of life, but a shedding of the entire "old age" dominated by Satan. The baptized lived in the eschatological promise: assured of full future reconciliation in the general resurrection to come. Being baptized was not something for them personally—baptism was a sign to each other and to the world that they were willing to defy death and to pour themselves out for the world. Baptism joined them into the compassionate, being-reconciled community; it proclaimed the same eschatological vision of early proclamation and early table fellowship.

In the *patristic period*, sacramental theology lost its eschatological edge and moved toward doctrines of purity or perfection. The meal did not symbolize the eschatological banquet (consorting with the unclean) as much as it symbolized the church itself and the moral goodness of the believers who practiced; the nonbaptized were excluded from the celebration.[12] Confessions and creeds were being incorporated into the eucharistic liturgy to ensure proper attitudes toward the "sacred eucharistic mysteries."[13] Full-blown controversies over the real or symbolic presence of Christ in the meal don't occur until the eighth century debates between Radbertus and Ratramnus, but the origins were already evident. As early as the end of the first century the agape meal pattern diminished and priests began to worry about proper disposal of the eucharistic remains. The shift from a public agape feast toward a private meal for the holy demanded some guardianship of the table.

Baptismal understandings exhibited similar transformations. Before Nicea (325) it is practically impossible to find any liturgical reference to baptism actually accomplishing the remission of sins. However, after Nicea baptism shifted toward a familiar pattern. In baptism "original sin" was remitted. The notion of purging and purification underlie the penitential season of Lent, which was added onto the primitive calendar as a period of preparation for the catechumenates.[14] Baptism was seen in increasingly instrumental and objective ways, as the means through which original sin was mitigated. The martyr model of baptism was displaced by a more ascetic and flesh-denying model, where it was the flesh itself and not the old age that was being rejected.[15] Baptism, once a sign of civil disobedience and radical prophetic commitment, became the mark of the good and orderly Christian, obedient to the propositional formulations of the state religion.

The shift from prophetic messianic communities to episcopacies also institutionalized cultural biases against women. Women were probably edged out of leadership roles before the end of the first century. Schüssler Fiorenza claims that the shift toward a bureaucracy of role definitions had three dramatic and interlocking implications: The local church became more patriarchal, leadership moved from the local prophet to the local bishop, and women's leadership roles became marginalized to those that were *culturally* acceptable for women.[16] "Women's inability to represent Christ in the priesthood becomes an unchangeable 'mystery' that lies on a sacramental and metaphysical plane."[17] What Schüssler Fiorenza and others overlook is that these interlocking structural developments are all legitimated by the christological shift. The content and purpose of preaching, the theological interpretation and administration of the eucharist, and baptismal guidelines are all blessed by the inherent dualism of incarnational thinking and purity/pollution oppositions.

By the *medieval period*, Anselmian notions of sacrifice dominated in both directions. The eucharist was both symbolic of Christ's atoning act and the communicants' own sacrificial preparation for the meal. The two elements had dwindled to one; the sacrament in two kinds disappeared as the clergy worried that careless communicants might spill (and contaminate) the wine. During regular weekly services, priests celebrated the eucharist at the far end of a narrow chancel, while the laity stood at a distance and watched. By the end of the Middle Ages, people took the eucharist once a year, after they had made confession and restitution.

By the end of the Middle Ages, infant baptism had become so normative that liturgical books no longer included rites for adults.[18] Since baptism was now categorically associated with the remission of original sin, infant baptism was a moral necessity. Confirmation practices developed as a second stage of baptism, a completion that involved instruction and the informed assent of the candidate. The separation of baptism from confirmation and the introduction of informed consent would become more significant in the development of Reformation and Anabaptist theologies. Making christological confessions took on even more highly individualized understandings as Protestant theologies met up with Enlightenment humanism and rationalism.

During the *Reformation period*, Luther considered the eucharist as an act of receiving grace and a humble offering of gratitude to God. In *The Babylonian Captivity of the Church*, Luther argued that the system of penances and indulgences to ensure the purity of the eucharist was based on a mistaken notion that our works could satisfy God. "In attacking most concepts of the mass as sacrifice, Luther was challenging not just worship, but the accepted basis of the ordained priesthood and, ultimately, church finances."[19] Luther returned the eucharist to the laity and rejected theories of transubstantiation, which were necessary for a "pure" sacrifice.[20]

Luther interpreted baptism as the sacramental activity of God that created "a priesthood of all believers." Baptism marked the radicality of grace that united all believers in the ministry of the church. Confirmation, while still important, was not a sacrament manifesting God's promises, but the promises of believer and community to act in accordance with grace. Baptism was God's work, confirmation was our response. Again, this reinterpretation of salvation demanded that our good works be acts of gratitude and never of negotiation.

For Calvin, the sacraments were symbols of God's covenant with the church. His understanding of incarnation/salvation restored a biblical notion of God's use of material things to give us spiritual things and avoided the sacrificial interpretation of eucharist, as well as the problems of transubstantiation. The eucharist was, subjectively, a sign to the covenantal community of its gracious election. And in the eucharist, the community could feed on Christ, being objectively strengthened and edified for ministry. But by connecting grace to election, Calvin began to shift interpretations of eucharist back toward worthiness and perfection. He revived a highly penitential eucharistic liturgy and a public cataloging of sins. Believers who had failed to meet the moral demands (the impure) could be excommunicated or at least temporarily barred from the table.

For Calvin, baptism was entrance to the church and signified a commitment to a Christian vocation. Even though he would not have argued for any ontological difference between clergy and laity, he supported a system of pastoral oversight and discipline. While we may be rightly critical of the hierarchical assumptions behind Calvin's stress on election, we will also have to recognize his turn toward an ethical community whose identity was formed by baptism.

Much American Protestantism has inherited a eucharistic theology that is usually characterized as Zwinglian.[21] Zwingli radically rejected any notions of spiritual purification through the meal or of Christ's special presence in the eucharist. With Calvin, he understood that the "giving of Christ's body" in the eucharist was a reference to his surrender on the cross and not the objective offering of it to the communicant.[22] Subjectively, the meal was a reminder of the cross, but not as Luther would have it, an ongoing objective act of forgiveness. Zwingli's understanding of the ascension meant that Christ was emphatically "not here" and that the Holy Spirit was the immediate advocate, teacher, and presence. Some have characterized this approach as an "ecclesial transubstantiation," wherein the congregation becomes the body of Christ, offered up to God.[23] His emphasis on the eucharist as an expression of the community's faith led him to caution about its authentic (pure) celebration. In later writings, Zwingli recommended the celebration of eucharist only on Christmas, Easter, Pentecost, and on the festal days recognized in Zürich.

Zwingli didn't accept Luther's position on baptism as a conveyor of grace, or Calvin's association of baptism with election or entrance into the church. For Zwingli, no sacrament or act of human beings could convey grace. Only the spirit could do that, and could do so without human ritual behavior. Baptism didn't accomplish anything beyond its ability to witness to a past act of grace. This radical notion challenged Catholic and Lutheran theologies because it trivialized the operation of baptism as a remedy for original sin and eliminated even Calvin's "compromise" position of baptism as both the sign and the reality of forgiveness. Still, Zwingli supported infant baptism as a sign or expression of the community's covenantal identity. Baptism was the outward seal of that covenant and a public witness to the child's place within a being-saved community. Zwingli shifted from objective to subjective approaches, claiming that baptism does not objectively accomplish anything, but is a subjective reassurance to the believer, a demonstration of the community's responsibilities to raise the child in the faith, and a witness to the world at large about the vocation of the church.

By the beginning of the modern era, the sacramental understandings of the Protestant Reformation, the Radical Reformation, and the Catholic Counter-Reformation were fairly well inscribed. The church had made several shifts (in conformity with the christological shifts) that significantly weakened the eschatological thrust of ritual behaviors. Rituals that had begun as communal rehearsals for the coming reign of God had developed into more individualistic rituals that indicated the moral or spiritual state of the believer. Or, to phrase it another way, the sacraments shifted from world-directed signs of God's reconciling relationship to internal signs indicating the relationship of God to the church.

This is not to say that rituals were uniformly interpreted within denominations or faith communities, or that there was even significant coherence between eucharistic and baptismal understandings within identifiable traditions. What is consistent among all is that baptism and eucharist become gate-keeping activities to protect the "purity" of the church and to participate in the idealized presence of Christ. Across the board, sacramental theology had become an instrument of conceptual and moral control and the tool of church discipline, designating what constituted proper belief (orthodoxy) and proper behavior (orthopraxy). The rituals of eucharist and baptism followed the same christological developments that shifted from questions of Jesus/Christ's messianic vocation to questions of his special relationship with God. Christian rituals became signs of the Church's identity to the exclusion of its eschatological vocation. Christian rituals had become means by which the pure could be distinguished from the impure. After all, what kind of a church would we be if just anybody can participate? Or as a slightly different version of the old Groucho Marx joke suggests, "Who'd want to join a group that would have *them* as members?"

Rituals and Salvage: Rehearsing the Basileia

Salvation as the activity of salvaging includes Hannah Arendt's understanding that action is more than mere work; that actions also involve the human intending within certain practices. Certain actions communicate the person's or the community's intentions and values more than other actions. And if we interpret salvation as a world-oriented activity and not just a sign of individual status or Christian identity, we can move beyond the inclusion/exclusion questions about who is really worthy of the sacraments. The whole notion of salvation or justification as a status or identity is dualistic; it dislocates inner spiritual experience from activity and vocation.

The following discussion suggests ways of revitalizing our sacramental activities that are consistent with a world-oriented theology of salvage and still operate within the familiar symbols and language of the contemporary faith communities. The proposals are based on the recommendations of the World Council of Churches (WCC) to create common ground among Christian communities.

The WCC's Faith and Order Commission has been particularly attentive to liturgical development to provide "theological support for the efforts the churches are making towards unity."[24] Faith and Order Paper No. 111 is commonly referred to as the BEM document, since its major divisions are Baptism, Eucharist, and Ministry. The BEM document explores the major areas of theological convergence within the ecumenical community.[25] The BEM document is a brief treatment of models for each of the three areas, with recommendations for theological reflection and practice. We will explore primarily the models for baptism and eucharist, and particularly the ones that are most compatible with the christology of salvage and the basileia.

I have chosen to consider the World Council recommendations for a number of reasons. First, a christology of salvage presupposes that the fragmentation of the church is less than ideal. Diversity is not, in and of itself, problematic, but opposition and isolation between traditions is a problem. If salvage activity is a sign of God's realm, then remedial efforts within the broad Christian community are signs of salvage. Efforts toward unity within the whole Christian community recognize the fragility of the church as a human institution and call into question any notions of a perfect human community. At the same time, unity efforts recognize the presence of God within the human community and call communities to ongoing reform consistent with God's purposes for reconciliation.

Second, the BEM document offers strategies for women ministers who will have to work across denominational borders in order to pursue justice-making within the church and toward the world. Having a common liturgical language among ourselves will probably enhance efforts to bring about necessary liturgical revisions. Third, within many mainline Christian denominations, the WCC recommendations are respected, and it may reduce resistance if women use the practical strategy of citing WCC resources. Notice, I'm not arguing that WCC suggestions are inherently authoritative, but that they have a certain practical authority that may be helpful to local pastors. I realize, of course, that for many congregations and denominations, theological congruence with the World Council of Churches would be considered a disadvantage. Nonetheless, I think there are several advantages to working within the guidelines of the WCC.

One strong disadvantage of WCC perspectives should be noted. The recommendations frequently encourage local respect for the more restrictive approaches. For example, in my own fellowship, the Christian Church (Disciples of Christ), the eucharist is regularly presided over by nonordained elders. Presidency at the table is one of the characteristic practices of Disciples elders, who take their duties as a manifestation of the priesthood of all believers. However, in ecumenical activities, the WCC recommends practices that favor those denominations requiring ordination for presidency at the table. In an ecumenical gathering that includes Disciples, Catholics, Southern Baptists, and Presbyterians, the recommendation would result in the exclusion of Disciples elders from presiding at the table. This ecumenical strategy, which is surely a practical compromise, actually has the most detrimental effects on women. Women are excluded from ordination with more regularity than any other group. This ecumenical compromise may allow for ecumenical convergence among ordained males, but does not address the problems inherent in ordination theologies themselves. Within the ministry section, where ordained ministries are discussed, there is some attention given to the inequities that we unwittingly reinscribe in the name of ecumenical dialogue, but there is hesitancy to press these justice issues where they would hinder cooperation:

> Some churches ordain both men and women, others ordain only men. Difference on this issue raises obstacles to the mutual recognition of ministries. But those obstacles must not be regarded as substantive hindrance for further efforts toward mutual recognition…Ecumenical consideration, therefore, should encourage, not restrain, the facing of this question.[26]

All in all, the advantages of working within the WCC guidelines probably outweigh the disadvantages. Women preachers and pastors are encouraged to study the document and consider its strengths, perhaps in a local group of clergy and laywomen. The overall advantage of using WCC guidelines is similar to the advantage of working within biblical symbols and narratives; it operates from a common language that is shared by those at all levels of the church.

Baptism as a Sign of the Basileia

The BEM document devotes less discussion to models of baptism than to the practice of the eucharist. Nonetheless, we will explore the points of convergence between different understandings of baptism and a theology of salvage, with particular attention to the way that understandings of baptism undergird the ethical activity of the church's ministries. Since we generally understand baptism as the beginning of Christian life, it makes sense to consider theological understandings of baptism as foundational for other dimensions of Christian activity.

One of the primary ways that the early church understood baptism was in the apocalyptic claim that the baptized person had left behind the patterns, definitions, and commitments of the "old" realm to assume the patterns, definitions, and commitments of the "new" realm. The baptized individual joined a community whose loyalties were directed toward God's eschatological future. The apostolic language of death and rebirth signified that the individual was no longer constituted by the values of the world, defined by power-as-domination. The believer "put on Christ" and rejected the demonic domination of the world, without rejecting the world itself. This "death" to the old realm was a simultaneous "rebirth" into the new realm of God's justice-making. The symbolism of total water immersion was an imitation of full-body burial, indicating that the believer was so radically redefined as to be considered "dead" to the old ways. The surge upward from this watery grave symbolized the resurrection of Jesus/Christ and was a sign of God's radical hopes for the world. The baptized individual had become part of Christ's body, the church, whose communal vocation was the messy business of salvaging the world from its captivity to evil. This understanding of baptism is captured by the BEM model of baptism as the sign of the kingdom:

> Baptism initiates the reality of the new life given in the midst of the present world. It gives participation in the community of the Holy Spirit. It is a sign of the Kingdom of God and the life of the world to come. Through the gifts of faith, hope, and love, baptism has a dynamic which embraces the whole of life, extends to all nations, and anticipates the day when every tongue will confess that Jesus Christ is Lord to the glory of God the Father.[27]

Although we tend to think of baptism as a commentary on the individual, it indicates more about the nature of God's future already being manifested in the being-saved community. Participation in the community of the Holy Spirit does not necessarily involve supernatural activities, but the more miraculous activities that the New Testament refers to as fruits of the Spirit, all of which are defined in terms of the activities that undergird relationships of hospitality. We misread the Pauline author if we assume that the fruits of the Spirit are nothing more than inward feelings; clearly he refers to concrete behaviors that enhance corporate life. The baptized were called to manifest a new type of social life that anticipated the future of God. They were to practice acts of love, expressions of joy, interactions of peace, the exercise of patience, acts of kindness, goodness, and faithfulness.[28] Elisabeth Schüssler Fiorenza suggests that changed relationships of engendered power were among these basileia realities. They were living in salvation: in past-tense assurance, present-tense experience and future-tense expectation. Baptism into the community of the Spirit signifies that the believers no longer operate in the world according to the world's dominant methodology. They operate among themselves and in the world according to a methodology that practices peace, respect, and loving service. The baptized are nurtured *by* the Spirit, *in* the community, *for* the benefit of God's world.

This model of baptism as a sign of God's future includes the other images of baptism that have characterized the tradition and that are represented in the BEM document. The basileia model of baptism incorporates these other images but does not isolate them from God's purposes for all of creation. With respect to *participation in Christ's death and resurrection*, it identifies the believers and the whole community with an epistemology of the cross and a rejection of sinful human relationships. It sets this image of death and rebirth within the context of a world-oriented reconciliation that does not locate narrowly on the identity of the individual or the special status of the church. With respect to *conversion, pardoning, and cleansing,* this model respects the notions of captivity to the old world and takes the reality of evil seriously. If we turn toward God's future, that will necessitate some turning away from the future projected by the kingdom of death and its power-as-domination. I prefer not to interpret this at an intensely personal level, as if such conversion were not intimately tied up with the communal reality of "learning and practicing" a converted life. Revivalistic and evangelistic notions of an objective change in status for the individual believer have led to a myopic focus on the individual's capacity for making such an informed change. I want to suggest that baptism as rebirth is analogous to ordinary human birth, in that it marks a beginning of nurture and instruction. *The gift of the Holy Spirit* is received in baptism, in which God "marks them with a seal and implants in their hearts the first installment of their inheritance as sons and daughters of God."[29] Within the faith community, the Spirit nurtures the life of faith, teaching, comforting, and empowering.

By seeing baptism as the beginning of a faith process (which may either begin with confession or result in confession) we can embrace both dominant traditions: believer's baptism and infant baptism. Whether at the age of informed consent or in infancy, Christian baptism-as-birth marks the beginning of a process that is shaped most significantly by the fruits of the Spirit within the nurturing community.[30] In other eras, when the church and the culture were almost identical, infant baptism lost its distinctive character because the church had lost its distinctive character. Since we do not currently live in a Christian state, the problems of pro forma baptism simply do not emerge. Those who continue to worry about the ethical meaning of infant baptism may want to put more emphasis on confirmation as the point of individual responsibility.

However, understanding baptism as initiation into a particular kind of ethical community avoids truncating or losing the ethical dimension. As long as the community is defined with reference to God's future, with reference to loyalty to God above secular loyalties, and as long as we exercise Calvinist suspicions of human institutions, baptizing infants into a moral community of liberation and salvage is less problematic. Seen in this light, baptism (whether at the age of accountability or in infancy) takes on the ethical dimensions of the community dedicated to God's future. An infant baptized into this type of radical egalitarianism is *incorporated into the body of Christ* and will learn the virtues and fruits of the Spirit. An adult will willingly embrace them. As a ritual of incorporation, baptism grafts the individual into a community whose vocation is to salvage the world from the domination of evil and injustice.

The act of baptism symbolizes to all concerned that this person is to be understood within God's greater purposes of reconciliation. It is a status change not in the sense of an inner dimension, but with respect to the worlds (what the New Testament calls "generations") that define that individual's identity and purpose: a shift from the "old generation" to the "new generation." The baptized individual no longer belongs to the world dominated by coercive power, kyriarchy, injustice, and abuse. The baptized individual belongs, through the church, to God's future.

Within a ritual understanding, this baptized individual takes on a new status relative to the community, as one being salvaged and, in turn, learning the vocation of salvage. For baptized infants, the community performs the task of salvage, incorporating the child into the communal vocation by teaching it in classes, through worship and eucharistic rituals. Children learn ethical behavior by imitation, so one of the primary responsibilities of the community is to consistently manifest salvagic activity toward the baptized and toward the world.

The community's commitment in baptism is routinely overlooked within Protestantism. However, the BEM document and subsequent WCC discussions offer possibilities for renewing the Protestant understanding of community formation through sponsorship and intentional instruction toward confirmation. Liturgical suggestions for the sacrament of baptism allow for sponsors to make commitments to God's basileia on behalf of the infant. This sponsorship is a way for the Christian community to exercise its power for forming individuals in the fruits of the spirit.[31] Whether the baptized is an infant or a person at the age of accountability, the community's responsibility includes the ongoing practice of teaching, modeling, and including. In baptism, the Christian community manifests its vocation to salvage and to join together whatever has been neglected. The community of believers welcomes the baptized into the ethical community and joins that person (sooner or later) to the church's vocation in the world.

As we reflect on the baptismal symbols of water and rebirth, we gain a deeper understanding of the community's responsibility to midwife the baptized into newness of life. We will have to move beyond our understandings of purity and pollution, of clean and dirty individuals. Salvage work is messy work, and it always involves contact with those whom the world has rejected. Baptism is not a matter of the individual becoming pure by rejecting his or her own embodiment. Baptism is a matter of the community engaged in the dirty work of clean-up, of helping the baptized become freed from the structures of "purity-power" that contaminate the world. Baptism, like the ancient practice of footwashing, is a practice of hospitality. In the waters of baptism, the community liberates the individual from the powers that enslave and welcomes that person into an imaginative sphere of human existence that is not defined by the dominant forces at work in human society.[32] As we baptize, we salvage people from destruction, from coercive power, and from self-delusion. Like Jesus, we drop to our knees with basin and towel, ignoring protests of unworthiness, and we tenderly welcome the undeserving into the "already" but "not yet" of the basileia. Baptism is an act of humility, a service offered by the church for God's future.

James White, a respected liturgical scholar, calls baptism the great equalizer, the foundational "sacrament of equality." As the foundation for justice, baptism (especially in the Pauline understanding) makes our invisible common humanity visible. Within Christian communities, there is no longer Jew or Greek, male or female, slave or free, since in baptism, we share one body.[33] White claims that Paul uses baptism as his validation for resisting the human tendency to categorize other humans. "The easiest way to deny another his or her full human worth is to place that person in another category."[34]

White is probably accurate with his interpretation that baptism confers equality; that is, all Christians are equal to one another. This is helpful as a strategy for making ecclesiastical justice claims, since we can claim that women, by virtue of baptism, are fully equal to men.[35] White makes precisely this argument when he points out that our in-house justice issues are essentially sacramental issues:

> Are women, through baptism, identified with Christ and his priesthood, or are they not? One cannot be baptized halfway… Churches that refuse ordination to women, if they were consistent, would also deny them baptism.[36]

I agree with White's claim about Christian equality but want to exercise caution about how this relates to our practices and interpretations about those outside the Christian fellowship. I want to claim that baptism is a particular Christian form of symbolizing our fundamental human equality before God. This interpretation makes baptism a Christian ritual of solidarity with all the world. If Christian baptism is interpreted as a claim about "special" equality, then it seems to function against the purposes of the basileia, setting Christian baptismal status in opposition to the world. If Christian baptism is interpreted in a way that confers special privilege or benefit to Christians or to the church, then it is a kyriarchal strategy and must be reevaluated.

My own argument would be for the more universal understanding that Christian baptism, like the epistemology of the cross, humbles our pretensions to any special knowledge or to any special wisdom. Baptism may be a mark of the church, but it cannot be a mark only for the church. As a rebirth symbol, it must rebirth us into the basileia, where power-as-domination has been defeated, where the tender power of new life is nurtured, and where solidarity with all the world is proclaimed.

Imagine what a powerful symbolic action it would be to baptize our children into the claim that all life is precious to the God who gets the divine hands dirty, salvaging what others have seen fit to throw away.

Eucharist as Meal of the Basileia

The model most consistent with the basileia future and a theology of salvation is "eucharist as meal of the kingdom."[37] Besides its sympathies with the theology of salvation, it also suggests a form of practice that rehearses the activities of justice-making.

> The eucharist opens up the vision of the divine rule which has been promised as the final renewal of creation, and is a foretaste of it. Signs of this renewal are present in the world wherever the grace of God is manifest and humans work for justice, love, and peace. The eucharist is the feast at which the church gives thanks to God for these signs of renewal and celebrates the anticipated coming of the Kingdom in Christ.[38]

The BEM description of this model goes on to claim that the world (beyond the church) is present in the eucharistic celebration. That is, we imagine ourselves joined to the world in this activity, being reconciled not only to each other and to Christians around the world, but also called to be in reconciliation with *all* the world. In the eucharist, we become the body of Christ, who suffered in service to the world. Our service is not limited to our own immediate fellowship or to the broader Christian community, but is specifically directed to the world beyond the church. This service of joy, rendered by the church toward the world, continues the joy of the resurrection, is a witness to new life and is reminiscent of Jesus' own table fellowship with those who were outcast by religious authorities. In this model, the eucharist becomes a model of inclusion, since it anticipates the vision of God's peaceful realm. The meal "is an instance of the Church's participation in God's mission to the world."[39]

Celebration of the eucharist in this model gathers into the communal consciousness all those who are not present: past believers, present believers, future believers, and all those whom God so loves. In short, we imagine the table crowded with all the people we favor and those we don't favor. The table is a sign of radical diversity and inclusivity. As such, the eucharist

> brings into the present age a new reality which transforms Christians into the image of Christ and therefore makes them his effective witnesses...As it becomes one people, sharing the meal of the one Lord, the eucharistic assembly must be concerned for gathering also those who are at present beyond its visible limits, because Christ invited to his feast all for whom he died.[40]

Beyond the discussion in the BEM, there are advantages to this model that the WCC may not be in a position to promote, given its ecumenical strategy of favoring the more restrictive interpretations. One advantage that does seem clearly in conformity with WCC strategies is the plurality of interpretations this includes. In some ways, this model is the smorgasbord of models. One advantage of the eschatological inter- pretation is that it includes the ministry, death, resurrection, and the second coming in one gestalt. The era between resurrection and the sec- ond coming is the present, in which the spirit of Christ sustains us to salvage. Demythologizing the second coming as we have the resurrec- tion, we can claim an emphasis on novelty, inclusion, and a future whose limits are not yet established. To proclaim the second coming is a meta- phorical way of affirming that the work of reconciliation is not done and that Christ's business is not yet finished. To this extent, I think the WCC would support my appropriation of the model.

However, the subversive dimension of this model is its grounding in the messianic vocation of Jesus/Christ and of the church. By combin- ing all these traditional elements under the understanding of Jesus/ Christ's messianic vocation, the celebration of the eucharist becomes more than just a private meal for a select few. It becomes a model for enacting the messianic vocation of salvaging, gathering, feeding, and justice-making. It includes the elements of the other four eucharistic patterns, (thanksgiving to the Father, memorial of Christ, invocation of the Spirit, fellowship of believers) but avoids focusing on the church's special identity, the moral aptitude of the believers, the death of Jesus, or our own worthiness. This eucharistic model is not a witness to the special relationship between God and the church, or God and believers, but between God and the world. The relationship that it manifests is one of compassion for all those who are not present, the invitation to all who are outcast, and radical hospitality to those who are not worthy.

To the extent that an ideal future is projected in the eucharist, it is a world where saints and sinners celebrate by sharing food. The gath- ering at the table is not a sign of the church's purity, the inner qualifi- cations of the communicants, or doctrinal orthodoxy. The gathering at the table is a foretaste of the world as it should be: where folks share resources without discrimination, without power-brokering, and with- out religious arrogance. The gathering at the table does not necessarily have to be baptized, confessing, or even better-than-average. If God were throwing a party, who would be invited? That's the question that should allow us to be radically unconcerned about any kind of status. The wedding feast in Luke is the primary model for this eucharistic cel- ebration, which includes the social riff-raff from the street. The gather- ing of outcasts at the table is a mini-manifestation of the hoped-for promise, and a powerful sign of God's presence in salvaging what has been thrown away.

Since this radical interpretation of the eucharist is not grounded in claims about particular Christians and their status, it also calls into question the "problem" of including children and others who may not be fully capable of informed consent. The BEM document does include marginal reflections on these implications when it reflects on baptismal practices and their relationship to celebrating the eucharist. Again, the BEM document doesn't ever suggest that anyone other than baptized believers are the appropriate communicants. However, there are some theologians who are beginning to question the necessary relationship between baptism and eucharist. Using the requirement of baptism and consent as preludes to the proper celebration of the eucharist is a strategy of "fencing the table" that seems to be in opposition with the theological claim of radical grace or God's egalitarian future.

> To require such understanding, churches now contend, may be to fence the Lord's Table on the basis of a far-too-narrow standard (one that would exclude the mentally disabled and many of the elderly). In fact, if intellectual understanding is the criterion for participation in the Lord's Supper, people of all ages may feel unprepared to commune.[41]

We need to be clear that these radically egalitarian and prodigal practices are not directly or indirectly suggested by the BEM document. Such practices would be unpopular within the broad constituency of the WCC, since they clearly subvert power and status claims, undermine human standards of merit, and subvert the kind of coercive power at the heart of church discipline. This model would call into question the practice of excommunication or the withholding of sacramental power from those who do not conform to "the rules." As a radically egalitarian model, it will not support church kyriarchies or status privileges, and will probably never be ratified by those who have coercive power within ecclesial bodies. It defies ecclesiocentric models that attempt to legitimate themselves by virtue of their own strictness. This radical interpretation of the eucharist doesn't say anything special about us as Christians, but only claims that we have a common vocation to interact with the world in terms of justice-making and salvaging what has been thrown away. It is, however, a loophole in the model, and I'm willing to open it broad and wide.

Wolfhart Pannenberg has argued that this eschatological understanding of eucharistic piety operates as a symbol of the global village. He discusses our contemporary inheritance of penitential piety, whose primary purpose was to generate feelings of guilt and unworthiness. When the eucharist was an offering made by us, or by a priest on our behalf, it was considered necessary that the offering be perfectly worthy: offered by perfect or near-perfect individuals. The kind of eucharistic piety Pannenberg calls for is one where God's future already begins to take shape in ordinary human activities. The ideal future envisioned in the eucharist is a future where the less-than-ideal are included. Jesus enacted/celebrated this new social reality by taking meals "with his disciples, Pharisees, with tax-collectors and sinners, who by the intrinsic symbolism of the joint meal were accepted by Jesus as candidates and citizens of the future kingdom of God."[42] Where earlier eucharistic spiritualities had remained ecclesiocentric, or definitive of the church's special character, the focus was too narrowly on the merits of the believers or the community. However, Pannenberg claims that the eucharist points to the reconciliation of the world and not to the church itself. He claims that this eschatological understanding of the eucharist "provides the universal outlook that is inherent in eucharistic experience and that embraces society at large and all humankind."[43] When we prepare to celebrate God's past, present, and future, we should not ask ourselves, "Who is worthy to make a sacrifice?" or even "Who has demonstrated an understanding of the implied responsibilities?" Rather, we should ask, "Who would God include in the eschatological future?" The answer, of course, is everyone.

Issues of justice, both in-house and world-oriented, take significant cues from the ritual practices and the theological understandings they inscribe. Our ritual actions tell us and others what we value, how we think of ourselves and others, and what responsibilities are implied by such relationships. As James White writes, "Every act of worship is a political statement in the form of roles that people play."[44] Within the Christian community, we assign roles and relationships to people by virtue of sacramental participation. We associate certain categories of people and activities with notions of dirt, undesirability, and inadequacy. "Roles we play in worship often underscore a community's real beliefs about power and authority."[45] What we want to question is the desirability of having purity and the coercive power it suggests. Perhaps, through a rhetoric of folly, we should reject power/purity for powerlessness/pollution. Maybe getting involved in the nitty-gritty of the world is precisely what Christians should be doing, getting washed of their purity/power and sharing food with the undeserving.

World-oriented Practices: Public Theology in a Pluralistic World

Now we need to turn toward a discussion of our practices that are oriented toward the world, and particularly those practiced within the context of other religious groups. Our in-house ritual practices not only refer to relationships between and among Christians, they also underscore our real beliefs about Christian power and authority in the world by determining how Christians are to act toward and within the non-Christian world. In general, this is what theologians call "public theology," or what David Buttrick has called "faith's conversation with culture." Without developing a full public theology, it is still possible to sketch out the problems for women's christologies within a pluralistic world and to offer suggestions for a public theology that is appropriate to a christology of salvage, hospitality, and stewardship of the basileia.

Public theology may be defined as "the deliberate use of distinctively theological commitments to influence substantive public debate and policy."[46] Definitions of public theology vary, but for the purposes of this discussion, I am referring to the explicit theological discourse used by Christians, among Christians and non-Christians, for the purpose of bringing about social and political change. David Tracy has similarly identified these three interlocking publics that all Christian theologians participate in: the church, the academy, and the larger society.[47] Within the larger society, the three overlapping public realms include the realm of the technoeconomic structures that allocate goods and services, the political realm, which involves the control of power and the regulation of conflict, and the cultural realm, which involves art, religion, philosophy, and cultural criticism.[48]

Public theology is a critical part of the church's vocation as Christian communities engage the social structures that dominate our lives. For women preacher/theologians, public theology is the foundation for challenging the injustices within the church, injustices within local communities, and injustices within the global community. Women theologians have given sustained critical attention to the way religion functions as a tool of conceptual control that extends far beyond local congregations to influence economic policy and political structures. We have surveyed how conceptual ideas about women's inherent incapacities or "natural" carnality have led to interlocking structures of political and economic oppression for women. The interlocking nature of all these publics is critical for the woman preacher/theologian who would proclaim God's vision of a just world. As Victor Anderson writes, "religious communities are distinctive locations where moral, social, cultural practices are theologically criticized and legitimized through the apparatuses of doctrine, liturgy, and organization."[49] Women preachers make religious claims for ultimacy that critique and suggest specific courses of action on behalf of the world that God so loves. If we are to be in meaningful conversations about global justice for women, other disenfranchised peoples, and the earth, we will have to discover strategies for making our theological claims and our theological methods public and explicit.

The Dilemma of Pluralism and Critique

The problem emerges in the three overlapping areas of the larger society. Christian women theologians feel that their specific Christian beliefs about liberation, wholeness, and justice demand their interaction in this most public realm. In order to challenge injustices within the technoeconomic and political realms, women theologians confront the reality that religious beliefs are inextricably tangled in these structures.

Since religious narratives and symbols function to legitimize social and political oppression, religious critique becomes a necessary part of cultural analysis. As Maura O'Neill writes,

> Women are beginning to realize that religion is an essential part in their discussions of social structures…oppression and justice can't be adequately analyzed and changed without giving due consideration to religion.[50]

However, Christian women are particularly hesitant to engage in cross-cultural religious criticism. We've uttered a relieved farewell to the so-called Christian century, waving a postcolonial goodbye to the christological imperialism that justified centuries of colonization, the Holocaust, and the religious abuse of those considered to be "other." The "other" is no longer far away and alien. We live in a global village where our children attend public schools with Buddhists, Muslims, Baha'is, Hindus, Jews, herbalists, practitioners of Tarot, New Agers, and Wiccans. In ordinary daily living and in our religious communities, we have developed and promoted a nonjudgmental attitude of respect and tolerance. Whether we are part of the First World tradition of Western Christianity or part of the Two-Thirds World tradition where Christianity is a minority religion, we are sensitive to the particularities of other religions and we try to avoid imposing our own values on other cultures.

Maura O'Neill claims that Western Christian women in particular are so sensitive to the charge of imperialism that we become silent co-conspirators whose respect for "cultural relativism" allows oppression to continue. We have, as Pamela Dickey Young claims, a "collective fear of having to look critically both at ourselves and at others."[51] We may feel free to criticize our own tradition but hesitate to be critically engaged with women of other traditions. Since we find it presumptuous to critique another tradition by our own culturally and theologically specific norms, we place ourselves in a dilemma, unable to make theological claims about injustice within other contexts.

Mary Daly's watershed work on the metaethics of feminism exposed the ambivalence and moral paralysis many Western women experience in the face of conflicting loyalties. Daly described the "unspeakable" African tribal practices of female circumcision, clitoridectomy, and infibulation on pubescent girls. The rituals involve not only the removal of genitals and tissue, they frequently involve this "surgery" without anesthesia, disinfection, or sanitary procedures. It is common for the girl's legs to be bound together (accumulating execrement), for the bladder to be pierced, or for the rectum to be cut open. "These ritualized atrocities are unspeakable also in a second sense; that is, there are strong taboos against saying/writing the truth about them, against naming them. These taboos are operative both within the segments of phallocracy in which such rituals are practiced and in other parts of the Fatherland, whose leaders cooperate in the conspiracy of silence."[52] Caught between the claims of suffering women and the claims of cultural respect, many Western Christian women hesitate to speak bluntly about the anti-women biases and violence of non-Christian religious practices or religious control. At the time of her writing, Daly indicted the World Health Organization, the United Nations, UNICEF, the Y.W.C.A., anthropologists, and church organizations, who knew but would not speak. Women who feared being charged with cultural imperialism, Christian superiority, or white racism withheld criticism; they practiced the same strategy as the male-dominated power structures.

Iranian feminist Azar Tabari claims that during the decade of the eighties, as the Khomeini machine gained power, "many Western feminists silently watched the consolidation of a religious monstrosity. But why should geographical and cultural borders make what is conceived as oppression in one context an acceptable cultural norm in another?"[53] Carter Heyward's warning comes back to haunt us: When we try to avoid our own highly particular and passionate commitments, when we try to avoid christological claims, we create a "generic" God in the image of an objective humanist gentleman. This God is fairly neutral about any particular situation. Western Christian women were guilty of attempting cultural objectivity, rightly concerned that it was impossible to critique the kyriarchy in other cultures without being kyriarchal themselves.

Suggestions for Meaningful Hospitality

Pamela Dickey Young suggests four possible orientations in this era "after imperialism." First, of course, we can continue to claim Christian uniqueness and the exclusivity of our own revelation. *Christian exclusivism* insists that there is no salvation apart from Jesus/Christ and that our version of the truth is the only legitimate version. Second, we can make our Christian claims inclusively, recognizing the partial truth of all religious claims. In this position, we still use Christianity as a norm for evaluating other faith claims. *Christian inclusivism*, claims Young, is still subject to imperialism and triumphalism, since it recognizes no other norms and safeguards the tradition. *Christian pluralism*, Young says, is the position that all truth is radically relative and open to debate. Christians cannot use their own norms for evaluation, but must compromise in favor of universal or generic claims. The problem with this position is that it tends "to compromise the integrity of the Christian tradition by playing down its central symbols...[or to claim] that its truth, like all other truths, is simply relative to its context."[54]

Young opts for a slightly different position, which negotiates between central Christian symbols and universal norms. "One cannot be religious in the abstract. To be religious is to be religious somehow." Christian symbols must be explored for their claims of ultimacy, which must be translatable into universal understandings *as they inform particular courses of action.* The arena of universal claims and their particular concrete actions is where interfaith conversation occurs. In this position, we make our Christian claims as contextual "wagers" that are subject to revision in light of other religious traditions and feminism.[55] Young maintains that our *contextual approaches* are all related to the universal questions of God, humanity, and the rest of the world. We act in the world out of particular values, and those values are conveyed to religious communities through the aesthetic practices of ritual, story, and worship. "Religious symbol systems embody what a religious tradition takes to be ultimate."[56]

Marjorie Hewitt Suchocki suggests a strategy that is compatible with Young's call for exploring the relationship between religious symbols and their courses of action. She claims that women theologians can radically affirm religious pluralism and still engage a "critical consciousness of well-being in the human community."[57] She argues that establishing a norm of justice for critiquing other religions does not fall prey to simply introducing one universal in place of another. Suchocki recognizes that absolutizing a religious value and imposing it as a mandate is precisely the charge that women have made against the Christian tradition. However, women theologians can never expect to enter into dialogue without being "value-laden and value projecting."[58] The problem is not in possessing values, but in imposing them:

> What is called for is not a nonjudgmental dialogue with other religions in light of the relativism of belief systems, but a shift of judgment from ideological ground to ethical ground, along with an open recognition of the conditioned nature of the norm of justice we bring, and a commitment to critical exploration of the norm in the very dialogue wherein it is brought to bear.[59]

Suchocki calls for a fully honest and respectful dialogue where the meaning of justice itself is explored, through a comparative discussion at three levels. The first level involves the issues of fundamental physical well-being: access to food, water, shelter, work, and community. To what degree are women [and other disenfranchised] within a particular culture enjoying fundamental physical well-being? Are there gendered differences in the level of well-being enjoyed? The second level involves issues of self-naming and dignity. Where people are allowed to articulate their own identities and enjoy those named selves, a significant amount of diversity and autonomy is not only tolerated, but essential to the community. The third level extends this openness to diversity outside the boundaries of the immediate community to encourage the diversity between communities. Where these three levels of justice operate, the community is, in principle, one without boundaries. "The ultimate test of justice is precisely the degree to which it knows no boundaries to well-being."[60]

When a community establishes well-being within itself to the exclusion of the well-being of other communities, that community is unjust. Or, more viciously, when a community "establishes its own well-being through the exploitation of the well-being of those outside itself, that community is to that degree unjust."[61] Suchocki suggests that communities ask themselves to what degree the well-being of others within the community and others outside the community is part of intentional promotion. "Does it define the communal good as extending through and among communities without boundary throughout all existence?"[62] With this absolute criterion in mind, Suchocki claims that modes of Christianity that violate this norm are "poor forms of Christianity," and that modes of other religions that violate this norm are poor forms of those religions. The community's inability to extend care for well-being radically within its own boundaries or beyond its own boundaries is unjust. "Systems that incorporate social ill-being into that which is religiously and socially acceptable do so with a paradoxical understanding of justice."[63] Women theologians have critiqued Christianity according to these standards and can also critique other religions by the same. Critique, of course, does not mean that we would either control or exclude or withhold well-being from such poor forms. When critique becomes a justification for jeopardizing the well-being or self-naming of any group, it participates in injustice.

As a dialogical strategy, Suchocki recommends exploring these levels of justice and having women name their own well-being or lack thereof. One of the strategies that Pamela Dickey Young recommends along these lines is an exploration of social realities coupled with cultural notions of beauty, religious symbols, and narratives for what is good and true.[64] By attending to aesthetic questions of beauty and moral questions of goodness, we might be able to understand how cultures use religion to reinscribe attitudes toward women and their bodies. How do understandings of women's bodies, menstrual cycles, sexuality, and power get symbolized within that religiocultural system? I would also suggest that we pay particular interest to the symbols of purity and pollution. What ritual activities reinforce these characterizations? What does veiling suggest about women in one culture? What does circumcision suggest? Who officiates at what rituals? Why?

Another strategy suggested by Suchocki is for women to articulate what their particular traditions project as the ideal community. "Each religion's deepest valuation of what physical existence should be like, not in its coping with the exigencies of history, but in its projection of the ideal."[65] Suchocki recommends exploring traditions for their images of ideal life, what the perfect human community would look like, how we would recognize radical reconciliation. "By looking at each religion's vision of the ultimately perfect mode of existence for its saints or holy ones, whether that vision be otherworldly or not, we might find some echo of unanimity on the value of freedom from suffering."[66] This question shifts interfaith dialogue from questions of philosophical meaning to questions of real embodied justice, to the concrete expressions and realities of human life.

Along with Young and Suchocki, Maura O'Neill claims that women will have to learn to tell our own religious and cultural stories *critically* and to listen to other stories *critically*. According to O'Neill, this critical mode of telling and listening is the key to understanding the way religious symbols and narratives function to legitimize or subvert real social transformation. She would agree with Young's mandate:

> I would maintain that formal argumentation, searching for the general or universal within and through the specific, is indispensable for dealing with the particularities or specifics of our lives. I do not appeal to the formal to avoid the particular but to illuminate it. Communication and mutual comprehension depend on the ability to extrapolate from the particular.[67]

For women preachers, this ability to demonstrate critical argumentation, or rhetorical theology, is a key to helping congregations act out their commitments to the world. As they preach, women pastors "do theology" in front of their congregations, modeling and rehearsing what it would be like for ordinary Christians to "do theology" in their everyday lives. We engage the world from particular sets of values, and those values are conveyed to religious communities through the in-house practices of ritual, story, and worship. Women preachers engage particular congregations in critical reflection relative to specific symbols and the universal claims they imply, as well as what concrete actions might be promoted.[68]

Toward the Basileia: Salvage, Stewardship, and Hospitality

The theology of salvage has been developed as it relates to in-house practices of ritual behavior. Now we explore its relationship to public theology and public practices that contribute to God's reconciliation of the world. This discussion is informed by two similar metaphorical theologies that are particularly disclosive for world-oriented activity in a pluralistic context. The first is a theology of hospitality developed by Patrick Keifert, and the second is a theology of stewardship developed by Douglas John Hall. When combined with a theology of salvage, they become powerful symbols of hope in a fragile world.

Patrick Keifert is a Lutheran liturgical theologian who explores the "public character of Christian thought and life in a culture of pluralism…[by] developing a public theology that couples what common sense generally separates: liturgical renewal and effective evangelism; evangelism and respect for cultural diversity; theory and practice."[69] Keifert's project is a dialogue between the worlds of ritual studies and Christian theology. He values ritual for its formative and transformative communal potential, particularly united around the biblical metaphor of hospitality to the stranger.

Keifert claims that our current understanding of hospitality has taken the metaphorical shape of inviting strangers into a private, cozy, intimate world, "into our church family" or "into our church home." The goal of hospitality becomes a sentimentalized notion of making strangers into friends, of developing relationships of intimacy. We live in public worlds characterized by safe "role" relationships, and in private worlds characterized by vulnerable "intimacy" relationships. The problem is critical at the level of public worship, since the invitation to the private religious world of intimacy is almost always threatening to the stranger.

Keifert's argument is particularly interesting when expanded to the interreligious sphere. If Keifert is correct that our notions of in-house hospitality include the "violation" of enforced and unwelcome intimacy, then our world-oriented practices of hospitality have taken the same shape. We have assumed that hospitality to others in the world involves making them into Christian brothers and sisters, "bringing them into our house." Our notions of hospitality have taken the evangelistic twist of attempting to make non-Christian strangers into Christian friends.

Keifert's fundamental theological claim is that God's grace, and not our own intimacy or familiarity, unites us in spite of irreducible strangeness and otherness. Keifert claims that the power of the biblical notion of hospitality is that we come together not because we like each other, but precisely in spite of the fact that we do not like each other, do not agree with each other, and are fundamentally strangers to each other.[70] The source of hospitality is not our liking for each other, but God's radical commitment to *all* of us. Although Keifert is specifically interested in Christian worship, I think his claims about the radicality of grace serve as well for world-oriented practices. We can come together in interfaith dialogue and in interfaith projects, respecting the otherness and strangeness of those who are not Christian or those who are differently Christian. Our coming together, in spite of our differences, is a witness to God's basileia purposes. God's basileia is not a vision of a Christianized world, but a world where all human communities work together toward reconciliation, salvaging the excluded and actively pursuing justice. Hospitality is a metaphor for our way of relating to humanity. Hospitality goes beyond the barest form of salvage to include a reconfiguration of social relationships. Hospitality is far more radical than the kind of intimacy we have with friends and family; interfaith hospitality does not require that strangers come into our faith homes, but requires us to meet on neutral territory to engage in a hospitality where all of us are strangers.

If hospitality is a helpful way to think about our relationships to the rest of humanity, the metaphor of stewardship is a helpful way to think about our salvage work with regard to the rest of the created world. Douglas John Hall has written extensively on this biblical metaphor, tracing it through both testaments to claim that the fundamental "truth" of stewardship is "the earth is the Lord's and the fulness thereof." To understand the whole of creation as belonging to God, in relation to which humans can at most be stewards, is to relativize all human claims to mastery or domination. Stewardship does not mean mastery or domination, but the tender nurturing care for that which ultimately belongs to God. "As soon as God is pictured as the owner and sovereign of everything...institutions such as the holding of property, the hierarchic distribution of authority, the technocratic mastery of the natural world, and the like are thrown into a critical perspective."[71]

Hall appropriates stewardship as a christological category, claiming that the vocation of Christ was that of chief steward. Stewardship and servanthood interpret each other metaphorically. Jesus, he claims, is not the owner of the world, but the steward of God's creation. If we understand God's creation as moving toward the basileia vision, we can appropriate Hall's christology as stewardship of the future. The eschatological parables of the steward and of the vineyard all converge theologically in the vision of God's purpose to salvage the fragility of creation from the destruction of power-as-domination. We do not imitate Jesus/Christ just to be good stewards, but rather, we join in his vocation of stewardship for the future of the world.

Ecclesiologically, this means that the vocation of the church is to steward all life away from the kingdom of death and toward God's vision of abundant life for all. This future-oriented and world-oriented thrust contains an implicit criticism of the church as an end in itself. The church, as a stewarding community, is always in the service of God's basileia, a purpose that is infinitely greater than itself. The Christian community exists "to serve the God of a grace that is universally offered. It is to participate in the extension of that grace throughout the world. It is to be the harbinger of a reign in which it may or may not have a place—nothing can be assumed!"[72] In fact, I would add to Hall's ecclesiology: The vocation of church is to risk its own corporate identity and life (to risk institutional death) in pursuit of God's beyond-the-church future. Stewarding the creation takes us beyond the confines of Christian identity and community into the world. We are not called to conquer the world for Christ, but, with Christ, to join other religious companions in a global salvage operation to rescue the world for its own future. "The ultimate test of justice is precisely the degree to which it knows no boundaries to well-being."[73]

In a delightful look at the parables of the kingdom, Robert Farrar Capon explores the radical inclusivity and pluralism in the images of the sower, the weeds, the yeast, the pearl of great price, and the dragnet.[74] What is interesting and usually overlooked in these parables is the suggestion that evil and good coexist, sometimes indistinguishably among peoples and sometimes indistinguishably within any given person. Goodness and evil are all mixed up in the world, whether that parabolic world is represented by the ocean, the dirt, the bread dough, or the harvest. "In the parable of the Weeds he simply says that 'the field is the world' (Matt. 13:38). In the Net (Matt. 13:47) he says the kingdom catches *all* kinds. And in his later parables, he develops this technique of including everybody into something close to an art form."[75] The church's job is not apparently to sort sheep and goats before the Big Day, but to assume that the divine sorter can accomplish that task unimpeded by human interference. According to Capon, God sows the kingdom all over the place, on sidewalks, slippery slopes, back alley barrios, primitive rain forests, dumpsters, and rice fields. Or, to have it another way, the glorious treasure is hidden in a plot of ordinary dirt. Or, the bacterial leaven is dissolved in flour and water. The weeds grow next to the wheat.

The main idea, says Capon, is that God is apparently far more prodigal than we are or than we imagine. The seed *is* the kingdom, Capon insists, and the reign of God has "already been sown in this world, squarely in the midst of every human and even every earthly condition," unbelievably in contact with what we reject as contaminated and unworthy.[76] Good seed bears fruit, bad seed does not. Weeds and wheat look too much alike to risk a weeding operation. "By speaking only of one man's field, and by avoiding any hint of a partial sowing of that field, he clearly indicates that there are no places—and by extension, no times and no people—in which the kingdom is not already at work."[77] Our churchly vocation is to bear fruit, not to sort, since we cannot tell by outward appearances whether we see weeds or wheat, sheep or goats, fish or old tires. More bluntly, we can't even tell whether *we* are weeds, goats, old tires, or rotten fruit.

In the parables of the kingdom, Jesus makes the crowds gasp because he keeps things too "squishy," too loose, too open for their comfort. Narrow minds want narrow meanings, and the crowds and religious officials are suspicious that Jesus doesn't seem to reserve the kingdom for Israel alone:

> Of course, the parable [of the sower] could perfectly well be about God's relationship with the Jews alone, but for suspicious

minds, *could be* is never an acceptable substitute for *has got to be*. They want an airtight case, not a leaky one; what Jesus gave them has enough holes in it to let in all the Gentiles in the world.[78]

If we take Capon's interpretation seriously, this means that the early church presented the basileia vision of Jesus as a radically pluralistic ideal future. Inclusion in this sense does not mean inclusion in the church, but inclusion in the future of earthly existence, where there are no throwaway children, countries, or ethnic groups, no disposable rivers or rain forests. Alfred North Whitehead wrote that loss is the ultimate evil. The God we know in Jesus/Christ works against decay and entropy to maximize the good, to save the fragile, to bring life out of death. The vocation of the Christian community is the fragile and risky work of standing in solidarity with all of *mater* earth, of refusing to let anything stay on the rubbish heap.[79] Salvaging is the stewardly vocation of the community, which must operate with what Whitehead calls a divine image of redemption: a "tender care that nothing be lost."[80] Or as Douglas John Hall has written, "the intention is not to chastise our institutions for having been unworthy stewards...but rather to remind us of the breadth and depth of this ancient piece of wisdom about the human vocation."[81]

A Christology for Public Proclamation

I am convinced that Christian women preachers have a vital role within the local Christian community and within the larger pluralistic context. Women preachers are pressed on a regular basis to make their faith claims and their justice claims in terms of christological understandings. Local women pastors are on the theological front line in a way that few other religious practitioners or theologians regularly experience. Women preachers regularly do creative public theology that could bear enormous fruit within the broader community of ecumenical and interfaith dialogue. Even where women preachers have not satisfactorily worked out a systematic christology, they have at least clearly understood the rhetorical problems of negotiating explicitly theological commitments through contemporary discourse for wider social and political purposes.

I have tried to offer a metaphorical christology that honors the primary narratives and symbols of the tradition, but that will do so in ways that subvert oppression. I believe that women preachers have a particular opportunity to reimage christology for their local congregations in ways that actually form those congregations for radical ministry. My strategy is a "populist" political strategy of empowering ordinary believers with the theological perspectives and rhetorical strategies to challenge kyriarchal power, to offer radical hospitality within their own communities, and to work across ethnic and religious barriers for political change. Preachers should never underestimate the life-changing potential of a vision for the future. We can, through rhetorical strategies and sermonic illustrations, construct an imaginative ideal world where all of God's creation is being redeemed. We can name our Christian vocation toward the world and with the world that God so loves, imaging a pluralistic community where nothing is lost and where coming in contact with the messy world is a virtue rather than a vice.

Part of my task has been to identify some common ground between lay women and their preachers, between women preachers and women academics, between Christian and non-Christian women, for the singular purpose of bringing together as many around the table as possible. I don't object to honest critical discourse among women, but I am weary of intellectual or doctrinal one-up-woman-ship that silences perspectives. Elisabeth Schüssler Fiorenza is correct when she warns that feminist scholars in religion have to guard against reinscribing the opposition between "church and academy, [or] between theory and practice, that the malestream ruling center of academy and church has enacted and still seeks to reinforce today either by silencing or by co-opting our feminist work."[82]

If we are going to salvage women and other disenfranchised people, we will have to work together in spite of the fact that we may not like each other and may not agree with each other. We will have to give up "lording it over each other" as well as "making nice." We may have to tell dangerous memories of mismatched, disagreeable women who still managed to work for justice in spite of themselves. Women have to create spaces for honest and critical discourse. Schüssler Fiorenza has called this "the oratory of Euphemia," a "political counterhegemonic space where critical practices for change can become operative."[83] There is nothing wrong with debate and disagreement, especially when it is in the service of finding common ground. To the extent that Christian discourse fragments communities of women, it is demonic. To the extent that explicit Christian discourse enables conversation among women, it is redemptive. Women theologians must be ready to meet repeatedly to negotiate common ground and joint strategies. Even if the common ground we negotiate looks narrow and winding, maybe it will be just wide enough for us to follow each other into the future.

I have tried to develop this christology accordingly. It is my wager, a wager made as I sit at the imaginary table surrounded by strangers within and beyond the faith community. I have offered a proposal with a systematic integrity that should still be elastic enough for local adaptation. I have intentionally tried to construct a christology that would operate with what Thomas Thangaraj called "a local christology with a global perspective." I have offered a christology that makes strong, clear claims and whose central claims involve a pluralistic vision of God's future. The following sketch gathers together all the christological pieces, including traditional language and symbols, as well as universal claims. I have tried to maintain a number of classical theological insights that seem muted in other women's christologies: some notion of the universality of evil and sin, notions of God's radical grace, the epistemology of the cross, and the hope of resurrection. I have tried to avoid mind/body splits, ecclesiocentrism, and Christian superiority.

A Contemporary Christological Wager for Preaching

We preach the good news of the God we know in Jesus/Christ. We believe that this God loves the physical world and is in the never-ending process of drawing it toward justice and beauty. The world is a fragile creation, and all dimensions of the world are subject to destruction and evil desires. No living thing is fully free from evil. God's redemptive purpose is to create the best possible world for the pleasure of all. We believe that God's redemptive work knows no boundaries.

We know this God through the human activities of Jesus, who came to preach this better future so that we could participate in God's ongoing work of justice-making and reconciliation. In his teachings, in his prophetic criticism of power, in his parables of the kingdom, Jesus pointed to the world as it should be. Jesus modeled new relationships that subverted power structures. He came in contact with those the world wanted to ignore or exploit. He shared food with them, he healed them, he treated all men, women, and children as if God really cared about them.

He was arrested as a subversive and killed as a political criminal. In his crucifixion, we believe that he shared in the suffering of all powerless people, and that he refused to engage in counter-violence. The story of his resurrection teaches us that his ministry of radical hospitality and his way of nonviolence are stronger than the powers of violence. The presence of his ministry and teaching endures wherever new life emerges from crushing death. When we say that he will come again, we are admitting that the work of reconciliation is not yet complete, but we have hope for the future.

Christians are those who follow this way of salvaging the lost and extending indiscriminate hospitality to the world. Like Jesus, Christians point to God's future and treat every man, woman, and child as if God really cared about them. When we are baptized, we enter into a community that rejects the destructive forces of terror and that practices a new form of social life. We say that we have died to sin, and that we are reborn into a new understanding of life. When we break bread and drink wine, we remember the meals of Jesus, and we are reminded that everyone deserves a decent meal. We also remind ourselves of God's future, where justice-making and real physical abundance will be experienced by all the world that God loves. In this celebration, we remember the broken body and the spilled blood of Jesus on the cross. This reminds us that our ministry of hospitality and salvage could get risky, especially the dangerous and threatening activities of feeding, teaching, and welcoming powerless people. People in power do not want too many victims to become strong, smart, and united. Caring for the powerless and loving strangers is ultimately subversive: It is the power-of-love that is stronger than the power-of-domination.

We call ourselves the body of Christ. This means that we are ordinary humans who try to embody God's purposes in all our activities. Our vocation is to go into all the world and tell this story of the God we know in Jesus, so that powerless and oppressed people can be freed from their bondage and so that the natural world is nurtured toward its fullness of beauty. We tell this story in words, but we also tell the story in every act of compassion and every act of subversive hospitality. Our purpose is at one with Jesus' own ministry and with God's own purposes: to work gently and lovingly against the forces of destruction in order to free creation for its ultimate abundance.

We participate in communal life with strangers. We share home and table, not only with our friends and compatriots, but with strangers. And in so doing, we begin to join little islands of intactness to other little islands to form new archipelagoes of matter: new heaven and new earth, the eschatological banquet, the wedding feast of rejects and riff-raff. Like the good Samaritan, we find the bleeding on the road and we save them. But not content with a mere salvage operation, we go beyond the call of minimal duty to offer extravagant hospitality to those the world has seen fit to throw away.

As a whole symbol for practical communal ministry, a christology of salvage assumes that new life is characterized by a ministry of humility and service to humanity. It de-centers the self of the individual and the community without devaluing either; it demystifies the status of the clergy and the church, and calls the community of believers to task in the world. To follow in the way of Christ is *not* primarily an exercise in the disciplines of individual perfection, but a headlong and risky communal commitment to the messy work of justice: a sign of the inbreaking basileia.

Bibliography

Allen, Ronald J., and John Holbert. *Holy Root, Holy Branches: Christian Preaching from the Old Testament.* Nashville: Abingdon Press, 1995.

Allen, Ronald J., Barbara Shires Blaisdell, and Scott Black Johnston. *Theology for Preaching: Authority, Truth, and Knowledge of God in a Postmodern Ethos.* Nashville: Abingdon Press, 1997.

Anderson, Victor. "The Search for Public Theology in the United States," in Thomas G. Long and Edward Farley, eds., *Preaching as a Theological Task: World, Gospel, Scripture* (Louisville: Westminster John Knox Press, 1996).

Aulén, Gustaf. *Christus Victor.* New York: Macmillan, 1945.

_____.*Eucharist and Sacrifice.* Edinburgh: Oliver & Boyd, 1958.

_____. *The Faith of the Christian Church.* Philadelphia: Fortress Press, 1960.

Auster, Paul. *In the Country of Last Things.* New York: Penguin, 1987.

Borg, Marcus. *Jesus: A New Vision.* San Francisco: HarperCollins, 1987.

Bondi, Roberta. "Prayer in Friendship with God." *Christian Century,* January 29, 1997.

Brock, Rita Nakashima. *Journeys by Heart: A Christology of Erotic Power.* New York: Crossroad, 1995.

Brown, Alexandra R. *The Cross and Human Transformation.* Minneapolis: Fortress Press, 1995.

Brown, Joanne Carlson, and Carole R. Bohn, eds. *Christianity, Patriarchy, and Abuse: A Feminist Critique.* Cleveland: Pilgrim Press, 1989.

Brown, Kelly Delaine. "God is as Christ Does: Toward a Womanist Theology." *Journal of Religious Thought* 46, no. 1 (Summer/Fall 1989).

Buttrick, David G. *The Mystery and The Passion: A Homiletic Reading of the Gospel Traditions.* Minneapolis: Fortress Press, 1992.

Camp, Claudia. "Wise and Strange: An Interpretation of the Female Imagery in Proverbs in Light of Trickster Mythology." *Semeia* 42, 1988.

Cannon, Katie G. *Black Womanist Ethics.* Atlanta: Scholars Press, 1988.

Carmody, Denise L. *Christian Feminist Theology.* Oxford, U.K., and Cambridge, U.S.A.: Blackwell, 1995.

Cheney, Emily. *She Can Read: Feminist Reading Strategies for Biblical Narrative*. Valley Forge, Penn.: Trinity Press International, 1996.

Chung Kyun Hyung. *Struggle to Be the Sun Again: Introducing Asian Women's Theology*. Maryknoll, N.Y.: Orbis Books, 1994.

Collins, Patricia Hill. *Black Feminist Thought: Knowledge, Consciousness, and the Politics of Empowerment*. New York: Routledge, 1990.

Crossan, John D. *Jesus: A Revolutionary Biography*. San Francisco: HarperSanFrancisco, 1994.

Daly, Mary. *Gyn/Ecology: The Metaethics of Radical Feminism*. Boston: Beacon Press, 1978.

Douglas, Kelly Brown. *The Black Christ*. Maryknoll, N.Y.: Orbis Books, 1994.

Douglas, Mary. *Purity and Danger: An Analysis of the Concepts of Pollution and Taboo*. New York: Ark Paperbacks, 1966.

Driver, Tom F. *The Magic of Ritual: Our Need for Liberating Rites That Transform Our Lives & Our Communities*. New York: HarperCollins, 1991.

Farley, Edward. *Good & Evil*. Minneapolis: Fortress Press, 1990.

Farley, Wendy. *Tragic Vision and Divine Compassion: A Contemporary Theodicy*. Louisville: Westminster/ John Knox Press, 1990.

Fredriksen, Paula. *From Jesus to Christ: The Origins of the New Testament Images of Jesus*. New Haven: Yale University Press, 1988.

Fuller, Reginald H. *The Foundations of New Testament Christology*. New York: Charles Scribner's Sons, 1965.

Gebara, Ivone, and Maria Clara Bingemer. *Mary: Mother of God, Mother of the Poor*. Maryknoll, N.Y.: Orbis Books, 1989.

Gilson, Anne B. *Eros Breaking Free: Interpreting Sexual Theo–Ethics*. Cleveland: Pilgrim Press, 1995.

Goss, Robert. *Jesus Acted Up: A Gay and Lesbian Manifesto*. San Francisco: HarperSanFrancisco, 1993.

Grant, Jacquelyn. *White Women's Christ and Black Women's Jesus*. Atlanta: Scholars Press, 1989.

Hall, Douglas John. *Lighten our Darkness: Toward an Indigenous Theology of the Cross*. Philadelphia: Westminster Press, 1976.

_____. *The Stewardship of Life in the Kingdom of Death*. Grand Rapids, Mich.: Eerdmans, 1985.

Heyward, Carter. "Heterosexist Theology: Being Above It All." *Journal of Feminist Studies in Religion* 3, no. 1 (Spring 1987).

_____. *Speaking of Christ: A Lesbian Feminist Voice*. New York: Pilgrim Press, 1989.

_____. *Touching Our Strength: The Erotic as Power and the Love of God*. San Francisco: Harper & Row, 1989.

Hicks, John, and Paul F. Knitter, eds. *The Myth of Christian Uniqueness: Toward a Pluralistic Theology of Religions*. Maryknoll, N.Y.: Orbis Books, 1992.

Hilkert, Mary Catherine. *Naming Grace: Preaching and the Sacramental Imagination*. New York: Continuum, 1997.

hooks, bell. *Ain't I a Woman: Black Women and Feminism*. Boston: South End Press, 1981.

Hopkins, Julie M. *Towards A Feminist Christology*. Grand Rapids, Mich.: Eerdmans, 1994.

Isasi–Díaz, Ada María, and Yolanda Tarango. *Hispanic Women: Prophetic Voice in the Church*. Minneapolis: Fortress Press, 1992.

_____. *En La Lucha*. Minneapolis: Fortress Press, 1993.

_____. *Mujerista Theology*. Maryknoll, N.Y.: Orbis Books, 1996.

Johnson, Elizabeth. *Consider Jesus: Waves of Renewal in Christology*. New York: Crossroad, 1995.

Kanyoro, Musimbi R. A., ed. *In Search of a Round Table: Gender, Theology and Church Leadership*. Geneva: World Council of Churches, 1997.

Katoppo, Marianne. *Compassionate and Free: An Asian Woman's Theology*. Maryknoll, N.Y.: Orbis Books, 1980.

Kee, Howard Clark, ed. *Removing Anti–Judaism from the Pulpit*. New York: Continuum, 1996.

Keifert, Patrick. *Welcoming the Stranger: A Public Theology of Worship and Evangelism*. Minneapolis: Fortress Press, 1992.

Kennedy, Rodney. *The Creative Power of Metaphor: A Rhetorical Homiletics*. Lanham, Md.: University Press of America, 1993.

Loades, Ann, ed. *Feminist Theology: A Reader*. London: SPCK; Louisville: Westminster/John Knox Press, 1990.

Lorde, Audre. *Sister, Outsider: Essays and Speeches*. Trumansburg, N.Y.: Crossing Press, 1984.

Malherbe, A., and W. Meeks, ed. *The Future of Christology: Essays in Honor of Leander Keck*. Minneapolis: Fortress Press, 1993.

McClure, John S. *The Four Codes of Preaching: Rhetorical Strategies*. Minneapolis: Fortress Press, 1991.

McFague, Sallie. *Metaphorical Theology: Models of God in Religious Language*. Philadelphia: Fortress Press, 1982.

_____. *The Body of God*. Minneapolis: Fortress Press, 1993.

McIntyre, John. *The Shape of Christology*. Philadelphia: Westminster Press, 1966.

McKenzie, Alyce M. *Preaching Proverbs*. Louisville: Westminster John Knox Press, 1996.

Newsom, Carol. "Woman and the Discourse of Patriarchal Wisdom: A Study of Proverbs 1—9," in *Gender and Difference in Ancient Israel*. Edited by Peggy L. Day. Minneapolis: Fortress Press, 1989.

O'Collins, Gerald. *Interpreting Jesus*. Mahwah, N.J.: Paulist Press, 1983.

_____. *Christology: A Biblical, Historical, and Systematic Study of Jesus*. London: Oxford University Press, 1995.

O'Neill, Maura. *Women Speaking, Women Listening: Women in Interreligious Dialogue*. Maryknoll, N.Y.: Orbis Books, 1990.

Ortega, Ofelia, ed. *Women's Visions: Theological Reflection, Celebration, Action*. Geneva: World Council of Churches, 1995.

Ottati, Douglas. *Jesus Christ and Christian Vision*. Louisville: Westminster John Knox Press, 1996.

Pagels, Elaine. *The Gnostic Gospels*. New York: Vintage Books/Random House, 1981.

Pelikan, Jaroslav. *Jesus Through the Centuries: His Place in the History of Culture*. New York: Harper & Row, 1987.

Pobee, John, and B. von Wartenburg–Potter, eds. *New Eyes For Reading: Biblical and Theological Reflections by Women from the Third World*. Geneva: World Council of Churches, 1986.

Purvis, Sally B. *The Power of the Cross: Foundations for a Christian Feminist Ethic of Community*. Nashville: Abingdon, 1993.

Ray, Darby K. *Deceiving the Devil: Atonement, Abuse, and Ransom Reconsidered*. Cleveland: Pilgrim Press, 1998.

Ricoeur, Paul. *The Symbolism of Evil*. New York: Harper and Row, 1967.

Rose, Lucy Atkinson. *Sharing the Word: Preaching in the Roundtable Church*. Louisville: Westminster John Knox Press, 1997.

Ruether, Rosemary Radford. *Sexism and God–Talk: Toward a Feminist Theology*. Boston: Beacon Press, 1983.

Russell, Letty, Kwok Pui–lan, Ada María Isasi–Díaz, and Katie Cannon, eds. *Inheriting Our Mothers' Gardens: Feminist Theology in Third World Perspective*. Louisville: Westminster, 1988.

Schreiter, Robert J., ed. *Faces of Jesus in Africa*. Maryknoll, N.Y.: Orbis Books, 1995.

Schüssler Fiorenza, Elisabeth. *In Memory of Her: A Feminist Theological Reconstruction of Christian Origins*. New York: Crossroad, 1983.

_____. *Revelation: Vision of a Just World*. Minneapolis: Fortress Press, 1991.

_____. *Jesus: Miriam's Child, Sophia's Prophet*. New York: Continuum, 1995.

Smith, Christine M. *Preaching As Weeping, Confession, and Resistance: Radical Approaches to Radical Evil*. Louisville: Westminster/John Knox Press, 1992.

Sobrino, Jon, S. J. *Christology at the Crossroads*. Maryknoll, N.Y.: Orbis Books, 1984.

Solberg, Mary M. *Compelling Knowledge: A Feminist Proposal for an Epistemology of the Cross*. Albany, N.Y.: State University of New York Press, 1997.

Song, C. S. *Jesus, the Crucified People*. Minneapolis: Fortress Press, 1996.

Stevens, Maryanne, ed. *Reconstructing the Christ Symbol: Essays in Feminist Christology*. New York: Paulist Press, 1993.

Suchocki, Marjorie Hewitt. "In Search of Justice: Religious Pluralism from a Feminist Perspective," in *The Myth of Christian Uniqueness: Toward a Pluralistic Theology of Religions*. Edited by John Hick and Paul F. Knitter. Maryknoll, N.Y.: Orbis Books, 1992.

Sugirtharajah, R. S., ed. *Asian Faces of Jesus*. Maryknoll, N.Y. Orbis Books, 1995.

Sun Ai Lee–Park, "A Short History of Asian Feminist Theology," in Ofelia Ortega, ed. *Women's Visions: Theological Reflection, Celebration, Action*. Geneva: World Council of Churches, 1995.

Tabari, Azar. "The Women's Movement in Iran: A Hopeful Prognosis." *Feminist Studies* 12 (Summer 1986).

Thangaraj, M. Thomas. *The Crucified Guru: An Experiment in Cross–Cultural Christology*. Nashville: Abingdon, 1994.

Thistlethwaite, Susan Brooks, and Mary Potter Engel, eds. *Lift Every Voice: Constructing Christian Theologies from the Underside*. San Francisco: Harper and Row, 1990.

Tisdale, Leonora Tubbs. *Preaching as Local Theology and Folk Art*. Minneapolis: Fortress Press, 1997.

Townes, Emilie M., ed. *A Troubling in My Soul: Womanist Perspectives on Evil & Suffering*. Maryknoll, N.Y.: Orbis Books, 1993.

Tracy, David. *The Analogical Imagination: Christian Theology and the Culture of Pluralism*. New York: Crossroads, 1981.

Weems, Renita J. *Just a Sister Away: A Womanist Vision of Women's Relationships in the Bible*. San Diego: LuraMedia, 1988.

Welch, Sharon D. *A Feminist Ethic of Risk*. Minneapolis: Fortress Press, 1990.

White, James M. *Sacraments as God's Self–Giving*. Nashville: Abingdon, 1983.

_____. *Protestant Worship: Traditions in Transition*. Louisville: Westminster/John Knox Press, 1989.

Williams, Delores S. *Sisters in the Wilderness: The Challenge of Womanist God–Talk*. Maryknoll, N.Y.: Orbis Books, 1993.

Williamson, Clark, and Ronald J. Allen. *Interpreting Difficult Texts: Anti–Judaism and Christian Preaching*. Philadelphia: Trinity Press International, 1989.

Wilson, Nancy. *Our Tribe: Queer Folks, God, Jesus, and the Bible*. San Francisco: HarperCollins, 1995.

World Council of Churches. *Baptism, Eucharist and Ministry*. Faith and Order Paper No. 111. Geneva, Switzerland: World Council of Churches, 1982.

Young, Pamela Dickey. *Christ in a Post–Christian World: How can we believe in Jesus Christ when those around us believe differently—or not at all?* Minneapolis: Fortress Press, 1995.

Notes

Introduction

[1]See C. M. Smith, *Preaching as Weeping, Confession and Resistance: Radical Approaches to Radical Evil* (Louisville: Westminster/John Knox Press, 1992), "Crosses Reveal Privilege: Classism," especially 153–57.

[2]C. M. Smith, *Weaving the Sermon: Preaching in a Feminist Perspective* (Louisville: Westminster/John Knox Press, 1989), 89–90.

[3]This comment was made in 1990 when Dr. Proctor was the Anne Potter Wilson Visiting Professor at Vanderbilt. I was beginning my doctoral studies by taking his class on "Preaching the Teachings of Jesus."

Chapter 1. The Christological Crisis of Women Preachers

[1]Julie M. Hopkins, *Towards a Feminist Christology* (Grand Rapids: Eerdmans, 1994), 18, 19.

[2]Women in parish ministry are always marginal figures in ways that minority men will never be. African American males suffer rejection in socially mixed situations but are "at home" when they preach before black congregations. African American women who pursue ordination and attain positions of ecclesiastical authority frequently feel exiled within their own worship communities. Women who preach are second–class religious citizens whether they are "at home" or not.

[3]See Ronald J. Allen, Barbara Shires Blaisdell, and Scott Black Johnston, *Theology for Preaching: Authority, Truth, and Knowledge of God in a Postmodern Ethos* (Nashville: Abingdon Press, 1997), 18–20. Allen identifies the postliberal perspective particularly with narrativists and traditionalists Hans Frei, George Lindbeck, Stanley Hauerwas, William Placher, and William Willimon.

[4]Ada María Isasi–Díaz, *Mujerista Theology* (Maryknoll, N.Y.: Orbis Books, 1996), 4.

[5]Isasi–Díaz, *Mujerista Theology*, 131.

[6]Patricia Hill Collins, *Black Feminist Thought: Knowledge, Consciousness, and the Politics of Empowerment* (New York: Routledge), 1990, xii.

[7]The term *tradition–constituted* is from Alasdair MacIntyre's work. He defines tradition–constituted communities as those whose primary identity refers to a narrative tradition, whether of religion, science, philosophy, or history. All vantage points have a "tradition" that is taken to be the normative reference point for negotiating what is true, rational, or just. See his *Whose Justice? Which Rationality?* (Notre Dame: University of Notre Dame Press, 1988), especially chapter 18, "The Rationality of Traditions," pp. 349–69.

[8]Allen et al. *Theology for Preaching: Authority, Truth, and Knowledge of God in a Postmodern Ethos* (Nashville: Abingdon Press, 1997), 19–20.

[9]MacIntyre, *Whose Justice? Which Rationality?* 350.

[10]I am indebted to Teresa Lockhart Stricklen for suggesting this approach to me. A fine theologican and homiletician, she is currently working on a project to articulate what kind of theology homiletics is.

[11]Walter Brueggemann, *The Prophetic Imagination* (Minneapolis: Fortress Press, 1978), 13.

[12]I am borrowing Carter Heyward's use of "Jesus/Christ" and her rationale for it. Heyward intends to avoid the dualism between the historical Jesus and the Christ of faith. "I have not argued seriously with the classical doctrine that Jesus Christ was and is both divine and human. I still do not. The classical framework has given me both an ideological target for my frustrations with the hierarchical, dualistic foundations of Christian thought and a pastoral and liturgical ground upon which to stand in sharing the language

189

of faith with other Christians." In *Speaking of Christ: A Lesbian Feminist Voice* (New York: Pilgrim Press, 1989), 15.

[13]Elisabeth Schüssler Fiorenza, *Jesus: Miriam's Child, Sophia's Prophet* (New York: Continuum, 1995), 54.

[14]Carter Heyward, "Heterosexist Theology: Being Above It All," *Journal of Feminist Studies in Religion* 31 (Spring 1987), 34.

[15]See also an intriguing book by Robert Goss, *Jesus Acted Up: A Gay and Lesbian Manifesto* (San Francisco: HarperSanFrancisco, 1993).

[16]Annie Dillard, *Living By Fiction* (New York: Harper & Row, 1982), 167–68. Dillard addresses the necessity for symbol and its ambiguity in her chapter "About Symbol, and With a Diatribe Against Purity."

[17]*Kyriarchy* is an alternative term to either patriarchy or hierarchy. Patriarchy is a gendered construct and consequently masks the participation of women in power schemes. Hierarchy designates levels of status but does not always suggest the power–as–domination involved. *Kyriarchy*, based on the word "kyrios" or lord, is a term preferred by Elisabeth Schüssler Fiorenza to indicate structures of relationships of unequal status and the exercise of power (lording it over) involved. See Schüssler Fiorenza, *Jesus: Miriam's Child, Sophia's Prophet*, 14.

[18]Dillard, *Living By Fiction*, 136. The pendulum swing of the mind/body split may be showing up again in postmodern American spirituality. The immediate trend might, in fact, be to "re–spookify" religion. According to recent polls, about 90 percent of American Christians believe in literal angels. And we may also want to pay close attention to the New Agers, the alternative spirituality folks, and the alien–watchers. Recently, thirty–nine members of a religious group called Heaven's Gate committed mass suicide, apparently on the assumption that a UFO was coming to "relieve them of the earthly bodies," which they believed to be illusory. Gnosticism is alive and well. One of the best short pieces on the Heaven's Gate group is John Taylor's "Heaven Couldn't Wait," *Esquire* (June 1997), 40–46. Taylor's interpretation of the group plays on Augustinian critiques of masochistic martyrdom and is astonishingly similar to Elaine Pagels' interpretation of postmodern gnosticism in *The Gnostic Gospels* (New York: Vintage Books/Random House, 1981).

[19]Dillard, *Living By Fiction*, 136.

[20]Pagels, *The Gnostic Gospels*, xxxii–xxxiii. Pagels credits Hans Jonas with this initial connection, noting that Jonas came to this conclusion after reading Heidegger.

[21]Grant identifies two reformist or revisionist strategies that she calls biblical feminism and liberation feminism. A third strategy is the rejectionist posture, which moves beyond christological symbols and narratives altogether. I've added a third revisionist posture by identifying historical strategies as distinct from, though related to, both biblical and liberationist strategies. See Grant, *White Women's Christ and Black Women's Jesus* (Atlanta: Scholars Press, 1989).

[22]Schüssler Fiorenza, *Jesus: Miriam's Child, Sophia's Prophet*, 88.

[23]John S. McClure, *The Four Codes of Preaching: Rhetorical Strategies* (Minneapolis: Fortress Press, 1991), 9.

[24]Allen et al., *Theology for Preaching*, 21–23.

[25]Ibid., 20–22. He cites David Ray Griffin, *God and Religion in the Postmodern World* (Albany: State University of New York Press, 1989), xi.

[26]Joanne Carlson Brown and Rebecca Parker, "For God So Loved the World?" in Joanne Carlson Brown and Carole R. Bohn, eds., *Christianity, Patriarchy, and Abuse: A Feminist Critique* (Cleveland: Pilgrim Press, 1989), 1.

[27]See Katie Cannon, *Black Womanist Ethics* (Atlanta: Scholars Press, 1988); bell hooks, *Ain't I a Woman: Black Women and Feminism* (Boston: South End Press, 1981); Delores S. Williams, *Sisters in the Wilderness: The Challenge of Womanist God–Talk* (Maryknoll, N.Y.: Orbis Books, 1993).

[28]*Ecumenical* refers to diverse groups of Christians, while *interfaith* refers to groups that include other faiths besides Christianity. In a later chapter we will explore distinctions between ecumenical diversity and interfaith diversity, since the two are frequently conflated.

[29]Brown and Parker, "For God So Loved the World?" 2.

[30]We will note in the next chapter that this charge against Anselm is misplaced. He did not support the punitive aspects that Aquinas, Luther, and Calvin later introduced.

[31]Brown and Parker, "For God So Loved the World?" 3.

[32]Rita Nakashima Brock, *Journeys by Heart: A Christology of Erotic Power* (New York: Crossroad, 1995), 55.

[33]Williams, *Sisters in the Wilderness*, 162.

[34]Mercy Amba Oduyoye, "Churchwomen and the Church's Mission," in J. Pobee and B. von Wartenburg–Potter, eds., *New Eyes For Reading: Biblical and Theological Reflections by Women from the Third World* (Geneva: World Council of Churches, 1986), 78.

[35]Schüssler Fiorenza, *Jesus: Miriam's Child, Sophia's Prophet*, 55.

[36]Patrick Keifert, *Welcoming the Stranger: A Public Theology of Worship and Evangelism* (Minneapolis: Fortress Press, 1992), 24.

[37]Grant, *White Women's Christ, Black Women's Jesus*, 191; and Jacquelyn Grant, "Come to My Help, Lord, For I'm in Trouble," in Maryanne Stevens, ed., *Reconstructing the Christ Symbol: Essays in Feminist Christology* (Mahwah, N.J.: Paulist Press, 1993), 65.

[38]Smith, *Preaching as Weeping*, 46–47.

[39]Smith, *Preaching as Weeping*, 54.

[40]Sallie McFague, *The Body of God* (Minneapolis: Fortress Press, 1993), 22.

[41]I am indebted here to Ed Farley's discussion of the ambiguity of the human condition. Farley distinguishes the "benign alienation" of ordinary human existence from the corrupting agency of that which diminishes being. See his *Good & Evil* (Minneapolis: Fortress Press, 1990). His distinctions between the suffering of ordinary finitude and the suffering caused by active wickedness would probably enhance women's embodiment theologies in a way that allows us to say that some concrete events and experiences are not revelatory of divine compassion.

[42]Sallie McFague's *Body of God* is a happy exception to this problem. Unfortunately, not many of the contemporary christologies deal with McFague's helpful discussions of christology, suffering, sacraments, and ecclesiology. Her "organic christology" does, I think, overcome many of the problems of classical Anselmian notions of suffering, while still calling for the church to be the body of Christ in solidarity with the cosmos.

[43]Douglas John Hall, *Lighten our Darkness: Toward an Indigenous Theology of the Cross* (Philadelphia: Westminster Press, 1976), 74.

Chapter 2. Christological Blunders of the Tradition

[1]Elizabeth Johnson, *Consider Jesus: Waves of Renewal in Christology* (New York: Crossroad, 1995), 1.

[2]Denise L. Carmody, *Christian Feminist Theology* (Oxford: Blackwell, 1995), 50.

[3]See also Jon Sobrino, S. J., *Christology at the Crossroads* (Maryknoll, N.Y.: Orbis Books, 1984), 338–39.

[4]John McIntyre, *The Shape of Christology* (Philadelphia: Westminster Press, 1966), 54. I use the word *gestalt* to indicate a phenomenon so integrally related that it should be considered a unitary whole whose discrete elements should not be interpreted without reference to the other elements.

[5]C. S. Song, *Jesus, the Crucified People* (Minneapolis: Fortress Press, 1996), 10.

[6]Johnson, *Consider Jesus*, 73–78. Johnson discusses Sobrino's typology and the major symbols of each type.

[7]Sobrino, *Christology at the Crossroads*, 338.

[8]I use the New Testament Greek term *basileia* to refer to what has traditionally been called the kingdom of God. I prefer basileia, or reign of God, or God's future, since they do not carry implicit gender or imperial connotations.

[9]According to Douglas Ottati, there are between thirteen and seventeen different christologies within the canon itself, including Son of God, Son of man, second Adam, Logos, son of David, etc. See Ottati, *Jesus Christ and Christian Vision* (Louisville: Westminster John Knox Press, 1996), 16.

[10]See Charles Talbert, "'And the Word Became Flesh': When?" in A. Malherbe and W. Meeks, *The Future of Christology: Essays in Honor of Leander Keck* (Minneapolis: Fortress Press, 1993), 43–52.

[11]It is virtually impossible to assume anything about Jesus' own self–understanding except as it is interpreted by the early church. What we have are several versions of the church's assumptions about Jesus' self–identity. There are also several strands of Jewish

messianism, but I am referring to general characteristics of intertestamental Judaism. I am using the terms *messianic prophet* and *prophetic messiah* interchangeably. The emphasis varies across the New Testament writings, with some placing more emphasis on the messianic nature of Jesus' ministry and others placing more emphasis on the prophetic nature of his ministry. This conflation of terms allows for a discussion of identity and vocation relative to similar terms as they appear in the different writings, since both dimensions appear in all the gospels. Marcus Borg, a Jesus Seminar scholar, has devoted an entire chapter to the prophetic nature of Jesus' identity and ministry in *Jesus: A New Vision* (San Francisco: HarperCollins, 1987), 151–71; and Gerald O'Collins has an extensive discussion of the messianic overtones of Jesus' ministry in *Interpreting Jesus* (Mahwah, N.J.: Paulist Press, 1983), 65–67.

[12]Marinus de Jonge, "The Christological Significance of Jesus' Preaching of the Kingdom of God," in Abraham Malherbe and Wayne A. Meeks, eds., *The Future of Christology:Essays in Honor of Leander E. Keck* (Minneapolis: Fortress Press, 1993), 3–17. De Jonge argues that the three types of early Christian explanations for Jesus' death are all found in the Hebrew Bible. They are the prophetic messenger, the suffering servant, and the martyr. All three of these roles are related to the eschatological symbol of the reign of God.

[13]Reginald H. Fuller, *The Foundations of New Testament Christology* (New York: Charles Scribner's Sons, 1965), chapter 5, "The Historical Jesus: His Self–Understanding," 102–30.

[14]Fuller, *The Foundations of New Testament Christology*, 130.

[15]Ibid.

[16]Gerhard von Rad, *The Message of the Prophets* (San Francisco: HarperCollins, 1965), 142.

[17]We tend to read Isaiah's servant songs and messianic visions through later christological doctrines, but the reverse reading is more apt. Isaiah's reinterpretation of this messianic figure can help us hear the announcement in a fresh way. Isaiah emphatically uses the language associated with the Zion tradition and the Davidic tradition and blends them into a prophetic messianism.

[18]James L. Mays, "Isaiah's Royal Theology and the Messiah," in Christopher R. Seitz, ed., *Reading and Preaching the Book of Isaiah* (Philadelphia: Fortress Press, 1988), 43–48.

[19]Mays, "Isaiah's Royal Theology and the Messiah," 41.

[20]Fuller refers to the suffering sayings in Mark. See *Foundations of New Testament Christology*, 120.

[21]According to Fuller, only a passage in Acts 7:56 can pass scholarly muster as an independent use of the title. See *Foundations of New Testament Christology*, 121.

[22]Fuller, *The Foundations of New Testament Christology*, chapter 4, "The Kerygma of the Earliest Church: The Two Foci Christology," 142–81.

[23]Paula Fredriksen, *From Jesus to Christ: The Origins of the New Testament Images of Jesus* (New Haven: Yale University Press, 1988), xii.

[24]Gustaf Aulén, *Christus Victor* (New York: Macmillan, 1945), 20–23.

[25]Aulén, *Christus Victor*, 21–22.

[26]See Gerald O'Collins' discussion of Aulèn's characterization in *Interpreting Jesus*, chapter 5, "Jesus the World's Redeemer," 142–67. O'Collins considers Aulèn's interpretation correct, that the primitive Christus Victor model was a liberation model whose thematic antecedents included the exodus and whose Christian connections involve the Passover symbolism and the warfare and struggle motifs of Revelation and Pauline rhetoric. While O'Collins prefers an "invincible love" model, he claims that the primitive atonement theory is both scripturally warranted and morally plausible. He rejects Anselmian atonement and its permutations as failing both criteria.

[27]Most of the New Testament writers use messianic or prophetic categories to interpret Jesus' life, death, and resurrection. However, it would be short–sighted to think that they did not also carefully distinguish Jesus/Christ from these models. Jesus was prophetic, but he was more than just a prophet. Jesus was messianic, but not messianic according to traditional expectations of a national imperial or political leader.

[28]See Paul D. Hanson's *Isaiah 40–66*, Interpretation (Louisville: John Knox Press, 1995), 217ff. Hanson claims that Third Isaiah radically shifted the messianic expectations by adding the dimension of martyrdom and suffering. This was not a vicarious suffering

to appease God (Old Testament Jews were not Anselmian), but the inevitable suffering of justice at the hands of human evil. Isaiah's vision of the New Jerusalem is a city that welcomes all nations and ethnoi. The inclusiveness of the vision was likewise offensive to the faithful of Isaiah's day.

[29]Rosemary Radford Ruether, *Sexism and God–Talk: Toward a Feminist Theology* (Boston: Beacon Press, 1983), 123.

[30]Ibid., 122.

[31]J. N. D. Kelly, *Early Christian Doctrines* (New York: Harper and Brothers, 1960), 223.

[32]See John H. Leith's *Creeds of the Churches* (Atlanta: John Knox Press, 1977), 30–31. The Council of Nicea was convened in 325 C.E. under the authority of Constantine. See Douglas Ottati's discussion of the councils and creeds and the problems that proceeded from the dubious shift to metaphysical language and incarnational christology. In *Jesus Christ and Christian Vision*, 23–23.

[33]Ottati, *Jesus Christ and Christian Vision*, 39–48.

[34]It was probably not very successful, since only a few years passed before the creedal competition between Nicea and Chalcedon erupted over the dinner table. In 473, Nicea was promulgated as a eucharistic test by Peter the Fuller of Antioch, who wanted to guard the table against the humanizing of Jesus. This debate over the material and substantial participation in the godhead sets the theological stage for centuries of weird christology and probably dominates most popular faith understandings today.

[35]Aulén, *The Faith of the Christian Church* (Philadelphia: Fortress Press, 1960), 194–95.

[36]Gerald O'Collins, *Christology: A Biblical, Historical, and Systematic Study of Jesus* (London: Oxford University Press, 1995), 155.

[37]Augustine's reformulation of the garden of Eden story is notable for its departure from traditional Jewish understandings of the same story. Pauline interpretations of Christ as the New Adam implied some of the notions that Augustine (and later, Luther) formalized in his doctrine. Pauline notions of the Adamic Christ had more to do with the inauguration of the New Creation than with the origins of sin. James Barr has argued against the Augustinian interpretation in recent work. "This narrative is not, as it has commonly been understood in our tradition, basically a story of the origins of sin and evil, still less a depiction of absolute evil or total depravity: it is a story of how human immortality was almost gained, but in fact was lost." In *The Garden of Eden and the Hope of Immortality* (Minneapolis: Fortress Press, 1993), 4.

[38]See Carmody's discussion of Eve and Mary as Augustinian "types," *Christian Feminist Theology*, 51.

[39]See Genevieve Lloyd's discussion of Augustine in *Feminist Theology: A Reader*, ed. Ann Loades (Louisville: Westminster/John Knox Press, 1990), 90–93.

[40]See O'Collins' discussion of the problems with the mind/body analogy for the two natures of Christ. Humans are fully human when endowed with mind and body, two natures united into one historical event. The analogy breaks down when used to describe the divine and human nature of Christ, since two independently complete entities are united in one event. In O'Collins, *Christology*, 185.

[41]*Enchiridion*, 108.

[42]Ottati, *Jesus Christ and Christian Vision*, 52.

[43]See Matthew Fox's *Original Blessing: A Primer in Creation Spirituality* (Sante Fe: Bear & Co., 1983) with its cheerful reclamation of Irenaean anthropology and its condemnation of the doctrines of human depravity. Fox's approach is helpful for its challenge to Augustinian notions of original sin, but probably reverts to an unsustainably romantic "faith in human nature."

[44]This high ecclesiology also tends to show up in Protestant episcopal structures: Lutheran, Methodist, Anglican, and others. Even within the so–called "low–church" ecclesiologies of the congregational denominations (Baptists, Christian Church [Disciples of Christ], Churches of Christ, Pentecostal, and Holiness churches), the incarnational bias is reinforced by high biblical authority. In this thinking, there is a strict double standard for clerical morality and the maintenance of cultural marriage and family stereotypes. The role of "ideal husband/father" has displaced the "ideal celibate" with relatively little difference. Sexuality is still strictly proscribed, and gender roles remain fairly rigid. And in

many Protestant denominations, women continue to be excluded from ordained ministry because they do not conform to the incarnation of God into male humanity.

[45]Mary Daly, *Gyn/Ecology: The Metaethics of Radical Feminism* (Boston: Beacon Press, 1978), 37.

[46]Schüssler Fiorenza, *Jesus: Miriam's Child, Sophia's Prophet*, 47.

[47]Guardianship of the faith almost always involves similar patterns of moralistic preaching, restrictive discipline, and antagonism against "unbelievers." Consider the contemporary Southern Baptist controversies over doctrine and the purging of seminary faculty members who will not make creedal confessions. Among the implicit villains are feminist theologians. At the time of this writing, the Presbyterian Church (USA) has publicly demanded celibacy for its unmarried ministers and fidelity for its married clergy. Those who don't comply are threatened with loss of ordination status. The flap was raised by controversy over the ordination of gay, lesbian, and bisexual candidates for ministry.

[48]I will not deal at all with the atonement theory of Peter Abelard (1079–1142), Anselm's younger contemporary. Abelard's atonement theory has been called the "moral influence" theory, since it interpreted Jesus/Christ's crucifixion as a "lesson" in sacrificial love whose purpose was to move us to guilt and repentance. See O'Collins, *Christology*, 202–3, and chapter 12; O'Collins, *Interpreting Jesus*, 157–60; see also Brown and Parker, "For God So Loved the World?" in Joanne Carlson Brown and Carole R. Bohn, eds., *Christianity, Patriarchy and Abuse: A Feminist Critique* (New York: Pilgrim Press, 1991), 11–13. See also Darby K. Ray, *Deceiving the Devil: Atonement, Abuse, and Ransom Reconsidered* (Cleveland: Pilgrim Press, 1998). Ray deals extensively with Anselm and Abelard, forging a critical synthesis for feminist reflections.

[49]Cited in O'Collins, *Christology*, 199, this is from Gregory of Nyssa's *Oratio Catechetica*, 21–24. Some of the earliest New Testament writings use this metaphorical language, especially the semi–mocking lines from 1 Corinthians 15:55 ("Where, O death, is your victory? Where, O death, is your sting?"). O'Collins argues that these two theories of redemption prevailed prior to Anselm. Origen, Augustine, and John Chrysostom had some sympathies for the ransom theory. The ransom or mousetrap theory follows classic trickster tale paradigms whereby the weaker member of a pair dupes the stronger member into some inescapable dilemma. The narrative theology behind the ransom theory assumes that the devil expected to get Christ's soul at death. The resurrection fooled Satan by allowing Christ to die and yet still escape the devil's clutches.

[50]Jaroslav Pelikan, *Jesus Through the Centuries: His Place in the History of Culture* (New York: Harper & Row, 1987), 107.

[51]See Alasdair MacIntyre's *Whose Justice? Which Rationality?* He argues that what constitutes morality or justice or rationality changes from age to age. Our language must be constantly renegotiated so that such words have shared meaning.

[52]Brown and Parker, "For God so Loved the World?" *Christianity, Patriarchy, and Abuse*, 8.

[53]See C. W. Bynum, *Jesus as Mother* (Berkeley: University of California Press, 1982). Gerald O'Collins points out that these associations were not peculiar to Anselm, but were also present in the writings of Origen, Clement of Alexandria, John Chrysostom, Ambrose, and Augustine. See O'Collins, *Christology*, 203.

[54]Carmody, *Christian Feminist Theology*, 248.

[55]Emily Cheney, *She Can Read: Feminist Reading Strategies for Biblical Narrative* (Valley Forge, Penn.: Trinity Press International, 1996), 43. Cheney's work should be used carefully, since many of her strategies actually reverse what I take to be legitimate Christian interpretations. I suspect that the gender reversal strategy may not be as subversive of cultural stereotypes as she hopes. There are probably occasions where the disruption is essential to proclamation and should not be avoided. Some stereotypical female behavior may indeed be more Christian than stereotypical male behavior.

[56]Gerald O'Collins, *Interpreting Jesus*, 142ff.

[57]For a clear discussion of the classical problems of doctrines of God and theodicy, see Charles Hartshorne's *Omnipotence and Other Theological Mistakes* (Albany, N.Y.: State University of New York Press, 1984).

[58]Readers who want to pursue a full investigation of Aquinas on this point are encouraged to read Question 92, "The Production of Woman (In Four Articles)," in *Summa*

Theologiae. See also works by Kari Elizabeth Børrensen, *Subordination and Equivalence: The Nature and Role of Women in Augustine and Thomas Aquinas,* trans. C. Talbot (Washington, D.C.: University Press of America, 1981), and Genevieve Lloyd's essay, "Augustine and Aquinas," in Ann Loades, ed., *Feminist Theology: A Reader,* 91–98.

[59]O'Collins, *Interpreting Jesus,* 150.

[60]Ibid., 21.

[61]Johnson, *Consider Jesus,* 101.

[62]Ruether, *Sexism and God–Talk,* 125.

[63]Aulén, *Christus Victor,* 111.

[64]Aulén, *The Faith of the Christian Church,* 108.

[65]Schüssler Fiorenza, *Jesus: Miriam's Child, Sophia's Prophet,* 34–57.

[66]Rosemary Radford Ruether, "The Liberation of Christology from Patriarchy," in Ann Loades, ed., *Feminist Theology: A Reader* (Louisville: Westminster/John Knox Press, 1990), 147.

[67]The Catholic Church underwent a similar period of revision that is usually referred to as the Counter Reformation. Many of the theological problems identified by Luther were subsequently addressed, especially reformulations of eucharistic theory and practice. We will not pursue the Catholic trajectory beyond this point, but must at least avoid any impressions that the Catholic Church is still operating with the theology Luther repudiated.

[68]M. Thomas Thangaraj, *The Crucified Guru: An Experiment in Cross–Cultural Christology* (Nashville: Abingdon Press, 1994), 121. See also a discussion of Luther's christology as functional, in O'Collins, *Christology,* 210.

[69]Calvin's emphasis on the work of the human Christ was partly an attempt to mitigate this tendency to spiritualize and personalize the benefits of Christ for the believer. Calvin apparently worried that too much emphasis on the divine activity in salvation would weaken the ethical impulse of the faith.

[70]See Eleanor McLaughlin's discussion of Luther in "Women, Power and the Pursuit of Holiness in Medieval Christianity," in Loades, *Feminist Theology: A Reader,* 99–123.

[71]Merry Weisner, "Luther and Women: The Death of Two Marys," in Loades, *Feminist Theology: A Reader,* 126.

[72]*Institutes,* II, 12, 1.

[73]François Wendel, *Calvin: The Origins and Development of His Religious Thought,* trans. Philip Mairet (London: William Collins Sons & Co. Ltd., 1963), 216.

[74]*Institutes,* III, 11, 23.

[75]Ibid, 8, 1.

[76]For a thorough discussion of the "extra calvinisticum" see the work of François Wendel, *Calvin: The Origins and Development of His Religious Thought,* 223–25. Wendel's work is a standard text for Calvin scholars.

[77]O'Collins, *Christology,* 211; O'Collins, *Interpreting Jesus,* 21, 150.

[78]Aulén, *Christus Victor,* 67. Aulén also argues that Luther's metaphors leaned toward the classical dramatic theory and the ransom theory, where human captivities to sin/death/Satan are broken and overcome by God's activity on the cross. See his discussion in the section on Luther, 117–38.

[79]Wolterstorff, *Until Justice and Peace Embrace* (Grand Rapids, Mich.: Eerdmans, 1983), 21.

[80]Many feminists and women theologians reject selflessness as a theological virtue. Their concern for self–abnegation is appropriate when considered in intimate and interpersonal relationships, but does not allow any discernment for corporate unselfishness as a proper virtue. In a following chapter we will explore the distinctions between self–abnegation and unselfishness and their implications for community ethics directed toward the rest of society.

[81]*Calvin's New Testament Commentaries,* 3:116–17.

[82]Karen L. Bloomquist, "Sexual Violence: Patriarchy's Offense and Defense," in Brown and Bohn, eds., *Christianity, Patriarchy, and Abuse,* 68.

[83]Sheila Redmond, "Christian 'Virtues' and Child Sexual Abuse," in ibid. 73–74.

[84]Rita Nakashima Brock, "And a Little Child Will Lead Us," in ibid., 52–53.

Chapter 3. Women and Contemporary Christological Options

[1]Phoebe Palmer, "The Great Army of Preaching Women," from *The Promise of the Father* (New York: W. C. Palmer, Jr., 1872), 21–33; cited in Richard Lischer, *Theories of Preaching: Selected Readings in the Homiletical Tradition* (Durham, N.C.: Labyrinth Press, 1987), 71–72.

[2]My own location as a white Protestant American in the liberal and post–modern tradition needs to be claimed. I am not pretending to offer suggestions to all women preachers everywhere. My primary interest is to equip American women with a breadth of perspective, so that their preaching will be more sensitive to issues of gender, ethnicity, cultural context, and ecumenism.

[3]A word about language is important here. First, I will use Sophia and Wisdom interchangeably, although Wisdom clearly refers to Hebrew Bible contexts and Sophia to the Greek New Testament language–world. I want to be cautious, however, about using the familiar descriptive phrase "Judeo–Christian tradition." Although used frequently in contemporary Christian discourse, it probably masks the distinctively Christian perspective of such a characterization.

[4]Tonya Burton has directed me to Elizabeth Huwiler's discussion of the development of male monotheism within the pluralistic and polytheistic context of primitive Yahwism. The argument assumes that in the process of eliminating polytheism and promoting a growing caste of male clergy, primitive Yahwism subsumed the attributes of local goddess figures under the symbol of the male divinity. Huwiler asks if the demise of polytheism, especially goddess–oriented types, could be the source of patriarchy. In *Biblical Women: Mirrors, Models and Metaphors* (Cleveland: United Church Press, 1993), especially chapter 6, "Gender and God: Constructive Biblical Theology."

[5]It would be an interesting study to trace the similarities between Wisdom/harlot, virgin/whore, monotheism/idolatry oppositions. All three sets of oppositions function relative to a purity/pollution model that Mary Douglas discusses in terms of body metaphors and ethics. See her *Purity and Danger: An Analysis of the Concepts of Pollution and Taboo* (New York: Ark Paperbacks, 1966).

[6]Schüssler Fiorenza, *Jesus: Miriam's Child, Sophia's Prophet*, 136.

[7]Fredrikson, *From Jesus to Christ*, 86. See also Elaine Pagels, *The Gnostic Gospels*.

[8]McFague actually ratchets up the intensity when she displaces king/kingdom language with her organic cosmic christology and may be even more radical than Schüssler Fiorenza. McFague's cosmic approach is certainly friendly to cosmic dimensions of apocalyptic language and symbols, though I wouldn't want to attribute such connections to her work. See *The Body of God*, chapter 6, "Christology."

[9]Schüssler Fiorenza, *Jesus: Miriam's Child, Sophia's Prophet*, 93.

[10]Ibid. John Dominic Crossan has also written extensively on the open commensality of the early Jesus community. Writing about the parable of the great banquet (Luke 14:21b–23, Matthew 22:9–10, and in the Gospel of Thomas), Crossan defines open commensality as "an eating together without using table as a miniature map of society's vertical discriminations and lateral separations. The social challenge of such equal or egalitarian commensality is the parable's most fundamental danger and most radical threat." In Crossan, *Jesus: A Revolutionary Biography* (San Francisco: HarperSanFrancisco, 1994), 67.

[11]An interesting politicized interpretation of the Markan "Stilling of the Storm," would cash in on the sociopolitical storms and calm a nervous batch of post–resurrection disciples; certainly an alternative to the highly spiritualized homiletic approaches where Jesus stills our inner fears.

[12]Johnson, *Consider Jesus*, 111.

[13]Ibid., 112.

[14]Similarly, homiletician Alyce M. McKenzie has focused attention on the subversive nature of wisdom literature as it surfaces in the teachings and sayings of Jesus. McKenzie characterizes the Jesus sayings (not just the parables) as "wisdom which subverts" and claims that we do not have to choose between Jesus the sage and Jesus the apocalyptic prophet to faithfully preach Jesus' subversive aphorisms. Like Schüssler Fiorenza and Johnson, McKenzie argues against any interpretive approach that would reinforce the "wisdom of the world." See her *Preaching Proverbs* (Louisville: Westminster John Knox Press, 1996), especially Part Two, "Proverbs that Create and Subvert Order."

[15]See Newsom's "Woman and the Discourse of Patriarchal Wisdom: A Study of Proverbs 1–9," in Peggy L. Day, ed., *Gender and Difference in Ancient Israel* (Minneapolis: Fortress Press, 1989), 142–60.

[16]Lucinda Nelson, unpublished review of Newsom essay, Vanderbilt Divinity School, March 10, 1997.

[17]Emily Cheney has written a helpful book on reading strategies for biblical texts to "test" their friendliness to feminist theological concerns. Cheney claims that several feminist scholars use reader–response strategies that do not deconstruct the literary convention of the "ideal male reader." "The strategy of putting the female character in the center of the analysis reveals her significant role in conveying the perspective of the text but does not remove her subordinate status in the story." Some female biblical characters are water–carriers for the good old boys. See *She Can Read: Feminist Reading Strategies for Biblical Narrative* (Valley Forge, Penn.: Trinity Press International, 1996), 37.

[18]See Schüssler Fiorenza on the development of Mariology as an alternative to underdeveloped doctrines of the Holy Spirit, *Jesus: Miriam's Child, Sophia's Prophet*, 178–82.

[19]Schüssler Fiorenza, *Jesus: Miriam's Child, Sophia's Prophet*, 186, 187.

[20]I am indebted to Leslie Linder for drawing my attention to the work of Claudia Camp and the trickster dimension of the Wise Woman. Camp argues that the binary opposition of women characters of Proverbs function like trickster figures in other folk systems, appearing to support and explain the dominant order at the same time they are subverting it. The Wise Woman and the Strange/Foreign Woman are both bearers of knowledge in Israelite culture; one bears good knowledge and one bears evil knowledge. Each type presupposes the other. See Camp's "Wise and Strange: An Interpretation of the Female Imagery in Proverbs in Light of Trickster Mythology," *Semeia* 42 (1988), 14–35.

[21]Alexandra Brown argues for just such a reversal within Pauline discourse on wisdom and folly, suggesting that Paul actually uses an apocalyptic strategy to oppose worldly success to the way of the cross. See her *The Cross and Human Transformation* (Minneapolis: Fortress Press, 1995), 75–80, 111–21. Rodney Kennedy has written persuasively on the Pauline rhetoric of folly and its reversal of inherited patterns of wisdom. See *The Creative Power of Metaphor: A Rhetorical Homiletics* (Lanham, Md.: University Press of America, 1993), 31–58.

[22]Jacquelyn Grant, *White Women's Christ, Black Women's Jesus: Feminist Christology and Womanist Response* (Atlanta: Scholars Press, 1989), 5.

[23]Grant, *White Women's Christ, Black Women's Jesus*, 6.

[24]Ibid., 212.

[25]Ibid., 220.

[26]There are a number of books that help Christian preachers negotiate christological options for preaching. Both the New Testament and the tradition contain implicit and explicit anti–Judaism, and careful preachers don't want to homiletically reinscribe such biases. See Williamson and Allen's *Interpreting Difficult Texts: Anti–Judaism and Christian Preaching* (Philadelphia: Trinity Press International, 1989); Allen and Holbert's *Holy Root, Holy Branches: Christian Preaching from the Old Testament* (Nashville: Abingdon Press, 1995); and Howard Clark Kee, ed., *Removing Anti–Judaism from the Pulpit* (New York: Continuum, 1996).

[27]See also Grant's essay on the servanthood model and its support of hierarchical structures, "The Sin of Servanthood," in Emilie M. Townes, ed., *A Troubling in My Soul: Womanist Perspectives on Evil & Suffering* (Maryknoll, N.Y.: Orbis Books, 1993), 199–216. Grant suggests replacing the servanthood model with discipleship, which includes care and support but does not reinforce power inequities.

[28]See also Elsa Tamez's interpretation of Hagar from a Central American point of view, in "The Woman Who Complicated the History of Salvation," in *New Eyes for Reading*, 5–17. Tamez reclaims Hagar as a strong heroic woman who assumes the burdens of single parenthood and manages to raise a son who refuses to "be dominated or domesticated, as his mother formed him." Tamez valorizes Hagar as one who complicates things as the poor frequently complicate the history of salvation. Note the reversal. For Williams, Hagar is a negative image, while for Tamez, she is positive. See also Renita J. Weems's *Just a Sister Away: A Womanist Vision of Women's Relationships in the Bible* (San Diego: LuraMedia, 1988), 1–19. In "A Mistress, A Maid, And No Mercy," Weems opens up the ambiguities in the story; she doesn't reject Hagar as a symbolic victim or valorize her as a symbolic heroine.

[29]Williams, *Sisters in the Wilderness*, 61.

[30]Ibid., 162.

[31]Ibid., 167.

[32]Ibid., 168.

[33]Kelly Brown Douglas, *The Black Christ* (Maryknoll, N.Y.: Orbis Books, 1994), 86.

[34]Douglas, *The Black Christ*, 107.

[35]Ibid., 109–10.

[36]Ibid., 108.

[37]Ibid., 110.

[38]Ibid., 21.

[39]Ibid., 24.

[40]Developing vocabulary is almost always a politically charged activity. Naming involves negotiation. In early work, Ada María Isasi–Díaz discussed the problems of definition within that Hispanic community of women. Hispanic, referring to the cultural influence of Spanish imperialism, is problematic for some women, because it is both derivative and gender–neutral. Latina, a feminine adjective or noun, generally refers to Latin American women and does not seem to capture the distinct Americanness of women who have never lived outside the United States. And both Hispanic and Latina overlook the real diversity within the broad category. There are Cuban women, Mexican women, Guatemalan women, Puerto Rican women, and so on. Isasi–Díaz's early work opts for Hispanic, which has stronger cultural connections to poverty than other vocabulary. See "A Hispanic Garden in a Foreign Land," in Letty Russell, Kwok Pui–lan, Ada María Isasi–Díaz, Katie Geneva Cannon, eds., *Inheriting Our Mothers' Gardens: Feminist Theology in Third World Perspective* (Louisville: Westminster Press, 1988), 97–98.

[41]Ada María Isasi–Díaz and Yolanda Tarango, *Hispanic Women: Prophetic Voice in the Church* (Minneapolis: Fortress Press, 1992), xii.

[42]Ada María Isasi–Díaz, *Mujerista Theology* (Maryknoll, N.Y.: Orbis Books, 1996), 60–61.

[43]Ibid., 65.

[44]Ibid., 71.

[45]Ibid., 129.

[46]Ibid., 130.

[47]Ada María Isasi–Díaz, *En La Lucha* (Minneapolis: Fortress Press, 1993), 74.

[48]Isasi–Díaz and Tarango, *Hispanic Women*, 47.

[49]Ibid., 36.

[50]Isasi–Díaz, "The Bible and Mujerista Theology," in Susan Brooks Thistlethwaite and Mary Potter Engel, eds., *Lift Every Voice: Constructing Christian Theologies from the Underside* (San Francisco: Harper and Row, 1990), 264.

[51]Ibid., 263.

[52]Again, we must note that language is politically and socially charged. "Third World" refers to the underdeveloped or developing countries of the world. It is frequently used in contrast or distinction to "First World," which indicates the countries that wield the greatest economic, political, and military power. Recently there has been a move to drop "Third World" in favor of "Two–Thirds World" to indicate the bias involved in ranking.

[53]Ivone Gebara and Maria Clara Bingemer, *Mary: Mother of God, Mother of the Poor* (Maryknoll, N.Y.: Orbis Books, 1989), 35. I am grateful to Leslie Linder for introducing me to the work of Gebara and bingemer and for leading classroom discussions exploring the productive dimensions of their argument.

[54]I am not suggesting that Hispanic men are more sexist than Anglo men, or any other group of men, for that matter. Isasi–Díaz claims that, as an attitude, machismo is ordinary male chauvinism that is not substantively different from sexism everywhere. She does suggest that what is different is the phenomenon of cultural support such sexism enjoys within Hispanic communities. If I understand her, she is simply making a claim that as a phenomenon, machismo is not considered "politically incorrect" within Hispanic contexts. See *En La Lucha*, 19–20.

[55]Grant, *White Women's Christ, Black Women's Jesus*, 6.

[56]Douglas, *The Black Christ*, 24.

[57]Donal Flanagan, "Eschatology and the Assumption," in Edward Schillebeeckx and Boniface Willems, eds., *The Problem of Eschatology* (New York: Paulist Press, 1969).

[58]Elisabeth Schüssler Fiorenza, *Revelation: Vision of a Just World* (Minneapolis: Fortress Press, 1991), 30.

[59]*Body–selves* is a term developed by Carter Heyward in *Touching Our Strength: The Erotic as Power and the Love of God* (San Francisco: Harper & Row, 1989), 94–99. She also uses the term in explicitly christological ways in *Speaking of Christ: A Lesbian Feminist Voice* (New York: Pilgrim Press, 1989).

[60]Audre Lorde, *Sister, Outsider: Essays and Speeches* (Trumansburg, N.Y.: The Crossing Press, 1984), 56. Mary Solberg questions this totalizing epistemological approach as a privileged way of knowing. Solberg's own experiences in El Salvador lead her to claim that suffering is the primary experience of Third World women and epistemologies located elsewhere are frameworks for avoiding questions of radical suffering. See *Compelling Knowledge: A Feminist Proposal for an Epistemology of the Cross* (Albany, N.Y.: State University of New York Press, 1997), 1–14, 110–11, 133. Solberg argues that the theological category of incarnation always needs to be qualified by the reality of human suffering. "God's decision to participate in the broken world—a world we recognize as ours, too—comes to a kind of physical and historical breaking point on the cross. It is there we glimpse the stuff God is made of," p. 133.

[61]Brock, *Journeys By Heart*, 25; and Anne B. Gilson, *Eros Breaking Free: Interpreting Sexual Theo–Ethics* (Cleveland: Pilgrim Press, 1995), 115.

[62]Carter Heyward, *Touching our Strength*, 3.

[63]With regard to the notion of "touch" as a theological category, see Paula M. Cooey's essay "The Word Become Flesh: Woman's Body, Language, and Value," in *Embodied Love: Sensuality and Relationship as Feminist Values*, ed. P. Cooey, S. A. Farmer, and M. E. Ross (San Francisco: Harper and Row, 1987), 17–32.

[64]Gilson, *Eros Breaking Free*, 111.

[65]Ibid., 110.

[66]See an excellent review essay of Gilson's work in James C. Waller, *Union Seminary Quarterly Review* 49, 3–4.

[67]Heyward, *Touching our Strength*, 189.

[68]Brock, *Journeys by Heart*, 50.

[69]For an extensive discussion of atonement theories and contemporary patterns of domestic abuse, see Darby K. Ray, *Deceiving the Devil: Atonement, Abuse, and Ransom Reconsidered*. Ray's position is similar to my own proposal to return to pre–Anselmian soteriologies. While I propose a return to a modified christus victor, she opts for a return to a modified ransom theory, demythologizing the dramatic narrative to avoid reinscribing literal claims about either Jesus or God.

[70]Rita Nakashima Brock, "Losing Your Innocence But Not Your Hope," in Maryanne Stevens, ed., *Reconstructing the Christ Symbol: Essays in Feminist Christology* (New York: Paulist Press, 1993), 49.

[71]Brock, *Journeys by Heart*, 69.

[72]Brock, "Losing Your Innocence But Not Your Hope," 50.

[73]For a stunning discussion of the fragility of creation and of the human condition, see Wendy Farley's *Tragic Vision and Divine Compassion: A Contemporary Theodicy* (Louisville: Westminster/John Knox Press, 1990), especially chapter 2, "The Rupture of Creation."

[74]Heyward, *Touching our Strength*, 187.

[75]Ibid., 103.

[76]Nancy Wilson, *Our Tribe: Queer Folks, God, Jesus, and the Bible* (San Francisco: HarperCollins, 1995), 55. See also Eleanor McLaughlin's essay "Feminist Christologies: Re–Dressing the Tradition," in Stevens, *Reconstructing the Christ Symbol*, 119–47. She calls for a literary critical paradigm of Jesus as transvestite, a transgressor and cross–dresser who defied the categories of gender as they were (and are) constructed throughout the tradition. "Jesus is the Trickster who peels us open to new depths of humanity, divinity, femaleness, maleness." He is the ultimate paradigm of boundary–violation and scandal.

[77]Heyward, *Speaking of Christ*, 47.

[78]Ibid., 50.

[79]Ibid., 37.

[80]Ibid., 45.

[81]Douglas, *The Black Christ*, 21.

[82]Farley, *Tragic Vision and Divine Compassion*, 39.

[83]Chung Kyun Hyung, *Struggle to Be the Sun Again: Introducing Asian Women's Theology* (Maryknoll, N.Y.: Orbis Books, 1994), 5.

[84]Ibid., 39.

[85]Ibid.

[86]Ibid., 41.

[87]See Beker's *Suffering and Hope: The Biblical Vision and the Human Predicament* (Grand Rapids, Mich.: Eerdmans, 1994), and Farley's *Tragic Vision and Divine Compassion*. Beker's work is highly autobiographical and traces his own experiences in a Nazi concentration camp. Farley's work is a phenomenological description of the domination that suffering exercises over the human spirit. See also Darby Ray's *Deceiving the Devil*, for similar discussions of emotional disassociation, denial, and depression relative to domestic abuse and child abuse.

[88]Chung Hyun Kyung, *Struggle to Be the Sun Again*, 43.

[89]Ibid., 66.

[90]Ibid., 77. See also Marianne Katoppo's excellent discussion of virginity in *Compassionate and Free: An Asian Woman's Theology* (Maryknoll, N.Y.: Orbis Books, 1980), 20–21. I am grateful to Terry Strachan–Terrell for bringing the reinterpretation of virginity to my attention.

[91]Kwok Pui–lan, "God Weeps with Our Pain," in John S. Pobee and Bärbel von Wartenberg–Potter, eds., *New Eyes For Reading: Biblical and Theological Reflections by Women from the Third World* (Geneva: World Council of Churches, 1986), 92.

[92]Ibid., 92; see also Lee Oo Chung's essay "One Woman's Confession of Faith," a meditation on the Markan version of the woman anointing Jesus with perfume. Her version assumes that the woman anointing Jesus understands his suffering more than the disciples do. Since she is a woman familiar with suffering, her own recognition of Jesus' impending suffering becomes an expression of solidarity. The woman was not a boundary–breaker, but a co–sufferer. Contrast this interpretation with Elizabeth Amoah's in the same volume. In *New Eyes For Reading*, 18–20.

[93]Bette Ekeya, "Woman, for How Long Not?" ibid., 64.

[94]Ekeya writes only of Iteso societies of Uganda and parts of Kenya. "Rather than generalize on African culture, I will give a brief description of the life and social position of the woman among the Iteso, although most of what I am going to say can be applied to the African woman in general," in "Woman, for How Long Not?" 59.

[95]Grace Eneme, "Living Stones," in *New Eyes for Reading*, 30.

[96]Ibid., 31.

[97]Elizabeth Amoah, "The Woman Who Decided to Break the Rules," in *New Eyes for Reading*, 4. Amoah is a Methodist from Ghana. Note how she follows fairly standard liberation feminist or early feminist homiletical strategy by making both Jesus and the woman into rebels and law breakers. Contrast this with the previous example of Lee Oo Chung's anointing at Bethany.

[98]Musimbi R. A. Kanyoro, "The Challenge of Feminist Theologies," in M. R. A. Kanyoro, ed., *In Search of a Round Table: Gender, Theology and Church Leadership* (Geneva: World Council of Churches, 1997), 177.

[99]Ibid., 179.

[100]Anne Nasimiyu–Wasike, "Christology and an African Woman's Experience," in Robert J. Schreiter, ed., *Faces of Jesus in Africa* (Maryknoll, N.Y.: Orbis Books, 1995), 70–85.

[101]See Charles Nyamiti's essay, "African Christologies Today," in Schreiter, ed., *Faces of Jesus in Africa*, 3–23, for a discussion of chief and medicine–man christology; and Francois Kabasélé's essays "Christ as Chief" and "Christ as Elder Brother," in the same collection.

[102]Oduyoye, "Be a Woman, and Africa Will Be Strong," in Russell et al., *In Search of Our Mothers' Gardens*, 39. Okomfo Anokye was a priest–politician who helped unify the Asante people into a nation. The Asenie group is one of the seven divisions of the Asante people, all seven of which were founded by women. Abena Gyata was the founder of the Asenie group. Oduyoye cites R. S. Rattray, *Ashanti Law and Constitution* (New York: Negro Universities Press, reprint 1969), 270–84.

[103]Oduyoye, "Churchwomen and the Church's Mission," 69.

[104]Ibid., 69.

[105]Oduyoye doesn't use the phrase "womb of the church," but it certainly seems to correspond to her metaphor of the church as bearer and sign of the New Humanity.

[106]Oduyoye, "Churchwomen and the Church's Mission," 69.

[107]Ibid., 74.

[108]Ibid.

[109]Ibid., 76.

[110]Oduyoye, "Be a Woman, and Africa Will Be Strong," in Russell, ed., *Inheriting our Mothers' Gardens.*

[111]Sun Ai Lee–Park divides Asian feminists into two broad categories, the EATWOT women (Ecumenical Association of Third World Theologians) and the AWRC women (Asian Women Resource Center for Culture and Theology). She claims that EATWOT theologians are more likely to view Jesus as feminist/liberator and Mary as a feminist/autonomous woman, and that AWRC theologians use more traditional categories like suffering and eschatology. Sun Ai Lee–Park, "A Short History of Asian Feminist Theology," in Ofelia Ortega, ed., *Women's Visions: Theological Reflection, Celebration, Action* (Geneva: World Council of Churches, 1995), 37–48.

[112]Virginia Fabella, "An Asian Woman's Perspective," in R. S. Sugirtharajah, ed., *Asian Faces of Jesus* (Maryknoll N.Y.: Orbis Books, 1995), 215.

[113]C. S. Song has discussed one dimension of this problem in *Jesus, The Crucified People* (Minneapolis: Fortress Press, 1996), 124–25; chapter 6, "An Interrupted Life." Song claims that the aggressive missionary impulse of Western colonialism functioned to de–historicize and therefore decontextualize Christian faith. He calls for a reclamation of the "historical" Jesus as a remedy to this spiritualizing function. Clearly, he is not calling for a historically proven Jesus in the positivist sense, but a historically plausible one. The history of missiology in the Third World has probably contributed to a bias for "historical" Jesus approaches, with all its corollary problems.

Chapter 4. A Metaphorical Christology of Salvage

[1]Heyward, *Speaking of Christ,* 45.

[2]Thangaraj, *The Crucified Guru,* 144.

[3]Ibid., 143, 145; citing Leonardo Boff's *Jesus Christ, Liberator* (Maryknoll, N.Y.: Orbis Books, 1979), 265.

[4]Farley, *Tragic Vision and Divine Compassion,* 121.

[5]Schüssler Fiorenza, *Jesus: Miriam's Child: Sophia's Prophet,* 89.

[6]Sallie McFague, *Metaphorical Theology: Models of God in Religious Language* (Philadelphia: Fortress Press, 1982), 15.

[7]McFague, *Metaphorical Theology,* 16.

[8]Kelly Delaine Brown, "God is as Christ Does: Toward a Womanist Theology," *Journal of Religious Thought* 46, no. 1 (Summer/Fall 1989), 7–16.

[9]It's helpful to distinguish between indicative and imperative claims, between the "is" and the "ought" of theological claims. Many incarnational christologians make what I would consider to be a category mistake, making claims about what ought to be rather than the way things actually are. To claim that *all of creation is holy* (an indicative claim) is to declare that nothing is less than divine. This means that every act and phenomenon is, by definition, perfectly good, including acts of murder, disease, tornadoes, etc. To claim that *all of creation should be suffused with divinity* (an imperative claim) is a recognition that created life is ambiguously full of both good and bad, and that the ideal situation is to increase manifestations of good and to decrease manifestations of evil. By grounding incarnational christologies on a faulty indicative (everything is great the way it is, or human beings are essentially oriented toward the good), some incarnational approaches lack a critical edge derived from the contrast between the indicative and the imperative.

[10]Johnson, *Consider Jesus,* 78.

[11]Paul Ricoeur, *The Symbolism of Evil* (New York: Harper and Row, 1967).

[12]David G. Buttrick, *The Mystery and The Passion: A Homiletic Reading of the Gospel Traditions* (Minneapolis: Fortress Press, 1992), 215. See Buttrick's fuller discussion of salvation meanings and metaphors in the epilogue, "The Promise of Salvation."

[13]Buttrick, *The Mystery and The Passion,* 215.

[14]Paul Auster, *In the Country of Last Things* (New York: Penguin, 1987), 36.

[15]Ibid., 133.

[16]She has one female lover and one male lover during the narrative chronology. She leaves with her male lover, Sam, her female lover having decided to stay behind and run covert "salvage" operations after the Woburn House folds. Victoria is Anna's first lesbian love and is probably the most emotionally stable and graciously ethical figure in the book. If anyone is an image of Mother Church in Auster's book, it is Victoria. "Woburn House was her only reality you see, and in the end there was nothing that did not give way to it." Auster, *In the Country of Last Things*, 164.

[17]The weather and the government are depicted as capricious and unavoidable, the great equalizers of the human condition. "If you happen to stay dry, then so much the better. But it has nothing to do with your attitudes or your beliefs. The rain makes no distinctions. At one time or another, it falls on everyone, and when it falls, everyone is equal to everyone else—no one better, no one worse, everyone equal and the same." Auster, *In the Country of Last Things*, 28.

[18]Ibid., 20.

[19]Douglas John Hall, *The Stewardship of Life in the Kingdom of Death* (Grand Rapids, Mich.: Eerdmans, 1985), 34. See also his expanded work on the same theme, *The Steward: A Biblical Symbol Come of Age* (Grand Rapids, Mich.: Eerdmans, 1990).

[20]Hall, *The Steward*, 94.

[21]Sally B. Purvis, *The Power of the Cross: Foundations for a Christian Feminist Ethic of Community* (Nashville: Abingdon Press, 1993), chapter 1, "One Face of Power: Power as Control," 19–36.

[22]Purvis, *The Power of the Cross*, 88.

[23]Virginia Fabella and Chung Hyun Kyung, in R. S. Sugirtharajah, ed., *Asian Faces of Jesus*, 212.

[24]Farley, *Tragic Vision and Divine Compassion*, 132.

[25]Ibid.

[26]Purvis, *The Power of the Cross*, 14.

[27]Aulén, *Christus Victor*, 21–22.

[28]Rodney Kennedy, *The Creative Power of Metaphor: A Rhetorical Homiletics* (Lanham, Md.: University Press of America, 1993), especially chapter 3, "The Rhetoric of 'Folly'"; see also Schüssler Fiorenza's *Revelation*, especially Part Three, "Theo–Ethical Rhetoric"; Purvis, *The Power of the Cross*, 48–54; Alexandra R. Brown, *The Cross and Human Transformation* (Minneapolis: Fortress Press, 1995), 25–30, 105 ff.

[29]Fredriksen, *From Jesus to Christ*, 86.

[30]Martin Luther, *Luther's Works*, vol. 31, 53.

[31]Solberg, *Compelling Knowledge*, 111.

[32]Ibid.

[33]Auster, *In the Country of Last Things*, 36.

[34]Aulén, *The Faith of the Christian Church*, 195.

[35]Douglas, *The Black Christ*, 24.

[36]Oduyoye, "Churchwomen and the Church's Mission," 69.

[37]Ibid.

[38]This was also Barth's position. Barth rejected any theological method grounded in philosophy, psychology, or sociology. He considered them all subject to pride and distortion. His radical biblicism was an attempt to maintain the authority of the scriptures over and above human authorities or experts.

[39]Oduyoye, "Churchwomen and the Church's Mission," 69.

[40]Jacquelyn Grant, "The Sin of Servanthood and the Deliverance of Discipleship," in E. Townes, *A Troubling of My Soul* (Maryknoll N.Y.: Orbis Books, 1993), 214.

[41]Isasi–Díaz, *Mujerista Theology*, 129.

[42]Heyward, *Speaking of Christ*, 50.

[43]Ibid., 37.

[44]Ibid., 45.

[45]Ibid., 37.

[46]Ibid., 44.

[47]From the videotape *Jesus and Generation X*, Harvey Cox, "Jesus at 2000," the 27th National Conference of Trinity Institute 1996, Office of Video Production, Parish of Trinity Church.

[48]Heyward, *Speaking of Christ*, 37.

[49]See Song's book *Jesus, The Crucified People* (Minneapolis: Fortress Press, 1996) for a highly contextualized Asian christology.

[50]Roberta Bondi, "Prayer in Friendship with God," *Christian Century*, January 29, 1997, 100.

[51]Hannah Arendt, *The Human Condition* (Chicago: University of Chicago Press, 1958), 189 ff.

[52]William James, *Pragmatism, and the Meaning of Truth* (Cambridge: Harvard University Press, 1975), 142.

[53]Kathleen Talvacchia, unpublished position paper at Wabash College, Workshop for Teaching and Learning in Religion and Theology, January 31, 1997. Dr. Talvacchia is the Assistant Professor of Ministry and Theology at Union Theological Seminary in New York.

[54]Ray, *Deceiving the Devil*, chapter 2, "Wrestling With God."

[55]Johann Baptist Metz, *Faith in History and Society: Toward a Practical Fundamental Society* (New York: Seabury Press, 1980), 77, 89, 236. Cited in Welch, *A Feminist Ethic of Risk*, 154–55. "Dangerous memory" has become a common theme for white feminist theologians. See also Rebecca Chopp, *The Praxis of Suffering: An Interpretation of Liberation and Political Theologies* (Maryknoll, N.Y.: Orbis Books, 1989), especially her discussion of Metz, 64–81.

[56]Sharon D. Welch, *A Feminist Ethic of Risk* (Minneapolis: Fortress Press, 1990), 60.

[57]Welch, *A Feminist Ethic of Risk*, 63.

[58]Farley, *Tragic Vision and Divine Compassion*, 129.

[59]Ibid.

[60]Ibid., 131.

[61]James H. Harris, *Preaching Liberation*, Fortress Resources for Preaching (Minneapolis: Fortress Press, 1995), 4. Harris also notes the theology carried in hymns and liturgy but still maintains the priority of preaching as the primary bearer of a community's theological reflection.

[62]Harris, *Preaching Liberation*, 4.

[63]Mary Catherine Hilkert, *Naming Grace: Preaching and the Sacramental Imagination* (New York: Continuum, 1997).

[64]From Bonhoeffer's Lectures on Preaching, Winter Semester 1935/36–1937, in Clyde Fant, ed. and trans., *Worldly Preaching: Lectures on Homiletics* (New York: Crossroad, 1991), 101, 104.

Chapter 5. Visions of the Basileia: Practicing What We Preach

[1]Tom F. Driver, *The Magic of Ritual: Our Need for Liberating Rites that Transform our Lives & Our Communities* (New York: HarperCollins, 1991), 91.

[2]Catherine Bell, *Ritual Theory, Ritual Practice* (New York: Oxford University Press, 1992), 26.

[3]Douglas, *Purity and Danger*, 63–69.

[4]Driver, *The Magic of Ritual*, 80.

[5]Ibid., 92.

[6]Ibid.

[7]Douglas, *Purity and Danger*, 5–6.

[8]Ibid., 35.

[9]Dillard, *Living By Fiction*, 171.

[10]Douglas, *Purity and Danger*, 35, 40.

[11]Ibid., 72.

[12]See Geoffrey Wainwright's discussion of the *Didache* liturgy, which called the holy to come partake and the unholy to repent, in *Eucharist and Eschatology* (New York: Oxford University Press, 1981), 68.

[13]Cheslyn Jones, Geoffrey Wainwright, Edward Yarnold, S.J., and Paul Bradshaw, eds., *The Study of Liturgy* (New York: Oxford University Press, 1992), 210–12.

[14]The development of the Lenten penitential season is fairly complex. One dimension of the development is the extension and integration of Pascha into Easter celebrations. As the church became more institutionalized, the pre–Paschal period of instruction

and preparation was extended. Thomas J. Talley indicates that a fairly established Lenten period may have been operative as early as the second or third century. In Thomas J. Talley, *Origins of the Liturgical Year* (New York: Pueblo Publishing 1986), 31–33.

[15]See Pagels' discussion of the early martyrs and the gnostic rejection of martyrdom as a foolish waste of life. Some gnosticism probably rejected an early version of Anselmian atonement theory, which demanded suffering as an offering to God. However, we probably need to be cautious about cheering on the gnostics, since their rejections were based on a lack of respect for bodily activities and not a desire to honor the body. In Pagels, *The Gnostic Gospels*, 97–122.

[16]Elisabeth Schüssler Fiorenza, *In Memory of Her: A Feminist Theological Reconstruction of Christian Origins* (New York: Crossroad, 1983), 288.

[17]Ruether, *Sexism and God–Talk*, 126.

[18]Jones et al., *The Study of Liturgy*, 151.

[19]James M. White, *Protestant Worship: Traditions in Transition* (Louisville: Westminster/John Knox Press, 1989), 39. See also Gustaf Aulén, *Eucharist and Sacrifice* (Edinburgh: Oliver & Boyd, 1958), 65–101. Any preacher who is still not convinced that preaching and language have the power to change group attitudes and loyalties should reread Luther. The ecclesiology he was resisting was driven by a thoroughgoing sacrificial worldview, reinforced in art, liturgy, and proclamation.

[20]For a careful look at Luther's theory of consubstantiation and its implications for salvation theory, see Gustaf Aulén, *The Faith of the Christian Church*, 344–49.

[21]See James F. White, *Protestant Worship*, 59–63; W. P. Stephens, *The Theology of Huldrych Zwingli* (Oxford: Clarendon Press, 1986); and Brian A. Gerrish, *Grace and Gratitude: The Eucharistic Theology of John Calvin* (Minneapolis: Fortress Press, 1993); and Gerrish, *The Old Protestantism and the New: Essays on the Reformation Heritage* (Chicago: University of Chicago Press, 1982).

[22]Gerrish, *Grace and Gratitude*, 11.

[23]Ibid., 184–85. Gerrish notes that the idea was not originally Zwinglian, but rather a debt to Luther's earlier eucharistic and ecclesial theology.

[24]*Baptism, Eucharist and Ministry*, Faith and Order Paper No. 111 (Geneva: World Council of Churches, 1982), vii.

[25]I use the term *ecumenical* quite specifically to refer to diverse Christian groups. I use the term *interfaith* to refer to the conversations and contexts that include religions beyond the Christian ecumenical setting.

[26]BEM, 32.

[27]BEM, 3. The last clause of this statement is problematic, since it suggests that the goal of the basileia is to make Christians out of the whole world. In the last section of this chapter we will consider appropriate understandings of Christian mission and evangelism within a pluralistic world.

[28]See Galatians 5:16–25 for lists that differentiate the practices of those who live in the old age and those who live in God's future. Paul's opposition between spirit and flesh is not the rejection of embodiment that we occasionally assume. The author of Galatians is differentiating two types of embodiment: one that takes its cues from the "flesh" of the old age, and one that takes its cues from the "spirit" of the coming reconciliation.

[29]BEM, 2.

[30]Many contemporary Christian communities would reject an interpretation of baptism that does not emphasize the personal dimension and commitment of an informed believer. Those who understand themselves as descendants of the Anabaptist Radical Reformation take the ethical dimension of baptism so seriously that it becomes, for them, unimaginable to baptize an infant into these ethical expectations.

[31]For additional suggestions on congregational study and liturgical assistance, see William H. Lazareth, *Growing Together in Baptism, Eucharist and Ministry* (Geneva: WCC, 1982); Max Thurian, ed., *Ecumenical Perspectives on Baptism, Eucharist and Ministry* (Geneva: WCC, 1983); Max Thurian, ed., *Baptism and Eucharist: Ecumenical Convergence in Celebration* (Geneva: WCC, 1983); and the Disciple resource by Keith Watkins, ed., *Baptism and Belonging: A Resource for Christian Worship* (St. Louis: Chalice Press, 1991). Several of these also have helpful bibliographies suited for specific denominational practices.

[32]David R. Newman, *Worship as Praise and Empowerment* (New York: Pilgrim Press, 1988), 19. Newman takes an eschatological perspective on worship, claiming the biblical language of powers and principalities seriously, if not literally.

[33]See Galatians 3:27–28 and a similar passage in 1 Corinthians 12:13.

[34]James F. White, *Sacraments as God's Self Giving* (Nashville: Abingdon Press, 1983), 96–97.

[35]This is precisely the issue that arose during U. S. colonial history with the conversion and baptism of slaves. The equality implied in baptism threatened the system of chattel slavery by eroding the question of ontological difference. Baptism, historically, always challenges ontological or natural order schemes. We should be especially cautious about invoking biological or developmental arguments relative to children and baptism. History suggests otherwise.

[36]White, *Sacraments as God's Self–Giving*, 99.

[37]BEM, 14–15.

[38]Ibid., 14.

[39]Ibid., 15.

[40]Ibid.

[41]Michael K. Kinnamon, "Children and Christian Baptism," in Keith Watkins, ed., *Baptism and Belonging* (St. Louis: Chalice Press, 1991), 126.

[42]Wolfhart Pannenberg, *Christian Spirituality* (Philadelphia: Westminster Press, 1983), 46.

[43]Ibid., 45.

[44]White, *Sacraments as God's Self Giving*, 103.

[45]Ibid.

[46]Victor Anderson, "The Search for Public Theology in the United States," in Thomas G. Long and Edward Farley, eds., *Preaching as a Theological Task: World, Gospel, Scripture* (Louisville: Westminster/John Knox Press, 1996), 20. A number of contemporary philosophers, theologians, and ethicists are currently working with definitions of public theology. See Ronald F. Thiemann, *Constructing a Public Theology: The Church in a Pluralistic Culture* (Louisville: Westminster/John Knox Press, 1991); William A. Beardslee, ed., *America and the Future of Theology* (Philadelphia: Westminster Press, 1967); Parker Palmer, *The Company of Strangers: Christians and the Renewal of America's Public Life* (New York: Crossroad, 1989).

[47]See Tracy's *The Analogical Imagination: Christian Theology and the Culture of Pluralism* (New York: Crossroad, 1981), particularly chapter 1, "A Social Portrait of the Theologian, The Three Publics of Theology: Society, Academy, Church."

[48]Tracy, *The Analogical Imagination*, 6–14.

[49]Anderson, "The Search for Public Theology," 21.

[50]Maura O'Neill, *Women Speaking, Women Listening: Women in Interreligious Dialogue* (Maryknoll, N.Y.: Orbis Books, 1990), 54.

[51]Pamela Dickey Young, *Christ in a Post–Christian World: How can we believe in Jesus Christ when those around us believe differently—or not at all?* (Minneapolis: Fortress Press, 1995), 15.

[52]Daly, *Gyn/Ecology*, 155.

[53]Azar Tabari, "The Women's Movement in Iran: A Hopeful Prognosis," *Feminist Studies* 12 (Summer 1986), 356–57, as cited in O'Neill, *Women Speaking, Women Listening*, 61.

[54]Young, *Christ in a Post–Christian World*, 4.

[55]I am borrowing the term *wager* from Lucy Atkinson Rose's *Sharing the Word: Preaching in the Roundtable Church* (Louisville: Westminster/John Knox Press, 1997), 5. Rose claims that a sermon is always a wager on the part of the preacher, a proposal about meaning that is made in the recognition of its own limitations and biases.

[56]Young, *Christ in a Post–Christian World*, 103.

[57]Marjorie Hewitt Suchocki, "In Search of Justice: Religious Pluralism from a Feminist Perspective," in John Hick and Paul F. Knitter, eds., *The Myth of Christian Uniqueness: Toward a Pluralistic Theology of Religions* (Maryknoll, N.Y.: Orbis Books, 1992), 149.

[58]Suchocki, "In Search of Justice," 150.

[59]Ibid.

[60]Ibid., 155.

[61]Ibid.

[62]Ibid.

[63]Ibid., 157.

[64]Young, *Christ in a Post–Christian World*, 103–5, and especially chapter 6, "Fullness of Existence and Beauty," 106–29.

[65]Suchocki, "In Search of Justice," 159.

[66]Ibid.

[67]Young, *Christ in a Post–Christian World*, 15.

[68]For a fine book on local congregational analysis, see Leonora Tubbs Tisdale's *Preaching as Local Theology and Folk Art* (Minneapolis: Fortress Press, 1997). Tisdale's book is focused on exegeting local congregations to discern their operative theologies.

[69]Keifert, *Welcoming the Stranger*, ix.

[70]Keifert uses "stranger" in three senses: (1) those who are culturally outsiders, in status, ethnicity, age,—those who don't fit our general demographic profile; (2) the "inside" strangers who are part of the cultural profile but do not belong to the intimate elite group of the congregation; and (3) the irreducible differences between human beings by virtue of personhood, that is, the stranger quality even between family members and friends.

[71]Douglas John Hall, *The Steward: A Biblical Symbol Come of Age* (Grand Rapids, Mich.: Eerdmans/Friendship Press, 1982), 42. See also his later work *The Stewardship of Life in the Kingdom of Death* (New York: Eerdmans, 1988).

[72]Hall, *The Steward*, 45.

[73]Suchocki, "In Search of Justice," 155.

[74]The parable of the sower (Mt. 13:1–8, Mk. 4:3–8, Lk. 8:5–8), the parable of the weeds (Mt. 13:24–30), the parable of the leaven (Mt. 13:33, Lk. 13:20–21), the parable of the pearl (Mt. 13:45–46), the parable of the dragnet (Mt. 13:47–50).

[75]Robert Farrar Capon, *Parables of the Kingdom* (Grand Rapids, Mich.: Eerdmans, 1985), 74.

[76]Capon, *Parables of the Kingdom*, 90.

[77]Ibid., 99.

[78]Ibid., 75.

[79]I am indebted to my husband for our ongoing conversations about the etymological relationships between mater/mother/matter.

[80]Alfred North Whitehead, *Process and Reality*, David R. Griffin and Donald W. Sherburne, eds. (New York: The Free Press, 1978), 346.

[81]Hall, *The Steward*, 17.

[82]Schüssler Fiorenza, *Jesus: Miriam's Child, Sophia's Prophet*, 11.

[83]Ibid., 24. The Oratory of St. Euphemia is the chamber where the Chalcedonian agreement was ratified. The bishops had met repeatedly and without compromise when finally, in this chamber named after a woman saint, the bishops agreed to a formula.

Index